CHRISTOPHER BERRY–DEE
AND ROBIN ODELL

PRIME SUSPECT

THE TRUE STORY OF JOHN CANNAN,
THE ONLY MAN POLICE WANT TO INVESTIGATE
FOR THE MURDER OF SUZY LAMPLUGH

D1323550

JB
JOHN BLAKE

Published by John Blake Publishing Ltd,
3 Bramber Court, 2 Bramber Road,
London W14 9PB, England

www.blake.co.uk

First published in paperback in 2008

ISBN: 978-1-84454–612-1

British Library Cataloguing-in-Publication Data:

A catalogue record for this book is available from the British Library.

Design by www.envydesign.co.uk

Printed and bound in Great Britain by Creative Print and Design,
Blaina, Wales

1 3 5 7 9 10 8 6 4 2

Papers used by John Blake Publishing are natural, recyclable products
made from wood grown in sustainable forests. The manufacturing processes
conform to the environmental regulations of the country of origin.

'Impressive... a detailed and balanced portrait of a murderer'

DIANA LAMPLUGH
The Suzy Lamplugh Trust

Christopher Berry-Dee is an investigative criminologist and author of 18 books, including the international bestseller Talking With Serial Killers. He is a freelance journalist and advises on television and movie production. He has interviewed over 30 of the world's worst serial and mass murderers. Chris consults with law enforcement including the FBI.

FOREWORD

John Cannan is an unlikely murderer. Handsome and charming in the traditions of the car salesman, which he was for a while, privately educated at an elite school and from a caring middle-class family, he had none of the obvious misfortunes and disadvantages that most people would expect of a man who turns to violent assault and brutal killing. Yet, as Christopher Berry-Dee and Robin Odell reveal as a result of their painstaking research and gentle but determined correspondence with John Cannan, he is quite likely to have been responsible for more than one murder, as well as the number of sexual assaults and the murder of Shirley Banks for which he was given a life sentence.

The authors, using skills that any psychotherapist would be proud of, encouraged Cannan to give a very full account of himself and his actions. By putting this account together with a detailed reconstruction of the known facts in the various cases, the authors are able to show that behind

John Cannan's charm and intelligence is a self-centred, frustrated and angry man who could have gone on to become a serial murderer.

This book therefore provides us with a microscopic account of the early stages and growth of the extremes of episodic violence. It allows us to watch the emergence of escalating acts of savagery and to judge for ourselves the validity of Cannan's own claims about these actions. Readers of this book are consequently in the rare situation of seeing both sides of rape and murder. On the one side are the accounts recorded by the police and victims; on the other the views of the offender himself.

A fascinating picture unfolds of Cannan, always at the centre of his own personal drama, driven by forces of which he is only dimly aware, constantly hiding from himself the enormity of his actions. We do not see here a profoundly evil man who enjoys the havoc he wreaks on other people's lives, but rather a person whose self-deception perpetuates ways of dealing with other people that can only lead to their exploitation and abuse. Here we can see the mind of a murderer probably more starkly than he can ever see it himself.

This book therefore makes an important contribution to our understanding of serial killers. It shows how one at least grew into the part he had implicitly written for himself. As the authors demonstrate, Cannan's actions have many chilling parallels to those of other men who went on to commit many more murders, most notably Ted Bundy, who was executed for his killing of a large number of young women. From my own studies, I can add that the steady increase of violence, from an attack on a loved one to the murder of a stranger, also mirrors closely the life story of John Duffy, the 'Railway Killer', sentenced to life for five rapes and three murders.

An understanding of the personal development towards serial murder, as revealed by Bundy and Duffy and so thoroughly documented here for the life plan of Cannan, further dispels the Hollywood mythology of the mad fiend who suddenly emerges at a full moon, or who is born committed to a life of evil. By allowing Cannan to speak so fully in his own words, this book also allows us to see that insanity is no necessary part of rape and murder. We can also see that there are episodes in a violent criminal's life that lead on to further violence or slow his movement along that path. Far from these actions being impulsive, almost random events, the authors show with admirable clarity the personal crises in Cannan's life that might have upset other people but for him were the precursors to brutality.

Further, the logic that John Cannan reveals in this book can be seen as a prerequisite to perpetuate the psychological processes that support his violence. Only a man as thoughtful as him could develop such sophisticated defences against the reality of his own excesses. That same intelligence also helped him to evade capture and continue his crimes.

The story of John Cannan's arrest and conviction is therefore also an important illustration of why the United States has a higher proportion of serial murderers than Britain. The British police are usually more effective in apprehending such men early in their violent careers. This book shows that there are likely to be many men in British prisons who would have gone on to commit a series of murders if they had not been arrested when they were.

In order to stop the trickle of British serial killers turning into a steady stream, then, men who have the potential for such violence have to be recognised and stopped before they proceed very far along this path. This book takes an important step in helping us to recognise and understand such men. As a consequence it assists the police, possible victims and potential murderers themselves, by helping them to identify the hidden and overt clues that would indicate the path of destruction along which they may be moving.

The authors summarise some of the current thinking on what creates a serial killer, but their own detailed account of John Cannan demonstrates that no simple formula will ever capture the complexity of any one individual, even less summarise the range of variations that distinguish one killer from another. The inner recesses of the psyche of people who commit the ultimate crime will continue to remain enigmatic for as long as murderers like Cannan continue to deny their crimes and defend themselves from the implications of their deeds. This book nonetheless does great service in removing some of the myths and confusions that continue to shroud the murder of strangers.

DAVID CANTER

Professor of Applied Psychology
University of Surrey

ACKNOWLEDGEMENTS

Carrying out the research for a book such as this and writing it can be both frustrating and distressing. But at the end of the task there is an opportunity to reflect on the journey and to acknowledge all those individuals and organisations who, in their various ways, helped to make it possible and also worthwhile.

Firstly, we thank John Cannan, whose errant life provided our inspiration and whose cooperation, even in the face of fiercely direct questioning, did not waiver. He has protested his innocence throughout but his arguments have little bearing on his guilt. He is destined to spend the rest of his life in prison and has nothing to gain from an examination of his life and crimes, except perhaps to be confronted by their grim reality.

We also thank Mrs Sheila Cannan, John's mother, who courageously faced up to the tragedy represented by her son's actions. She gave us valuable recollections of his childhood.

A note of special appreciation is accorded to Sharon Major, one of John's rape victims. She gave us valuable insights into the months she spent with him, during which she shared the best and the worst that his volatile nature could provide.

For information and advice on the legal, medical and police aspects of Cannan's offences, we are indebted to Detective Superintendent Bryan Saunders and his colleagues of the Avon and Somerset Constabulary, Chief Superintendent Anthony Miller of the Thames Valley Police, Assistant Chief Constable (Crime) T Meffen OBE of the West Midlands Police, Detective Chief Superintendent G. Heyhurst (Head of CID), Warwickshire Constabulary, and the Dorset Police.

John's solicitor, Jim Moriarty, of Blackham, Maycock & Hayward, provided us with copies of the case papers with his client's permission. He unfailingly responded to calls for further information and provided help wherever he could. We are also grateful to the former Lord Chief Justice of England, Lord Lane, for his helpful comments, and to John's trial judge, the Hon. Mr Justice Drake DFC.

For guidance on the forensic aspects of John Cannan's offences we turned to Mr D Neylan, Director of the Home Office Forensic Science Laboratory at Aldermaston, who was most helpful in giving clarification of procedures. We also extend our thanks to Dr B. Sheard, Director of the Metropolitan Police Forensic Science Laboratory at Lambeth.

The world of criminal psychology can be a minefield of confusion and contradictions. In an effort to resolve difficulties as they arose, we were fortunate to be able to call on the valued assistance of Dr Denis Power, Honorary Consultant psychiatrist to HM Prison Service, and David

Canter, Professor of Psychology at Surrey University. Dr Power has immense experience in the study of criminal offending and Professor Canter is recognised internationally for his pioneering work on offender profiling. We are deeply grateful to them for their valued guidance.

The Home Office provided us with open lines of communication to John Cannan, for which we express thanks to Trevor J Gadd, Governor of HMP Wakefield, to Mr P Buxton, Governor of HMP Frankland, and Mr WM Goodwin, Head of Custody at HMP Frankland. We also wish to acknowledge the speed and efficient manner in which the headquarters of the Prison Service dealt with correspondence. John Goodchild, Principal Local Studies Officer at Wakefield, provided us with information about the history of the prison.

Shirley Banks's former employers declined to provide any information, stressing that her murder had been an upsetting experience for her colleagues. Janet Eyles, wife of the late Tom Eyles, gave us details of her husband's private investigation practice, and Basil and Jill Hooper relived the painful experience of discovering Shirley's body while out for a walk with their family. We thank them all for their assistance. We are indebted also to a number of newspapers published in the West Midlands, particularly the *Birmingham News* and *Mail* and *Sutton Coldfield News* for local background reporting.

For their personal support throughout the project and for their patience in listening to hours of discussion we thank Al Barker, Tracy Berry-Dee and Joan Odell. Special thanks are extended to our agent, Peter Robinson, and to Gill Gibbins, Susanne McDadd and Peter Day for keeping faith and providing encouragement along the way. A big thank you too to Elfreda Powell, our editor, who applied a rationale which finally pulled everything together.

A final expression of thanks is extended to Elliott Leyton, Professor of Anthropology at the Memorial University of Newfoundland, Canada, who, on the basis of a chance meeting in a broadcast studio, agreed to look at the conclusions we had reached. We are fortunate to have had the opportunity to act on suggestions made by one of the foremost authorities on serial violence.

CHRISTOPHER BERRY-DEE
Robin Odell

CONTENTS

INTRODUCTION

This book is not for the faint-hearted. It is an account of a human predator, prone to serial violence, an arch-opportunist who trawled for victims in wine bars and car parks. The minds of such individuals are shaped by a variety of sociological, physiological and psychological factors, perhaps of a genetic origin but certainly acquired during their formative years. They know the difference between right and wrong, but simply don't care.

Such predators are difficult to detect because their behaviour is masked with protective cunning. They merge into society and appear to all intents and purposes normal and well adjusted. Yet they are loners, restlessly roaming from place to place in search of opportunities to fulfil their lusts. John Cannan was such an individual.

Nature endowed him with the good looks and easy charm of the 'ladykiller'. He conquered the hearts of attractive women with seemingly little effort and enjoyed his powers to the full. But nature had leavened her gifts with a fatal flaw that transformed him into a killer. John developed a destructive urge that he could not control.

He is currently serving a natural life sentence for the murder of Shirley Banks, a newly married young woman who disappeared from Bristol in October 1987 and whose body was found in Somerset the following year. This murder was the high point of violence in John's criminal career. What preceded it was a string of robberies, violent assaults and rapes, interspersed with a number of amorous affairs. He displayed increasingly tense and violent behaviour in his normal relationships and reached a stage where he began, like a serial murderer, to trawl for victims.

His adult life and the pattern of his behaviour bear all the hallmarks associated with serial killers. He was plausible, mobile, opportunistic and a manipulator. When he suffered rejection or humiliation, his mind turned to revenge and the kind of satisfaction that feeds on pain inflicted on others. In a sudden change of mood, he could swing from being an amusing companion to a human predator seeking a victim. Shirley Banks may not have been his only murder victim. Cannan's name has been linked with the disappearance of Suzy Lamplugh in 1986 and another murder – that of Sandra Court – which remains unexplained, although he has consistently denied any involvement in either case. There are, however, a suspiciously high number of coincidences to link him to them. Is John Cannan a serial killer? What is certain is that John was set on a violent path, in which the attacks were coming closer together and with increasing ferocity, inflamed with hatred and a desire to cause pain and suffering.

Despite all the evidence that convicted him, John

portrays himself as the luckless victim of circumstance and conspiracy. But it is a long chain of coincidence that binds him irrevocably to rape, abduction and murder – he had the misfortune, again and again, to be in the right place at the relevant time. If these occasions were simply coincidences, he must be an outstanding victim of chance and circumstance. And either chance or circumstance decreed that he would be at liberty and within striking distance of Suzy Lamplugh on the day she disappeared in London after meeting the mysterious 'Mr Kipper'. And was it also just a coincidence that 'Kipper' was one of John's nicknames?

This book is an account of John Cannan's life and crimes. It is written with his consent but without the benefit of his confession. He has steadfastly denied the offences for which he has been convicted in the teeth of the strongest evidence against him. The story is nevertheless punctuated with his own words and commentaries drawn from the explanations given by him in letters written to the authors.

He agreed that we should publish an account of his life and urged us to write it as we saw it. For his part, he promised to provide information and answer questions. He fulfilled this undertaking in large measure, making available details about himself and the events that consumed him. His correspondence shows him to be articulate and witty, with a liking for block capitals and repetition when he wants to make a point. He has tremendous recall of factual details such as names, dates and places but it is a talent that proves to be fallible. On many crucial issues, his memory conveniently fails him, although he has an answer of sorts for everything.

With John's help and, through him, that of his solicitor, Jim Moriarty, we gained access to his case documents. Other papers and photographs came through the cooperation of the Avon and Somerset and Thames Valley police. These two sources, which included the transcripts of John's many tape-recorded interviews with Detective Chief Inspector Bryan Saunders and Detective Inspector Terry Jones, are at the core of the book. We have used extracts from John's letters to represent his views and to provide his interpretation of events. On practically every issue he is at variance with the evidence given by witnesses and with officially recorded views. This is not surprising, bearing in mind that he denies all the charges made against him.

John regards himself as a wronged man who, from the outset of his adult life, was let down by the people around him. And when things went wrong for him, he was victimised by the system. His conviction, he believes, was contrived by people in influential positions, the police, the judiciary and the media who needed a scapegoat. He is embittered and far from being at peace with himself or with his circumstances. In this respect, he has much in common with the well-documented personality profile of the serial murderer.

We have sought to protect the feelings of the rape victims by not using their real names. Thus, 'Sharon Major', 'Jean Bradford' and 'Donna Tucker' are pseudonyms for the three women who experienced brutal attacks. These are the only names that have been changed. Here, the authors are at variance with John, who coldly maintains that, if these individuals made allegations against him, they should be publicly revealed. The other women who featured in

John's life, with some exceptions, did so willingly and saw something of the better side of his character.

As for John himself, he remains an enigma to the extent that he wishes to be one. We know that he has not told us everything, because he has said so. It is his view that information gives power and control. It may be a mistaken view in light of his present situation, but he holds to it nevertheless. Even without John's full admission, we understand enough about him to realise that his violent lapses made him a danger to society.

For all that, we have tried to ensure that he retains his dignity. It has not been one of our objectives to destroy his character; our aim has been to seek understanding. His acts have been brutal and the probability is that he would have gone on had he not been caught. He was driven by forces which he did not, and apparently still does not, comprehend and to that extent he is a victim himself.

Had the lottery of fate dealt John Cannan a different set of circumstances, he might well have used his natural gifts in ways that would have earned him praise instead of punishment. Such is the knife-edge that can turn one individual to destructive ends and another to creative acts. Yet, while circumstances may divide them, they remain united by their humanity. John is a member of the human race, even though he is set apart from society, and we demean ourselves if we too easily castigate individuals like him without at least trying to understand them.

John will not like our conclusions. They will be as unpalatable to him as they are odious to the rest of us. But we hope that in time the book will help him to come to terms with himself. We hope too it will help people to understand the pressures that society exerts on individuals who are not temperamentally equipped to cope with them except through violent means. Finally, we hope that vulnerable members of society who put themselves at risk through unthinking and incautious behaviour will realise that predators in an increasingly violent society all too often wear sheep's clothing.

C.B.-D.
R.O.

PRELUDE – A SUNNY AFTERNOON

A man's voice shouted, 'Come on, come on!' The tone expressed annoyance and urgency. It sounded as if a fight were taking place in the thickly wooded copse. There were no people to be seen – only the thumping of heavy blows as if someone were hitting a punch-bag.

Suddenly, the dark-clad figure of a man was highlighted by a shaft of sunlight breaking through the canopy of trees. He appeared to be holding something with one hand and punching it with the other. The object of this assault screeched in protest, leaving no doubt that the victim was human. The man shouted several times, 'I told you what I would do,' and continued to punch and kick his victim, who was now on the damp ground screaming in terror. After that, apart from a dreadful choking sound, there was an ominous silence.

Amelia Hart, accompanied by her husband George, witnessed this nightmarish incident on a sunny autumn afternoon while they were out for a drive. The elderly couple had left their home at Westbury Park, Bristol at about 2.15pm to visit some former neighbours who had moved to Clevedon. The Harts' route took them across the Clifton Suspension Bridge and into Bridge Road and Leigh Woods.

As they drove past a block of flats called Foye House, they saw smoke rising from the adjoining copse. Mrs Hart asked her husband, who was slightly deaf, to slow down. She was concerned because, while there were no flames visible, no one appeared to be supervising the seat of the fire. The copse was a triangular-shaped area of woodland with quite a few trees and dense undergrowth. She thought perhaps there were Boy Scouts camping in the woods.

As their Vauxhall Chevette slowed to a stop, Mrs Hart heard and then saw the man in the woods. She told her husband she thought something terrible was going on and she was frightened. The screaming was quickly over and the man who was crouched down became aware that he was being observed and looked over his shoulder.

Amelia Hart opened the car window and shouted to him, asking what he was doing. The man moved out of sight but then suddenly emerged from the copse on his hands and knees and loomed up on the pavement beside the car. Raising his hands, he yelled 'Cow!' at her. Mrs Hart saw a crazed look on his face and he appeared to be breathing heavily after his exertions. She quickly wound up the window and shouted to her husband to drive off.

The man had his back to them, his head slumped forward and he was holding on to a lamppost and some overhanging tree branches. As the Harts pulled away, he peered at them by bending his head under his arm.

All this took place on Friday, 9 October 1987, the day after a recently married young woman named Shirley

Banks had disappeared while shopping in Bristol's town centre. Her car was later found in one of the garages at Foye House and her thumbprint was discovered on a document in Flat 2. Both the flat and the garage were rented to John Cannan, a convicted rapist who had in his possession the excise licence disc from Shirley Banks's Mini car. The missing bride was found six months later lying naked and face down in a stream that meandered through a remote area of the Quantocks in Somerset. She had been battered to death.

Detective Chief Inspector Bryan Saunders of the Avon and Somerset Constabulary was the officer who eventually charged John Cannan with the murder of Shirley Banks. He is convinced that Amelia Hart witnessed the missing woman's attempt to escape from her abductor.

Shirley Banks was an attractive young blonde. As she mingled with evening shoppers in Bristol on Thursday, 8 October 1987, intent on buying a new dress, she was being observed without her knowledge, for her physical attributes had marked her out as a potential victim for a kidnapper and murderer. A sexual psychopath had noticed her and he was following her. At some point she was approached, whether with blandishments or menace, we will never know, and she was spirited away, probably in her own car.

Shirley's movements on the day she disappeared can be precisely recorded down to the minute until 7.26pm. After that she vanished entirely from the public domain; how she spent the remaining hours of her life is known only to her murderer. Her car, a recognisable part of her daily existence, also disappeared, although only as far as the garage at Foye House. There, hidden from public gaze, her orange Mini Clubman was crudely repainted blue. The vehicle was discovered in its bright new paint long before Shirley's ravaged corpse was stumbled upon by a family out for a Sunday afternoon walk.

The tenant of Flat 2 at Foye House liked to describe himself as a businessman. In reality he was a not-very-successful car-dealer who lived on his wits and the proceeds of theft. By the time he took up residence in the summer of 1987, John Cannan had begun to slide into a pattern of serial violence: he had committed three violent rapes, and may or may not have committed other murders. There are sound reasons for making these other connections because Cannan's *modus operandi* was very like that of a serial killer, and also fitted the circumstances.

John Cannan was someone who was always on the move and available. He enjoyed cars and travelled regularly, visiting towns in the West Midlands and the South and West, looking for opportunities. He carried with him the tools of coercion and restraint – an imitation handgun, handcuffs, a knife and lengths of rope.

On an emotional level, he was a man with a mercurial temperament: capable of normal, loving relationships, but finding them difficult to sustain. He could suddenly become mean and aggressive. A man of above-average intelligence, he was also a manipulator, obsessed with himself, a man who always had to have his own way. When events took a course other than the one he desired, particularly in his relationships, he resorted to threats and menaces. When his emotional equilibrium was disturbed, he was primed for violence and sought revenge, hunting down vulnerable female victims.

He needs to feel he is in command of every situation.

That desire to control led him down the path to serial violence, and bred within him the instincts of a predator.

'I AM IN CONTROL because information is power,' he wrote to the authors, mistakenly believing that, by not confessing to his crimes, he still held the whip hand. Eventually, though, by brilliant police teamwork, the case was to be proved otherwise.

1
JOHN

The motto of the Duc de Guise, 16th-century head of the Catholic League, was *A chacun son tour* (My turn will come). The Duke's surname was one of those given to John David Guise Cannan, born in Sutton Coldfield, Warwickshire, on 20 February 1954.

John was born to loving parents. His mother doted on him and, despite having an older sister and, in due course, a younger brother, it was 'little Johnnie' who occupied centre-stage in the Cannan home. His father, Cyril Cannan, was an exacting man with a quick temper. He had been a flight-lieutenant in the Royal Air Force during the Second World War and served as an instructor on aero engines. Cyril Cannan was widely respected in Sutton Coldfield and was well known in the motor trade throughout the Midlands, although he was considered by some to be an overbearing individual.

John's mother was short and fair-haired, neat in her personal appearance and also in the well-ordered way she ran her household. She provided a comfortable, stable home for her husband and their three children. John probably acquired his habits of personal neatness and sense of good taste from his mother.

'Little Johnnie' was a boy with dark hair and piercing blue eyes beneath dark eyebrows that would converge over his nose as he grew older. Like his father, he reacted quickly if he did not get his own way and soon became something of a young tyrant, with the whole household revolving round his whims and wants. John grew up expecting to have his own way in everything, while his father, a fractious man, always found fault.

Mrs Cannan was frequently the peacemaker between an ill-tempered husband and a wilful son. Her calming influence reflected an inner strength, which was to be amply tested by the tragedies that were to come. John may have interpreted his mother's acquiescence as weakness in the face of dominant forces. Certainly, he would grow up with an ambivalent emotional attitude towards women. They were something to be controlled, and, when they reacted independently, he took violent steps to control them. He was capable of loving relationships but, when he was thwarted, he preyed on female vulnerability as a means of releasing his frustration.

John was a loner with a strong sense of his own power. As an adult he would say, 'I always wanted to be "TOP GUN" and, because I was talented and worked hard, ALWAYS WAS TOP GUN.' He regarded his abilities as second to none and those associates in his working life as a car salesman who regarded him as insufferable he dismissed as 'B minus'. He despised weakness and the resentment he saw as projected by people who suffered from a sense of inferiority. He characterised himself as 'Big head – big mouth', while his colleagues called him 'Billy Liar'.

He also regarded himself as a sensitive personality and developed a liking for reading philosophy. Perhaps he realised that the power to be derived from knowledge would lend strength to his already burgeoning self-confidence. When he played truant from school, he did not waste his time but, with admirable self-motivation, spent hours in public libraries learning about the things that interested him. Others have indulged this kind of random education which can create specialised knowledge but often at the expense of structured learning.

John Cannan matured as a person with an unshakeable faith in his own abilities. He believed himself to be knowledgeable, aggressively competitive and with a taste for the finer things of life. He also became aware of the magnetism of his own personality. As we have seen, as a boy in his parents' home, he had always got his own way. As a youth he had enjoyed the power bestowed by driving fast, shiny motor cars and as an adult he discovered his sexual power. To his handsome looks and self-confidence, he added the civilities of good taste. He dressed well, favouring smart business suits, and, once he had acquired his own flat, he furnished it tastefully. He also knew how to charm his way to acceptance by his female companions with gifts of champagne and roses.

After a period in which he indulged all his considerable attributes of charm, knowledge and self-assurance – a time which he later described as consisting of 'a hundred one-night stands' – John's confidence was sky-high. He could do anything he wished. He was living in 'cloud cuckoo land'. In reality he had little ambition: he was a car salesman who portrayed himself as a businessman. Self-deception began to emerge and, with it, a fatally flawed personality who was never wrong about anything.

John's education began when he was four years old and his parents sent him to a private school for boys. They chose Keyse, situated high on a hill overlooking parkland, not far from his home. The school stood in spacious, well-tended grounds with secret paths threading their way through forests of mature scarlet rhododendrons. It was a place, he said later, where 'the better off sent their prodigal sons'. Among his first childhood memories were feelings of excitement about going to school. There were no tears over leaving his cosseted home life, just natural boyish high spirits which were borne out in conker fights, Dinky Toy swaps and improvised football games. In a nostalgic reference to these early school days, he spoke about his form teacher who had a weakness for eating biscuits during breaktime. In an early demonstration of his blue-eyed charm, John wheedled his way into the affections of the teacher who eventually shared her biscuits with him. 'She melted,' he said, 'and our morning breaks were nearly always spent sitting next to each other with yours truly chomping away at her "bikkies" and looking up at her adoringly. And adore each other, we did.'

Academic work was taken seriously and there was always plenty of prep. The rule on the sports field was that 'Keyse boys don't cry'. John loathed cricket but enjoyed his rugger, despite never doing anything well enough. Pupils were bawled at when they lost, on the grounds that they should have done better, and bawled at when they won, for not doing better still.

His mature recollections of the first years at Keyse were of happy times but of tough discipline. But then the headmaster at Keyse moved. His successor brought in a new regime and new staff to enforce it. Beatings became a regular part of the school routine and a threatening atmosphere pervaded the classrooms. But there was worse to come.

When John was seven or eight years old he suffered an experience that marked him badly. A teacher took him into a vacant classroom and told him to drop his trousers. He then touched him between the legs and wanted John to feel him as well. John was wary of the teacher anyway and, in total fear, did as he was told. 'It went on for months,' said John, 'and it was something I couldn't share with anyone. It was dirty and horrid and I felt ashamed.'

After that, school became a place of horror and, not surprisingly, John employed every dodge he could think of to avoid going there.

He became a nervous, highly strung child and developed a bad stammer. His mother took him to the family doctor and, at nine years of age, he was taken away from Keyse school and the misery it held for him. The experience had stigmatised him and more forcibly because he felt unable to discuss his feelings with his parents.

Many years later, writing from prison, he recalled the original headmaster at Keyse whom he described as a 'super bloke', and spoke of how things later went sour. During a visit to the family home in 1987 he had gone for a walk on his own and could not resist the temptation to amble up to the old school. The Victorian building which had stood at the top of Wyndley Lane had been demolished by then but the memories came flooding back: 'the fear, the canings, the assaults – everything'.

John had an uneasy relationship with his father, who was quick to criticise and had an unpredictable temper. The parental philosophy, like that at Keyse, was to bear up with life's trials. 'He was only ever proud of me when I came first,' John remarked of his father. Any complaints about ill treatment at school obviously did not fall into a prize-winning category.

John was 12 years old before he understood the unsavoury experience to which he had been subjected. He said that he began to feel 'somehow different and estranged from other people. It felt as if I had done something so terribly wrong.' There were times when he suddenly felt very low, unhappy and totally worthless. These feelings began to affect his behaviour and he found he could not apply himself consistently to any activity. Following another visit to the family doctor in his early teens, he was referred to a psychiatrist at Good Hope hospital. Of the consultation which took place, he said he was 'too embarrassed to really open up'.

He believed his problems went far deeper than willpower or strength of character. 'I realised,' he wrote later, 'that emotionally I had a problem and one which was tending me to hold people away at arm's length.' He did not have any close friends, and developed no close bonds with his brother and sister. He blamed what happened at Keyse for making him different from other people. 'Different,' he explained, 'because I'd been involved in something dirty despite being involuntary. From Keyse onwards, I've always harboured humiliation and shame and, arising from them, anger and a simmering resentment.'

Claims of child sexual abuse are one of the standard means that perpetrators of sexual violence use to justify their acts.

John's rationalisation of these events came after his life was shattered by his conviction for murder. In Wakefield prison, contemplating his chances of a successful appeal, he had plenty of time to examine those experiences that might have contributed to his failure. Blaming the system or the actions of others for his own misfortunes has been part of John's raison d'être since conviction. But there can be little doubt that he felt traumatised by those early events.

Denied a family environment in which his feelings of shame could be properly explained, he felt anxious and alone, a very unhealthy prospect for a young boy. 'It was after this period,' he said later, 'that I began to commit crime.'

A measure of his disorientation lay in the indecent assault which he committed when he was 14 years old. He accosted a young woman in a telephone kiosk and put his hand up her skirt. His parents were utterly shocked and their son was given 12 months' probation.

John continued his education, although he was frequently a truant. He was unhappy at home due chiefly to the overbearing attitude of his father. The time he spent in public libraries perhaps helped him to gain five Certificates of Secondary Education (CSEs) and three Ordinary Level General Certificates of Education (GCEs). His athletic prowess won him an offer of a Sports Council grant to train with the Birchfield Harriers, a leading athletic club, but John's father was against the idea.

John left school at the age of 17 and joined the Merchant

Navy. This was perhaps a bid to escape from his unhappy family life but lasted only three months. (We have no direct information on this and can only surmise that joining the Merchant Navy was an attempt to break the family bonds. But, having gone to sea, he probably found life too restrictive and subject to discipline.) He respected his father's engineering background and, through him, developed a life-long love of cars. Mr Cannan was general manager at Reeve & Stedeford, whose prestigious showrooms in Birmingham were filled with the latest models of the famous marques in British car manufacturing. Young John was taken on visits to car factories and later acknowledged his father's influence. 'Through him,' he said, 'I grew up enchanted with such names as Austin of England, Morris of Oxford and MG at Abingdon...'

John became a car salesman in his father's firm but at a difficult time for British manufacturers. Foreign imports, particularly from Japan, were affecting home sales. He regarded it as a matter of pride that he was selling British cars while many of his fellow salesmen had defected to sell imported models.

These were happy times and he enjoyed the glamour and the people associated with the motor trade. Nevertheless, as he acknowledged later, his real ambition was to have qualified for university entry at 'a really great university like Oxford or Cambridge. Academia is where I really at heart wanted to be.' (As we shall see in the final chapter, this unrealistic idea of one's own potential is frequently a characteristic of men committed to serial violence.)

The life of a car salesman had its advantages, of course, and access to cars was one of them. He recalled enjoyable times with the Sutton fast crowd, 'dancing at The Belfry and screaming through the back lanes of Sutton in our Jag, TR7 and company demonstrators'. John had not the slightest doubt about his abilities at this time. 'We were factory-trained sales executives conversant in finance depreciation, projection, motor engineering and responsible for six-figure sales turnovers.'

However, the sad account of his traumatic school abuse and his description of himself as a sales executive come only from the mind and pen of John Cannan. Perhaps he was abused at school: we can only take John's word for that. But when we read his own job description we catch another glimpse of John's inflated opinion of himself. In reality, he was simply a car salesman in the second-hand department. The finance depreciation he refers to can be found in the car dealers' reference book, *Glass's Car Guide*. Projection presumably is of a financial nature and a word used by John to dress up his own importance. He was not factory-trained in sales or motor engineering nor was he responsible for six-figure sales turnovers.

But these 'happy and vibrant times', as John described them in Biggles-like terms, came to an end when he married in May 1978. June Vale – a pretty, home-loving girl with light-brown hair – worked in a florist's shop near the garage. She was his one and only steady girlfriend and their engagement lasted for seven years.

John claimed later that he had suggested she had other boyfriends before committing herself to marriage, believing this might have alleviated later difficulties, the nature of which he does not explain. The unusually long engagement to June seems at odds with John's later promiscuous activities but he was very much a loner with few, if any, really close friendships.

When they married at Four Oaks Methodist Church, Birmingham, John's younger brother Anthony was the couple's best man. John had the customary stag-night celebration but those who attended were mainly Anthony's friends, not John's. Yet, if style was anything to go by, the couple had a good start. 'My marriage was motor-trade blessed,' said John, 'with two beautiful dark-blue Rolls-Royce Shadows provided by the company.' Such a blessing it was that no one from the motor trade attended his stag night.

In John's view, the couple were 'rushed into marriage', chiefly by June's parents. After seven years, this might be thought rather an odd statement. With all the benefits of hindsight, John claimed, 'I never would have married her but everybody was trying to hassle me into it, her side especially.' The newlyweds did not have a home of their own so they went to live with John's parents. Despite this, they came under pressure to start a family. John alluded to differences in status between the two families and suggested that his mother-in-law wanted to consolidate her daughter's position with the Cannans.

According to John's account, his wife became pregnant against his wishes and, while he acknowledged that pregnancies can be accidental, 'that one wasn't'. He claimed that June had been meticulous in taking the pill, so he thought it was strange that 'she "forgot" two weeks after her Mum had "asked me" about when we planned to start a family'. The couple were trying to buy a flat in nearby Minworth and John was seeking to establish a career for himself in the motor trade. 'I really could have done without all that extra trouble,' he said.

Later, writing from prison in November 1989, John recalled the pressures of marriage as a turning point in his life, one 'that ruined all those previous years of happiness and success'. He said that from a spiritual point of view things got on top of him at this point 'and I began to slide downhill'.

Instead of going home after work to join his wife and daughter, Louise, he would lock up the showroom and drive into Birmingham. There he would buy dinner at The Albany or go to the Opposite Lock, a nightclub and rendezvous for the motor trade. He was smoking and drinking heavily. As he put it, 'Booze there most certainly was, and a string of girls and one-night stands.' By 1980, at the age of 26, John was practically an alcoholic.

Apart from the bitter tragedy he was building for himself, he was also about to snare others in a web of violence.

2

'SHARON'

John had effectively deserted his wife and daughter by the end of 1979. He was working six days a week and frequently put in two evenings a week at the showroom as well. Social drinking became something more serious and he had begun to slide into alcoholism. 'If you've ever wondered why the Scots are so aggressive,' he wrote, 'it's because whisky has a capacity to affect and radically change your personality and behaviour. Gin, it's true, can make you depressed, whisky, however, just makes you plain nasty, at least to some people it can.'

In February 1980, John thought his fortunes had changed for the better. He walked into an off-licence in Sutton Coldfield and bought a case of wine. It was Valentine's Day and he and the girl behind the counter, Sharon Major, were immediately attracted to each other. She remembered John as 'the best-looking man I'd ever met and immediately I had a physical attraction towards him'.

They laughed and joked and agreed to meet after work.

He followed up by sending her roses at the shop and she was won over by his charm.

Sharon was a vivacious woman with an open, trusting face, framed by longish fair hair. Aged 32, she was six years older than John. She was married with two children but was on the verge of separating from her husband, although they continued to occupy the same house. When John asked her out, she accepted and he explained that he was divorced, which was not true at that time, and that he worked as a sales manager at a local car showroom, which was not strictly accurate either.

When his father learned of his son's extra-marital liaison, he took an uncompromising moral line, which John described as supercilious. There was a showdown. John left his job, and he left his wife and child.

'I packed my bags,' he said, 'and checked in at Sutton House [a guest house in Chester Road, Erdington].' He had stayed there before with one of his conquests from the 'hot spots of Birmingham'. He described his technique: 'Buy 'em a drink, tell 'em I love them, tell 'em they were the best thing since sliced bread then take them to the Sutton House Guest House for a cheap night of easily forgettable passion.' On this occasion, there were no cheap pleasures – he was broke and craving alcohol.

Despite his low state, he and Sharon hit it off and became regular companions. In April 1980, he left the guest house and went to live with Sharon and her children. By this time, her husband had left home. For the next six months or so, their relationship seemed to prosper. John had acquired a ready-made family with Sharon's two youngsters, a boy aged four and a daughter aged six. 'I took very seriously my role as their surrogate dad,' he said. He bought them toys occasionally and took the little boy to his first football game, Aston Villa v. Birmingham City. 'We sat munching hamburgers,' John recollected, 'and he learned how to call the referee a "pillock".' He said the girl was backward for her age and he and Sharon took her to see a specialist at the children's hospital.

They went on trips as a family, including a visit to Blackpool and to Sharon's parents at Ilfracombe. John discovered – as all dads, surrogate or otherwise, do – that entertaining children was expensive. He bought them each a bicycle for Christmas 1980; second-hand machines which he painted up, because funds would not run to new ones. Their financial problems became more acute when John lost his job through taking a vehicle without authority from the car firm that was employing him at the time.

In time Sharon came to realise that a great deal of what John had told her about his background was untrue. She encountered June Cannan in the local Safeway store and discovered that she was still married to John. She had baby Louise with her in a pushchair. Sharon did not challenge him about this immediately as he was busy looking for another job but she had a new slant on his character. She later described him as 'extremely plausible and convincing'.

Their sexual relationship was described by Sharon as being 'normal, healthy and active'. She regarded him as a demanding lover and he varied his technique. They did not use any sexual aids and bondage was never employed. 'John was what I would describe as a very physical lover,' she said after their affair had finished. More recently in an interview with one of the authors, she was to alter her previous accounts by stating that he was no great shakes in bed. Harsh words and accusations would later be voiced about the use of 'prosthetics', as John liked to call sexual aids, and of attempts to commit anal intercourse. But, by then, their relationship had long been over.

If John was an attentive lover, he was also a jealous one. He claimed that he became fed up with men telephoning Sharon at home while he was there and also with men calling at the house when he was out. One evening he became so incensed when a male acquaintance phoned Sharon from The Belfry that he leaped into his car and drove off to confront him. He walked into the golfers' lounge at the club and called out the man's name. He was told that he had left. According to John, the man turned up at the house on the following evening and a row ensued in the street. No blows were exchanged but John felt he had done enough to demonstrate that, as he put it, Sharon could not have her cake and eat it too.

In one of his letters written from prison, John talked of his strong desire to keep the family together, 'to forge a more constructive future for us all,' he claimed.

But the odds were not running in his favour. He took a job with a car firm in Bideford, Devon, which Sharon believed was in expectation of her moving to live near her parents in Ilfracombe. Indeed, John spent his weekday nights with her parents and commuted to Sutton Coldfield at weekends.

Sometimes John stayed with his mother in order to see his wife and daughter. The financial implications of sustaining this complicated existence were crippling him. He was, in effect, trying to support two families while living apart from both. He described it as 'Pressure with a capital P'. Something had to give and cracks began to develop in his relationship with Sharon.

John was besotted with Sharon and her maturity appealed to him. He was frank about his drinking but he lied to her over his finances. 'She was, or seemed to be, the answer to a prayer,' he said when he moved in to live with her in April 1980. But as his financial situation deteriorated, so his drinking accelerated. He claimed he was paying maintenance to June, supplementing Sharon's income when he could, while paying rent on a cottage in Devon in the hope of moving with Sharon and her children. 'Financially, I was trying to do the impossible, my income was falling considerably short of my outgoings and every month my bank overdraft was getting bigger.' In addition to this burden, he was having to finance his drinking which now amounted to a bottle of Scotch daily.

Circumstances took a toll on their relationship. They argued about the slightest thing and John was jealous of Sharon's other relationships. On one occasion he gave her a black eye and she began to realise that, while John could be loving and caring, he also had another, more sinister side to his character which frightened her. 'I realised that there was an extremely evil streak in him,' she said later. Sharon, by this time, wanted their relationship to finish but she did not know how to go about ending it: 'One part of me still wanted to be with him but common sense told me it had to end.'

Matters came to a head with the approach of Christmas. There was an argument because Sharon's husband was coming to the house to visit the children on Christmas Day and Boxing Day.

'He wasn't going to stay at my house,' said Sharon, 'just visit.'

John took exception to the idea that Sharon's husband, who, as he saw it, had walked out and left the family, had decided to spend the Christmas holiday at home and be a father again. 'That I strongly objected to,' he said, and he pleaded with Sharon to make a clean break with her husband. After much argument, he lost his case and, as he later described it, 'The upshot was that I spent that Christmas alone in a small hotel in Erdington.'

Sharon did not see John again until he turned up at the house on 30 December in the early afternoon with a bottle of wine. She said he suggested that 'as we'd always had such a lovely time together and been so close to each other ... that we have one more time in bed.' She yielded and he opened the bottle.

The way John put it was that Sharon did not want their relationship to end. 'It was me who alluded to it,' he said. 'We went to bed and tried to patch up our differences but we'd both been drinking and started to argue. She said the wrong thing and suddenly I snapped.' John's description of events seemed to take account of the brittle nature of his own temperament.

What followed was the subject of much bitterness and later recrimination. Sharon's account was that, during intercourse, John put his hands around her neck so that she had difficulty breathing. 'I told him to stop, saying, "Don't, you'll kill me doing that." He said, "I mean to kill you. I'm going to kill you. You've hurt me so badly, I'm going to hurt you too."' Sharon was terrified by the fierce expression on John's face. She tried to get off the bed but he held her down by placing his body across hers. She reacted by screaming and punching him about the head; she pleaded with him to stop and think about her children. 'I don't give a fuck about them,' was his menacing reply.

Sharon's recollection was that John then reached out for the plastic bag that he had brought with him into the bedroom and emptied the contents on to the bed. 'There was a vibrator,' she said, 'a gun and a pair of black rubber pants with a false male penis fitted to it.'

He picked up the gun, pointed it at her face and said, 'This is loaded.' Sharon was now convinced that he intended to kill her. She struggled to seize hold of the weapon and direct it away from her. 'Between us,' she said, 'we pulled the trigger.' As a result the gun fired an air pellet which lodged in the wall. She recognised the gun as an air pistol that they had used during the summer to shoot at targets in the garden. 'I knew that it fired one pellet at a time,' she said.

After Sharon had managed to throw the gun on to the floor, John tried a different tactic. 'I'm going to screw your backside,' he shouted. He failed in his attempts because she struggled furiously but he did succeed in twice penetrating her vagina with the vibrator. She began to bleed heavily but, undeterred, he had sexual intercourse with her wearing the false penis. 'He made extremely violent love to me with this thing which hurt me a great deal,' she claimed. Sharon's screams were heard by neighbours but they turned up their record-player to drown out the noise.

The couple were engaged in a grim struggle with Sharon several times trying to get off the bed. She was bleeding internally and also from the mouth and nose where he had struck her in the face. She grabbed his testicles to try to stop his continuous attack, 'but that just made him more violent than ever … John was so evil,' she said, 'looking almost possessed.'

At one point she lost consciousness and remembered coming to with John slapping her face and saying, 'I haven't finished with you yet.' He called her a whore and a bitch and renewed his attempts to achieve anal intercourse. Nearing exhaustion after two hours of trying to fend him off, Sharon consented to his demands provided she could use a lubricant. 'Let me get some Vaseline,' she asked. This was a ploy to get out of the bedroom in the hope of making a dash down the stairs.

With one arm across her neck and the other holding her arm across the back, John 'frogmarched me towards the other bedroom', said Sharon. She found the Vaseline and he began to manoeuvre her back to the main bedroom.

Thinking that he was going to kill her or at least subject her to further sexual abuse and physical attack, Sharon made her move at the head of the stairs. She said afterwards, 'I'd be better off dead or paralysed than face going back into that bedroom.'

Sharon pushed John, causing him to lose balance, and they both fell down the stairs. They tumbled into the stairwell and Sharon hurt her back. 'I couldn't have fought with him any more. I was so physically drained.' At this point, she recalled later, John reverted to his old self. He was caring and full of apologies. 'Oh my God,' he said. 'What have I done? I'm sorry.' While he telephoned for an ambulance, Sharon tried to stand up, thinking he was still going to kill her, then she blacked out.

On the way to hospital in the ambulance, she asked him, 'You really did mean to kill me, didn't you?'

'Yes, I did,' he replied.

Sharon was treated in the casualty department and John remained with her until the police arrived. She gave him her house keys and told him to remove 'all his horrible things'. She called a woman friend who drove to the hospital and took her home. By then, John had collected and removed the contents of his plastic bag, leaving the house keys behind.

Sharon said that she was battered and bruised with a swollen face and two black eyes. Her facial injuries necessitated dental treatment on her front teeth and she said that John had pulled out so much of her hair 'that you could have made a wig with what came out'. Her parents travelled up from Ilfracombe to look after her. 'I told both of them about the physical attack,' she said, 'but I omitted to tell them about the sexual side of the assault.' Her father was shocked at her appearance and hardly recognised her.

Sharon did not report the assault to the police on the grounds that she had no faith in the legal system. She felt that she had only just escaped being killed and that if she lodged any complaint against John 'he might get only a few years' imprisonment' and might 'track me down and finish off what he had started'.

She added that she was afraid he would try to get to her through the children. 'I was absolutely terrified of John.' She regarded the day of the attack as the end of their relationship and resisted John's subsequent attempts at reconciliation.

Her account of the stormy and painful conclusion of her affair with John Cannan came seven years after the event and at a time when he was in police custody. In even the most timid of lovers' tiffs, the partners will disagree over the circumstances. This far more serious encounter was to prove no exception and John's account differed substantially.

In correspondence with the authors, John referred on many occasions to the assault on Sharon, repeatedly denying that he made a sexual attack on her. He admitted making what he called a serious assault and acknowledged using sexual prosthetics in the course of lovemaking, which he thought probably accounted for the difficulties she subsequently encountered with her vaginal coil. 'The truth is,' he alleged, 'she was an instructive, older and enthusiastic partner...'

John called Sharon's version of events 'tripe', and maintained that she suffered 'terrible emotional insecurity and [sought] acceptance and comfort from as many people as possible, especially men, which tend[ed] largely to make her stray'. Sharon, he said, 'wasn't sugar and spice and all things nice ... but a devious and calculating woman, who frankly couldn't be trusted.' He maintained that her failure to report a sexual assault to the police in 1981 was because no offence had occurred.

His version of events was that he had been incensed over Sharon's decision to have her husband home at Christmas. He also claimed to have discovered that she had been 'a little more than just a friend', as he put it, to a male acquaintance. 'Never have I been so angry,' he said, 'I really slagged her off.' He told her their affair was over; they shouted at each other and blows were struck. 'I hit her and I hit her hard ... I wanted to hurt her, I did hurt her.'

John claimed that she exaggerated her injuries and denied that any of her hair was pulled out. 'So "serious" were her facial injuries,' he said sarcastically, 'that neither the ambulanceman, the hospital doctor or her doctor ... had any recollection of her condition.' He alleged she had 'told a tissue of lies and made herself sound and look extremely silly'. He believed that 'anybody with a modicum of common sense and experience of both people and life could not fail to deduce her malice and spitefulness'.

These recollections of events came in letters written by John from prison ten years afterwards while he was facing the prospect of serving a life sentence. He blamed Sharon for precipitating the end of their affair which 'occurred against the background of considerable provocation'. Yet he claimed that he had tried to repair their relationship, using what little money he had to hire a car to drive down to Ilfracombe to find her. 'What I wanted to do,' he claimed, 'was to apologise and get us back as a family together again.' His trip proved futile because Sharon was not at her parents' home. In February 1981, he returned to the house at Sutton Coldfield. 'We sat in the kitchen and I begged Sharon to forgive me for hitting her, I was truly sorry.'

Although John denied sexual assault, he acknowledged the use of 'prosthetics'. Why he chose to associate this word with sexual devices is unknown. Hardly an everyday term, the word describes the branch of surgery concerned with prosthesis, the replacement of a missing bodily part with an artificial substitute. He claimed that these devices, these sexual aids, were left at Sharon's home by a man friend who was the producer of pornographic video films in which they 'were used as props'.

He claimed that he was sexually inexperienced but Sharon introduced him to 'things I'd never known before'. He also alleged that to avoid any trouble with her husband, he agreed to store the sexual aids at his home where they were later discovered by the police, concealed in the attic

23

along with a large assortment of pornographic videos and magazines.

John also denied that anal intercourse had ever played a part in their relationship. Sharon claimed that he asked for anal sex on one occasion earlier in their relationship, which she had refused. He did not press the issue again until the day of his assault on her. She recalled 'that there was something quite different about him on that occasion.' She sensed in his demeanour that something was wrong. He was more physical than usual in the lovemaking that preceded the attack. She had consented to what she thought would be the final time together before their relationship ended. But from the moment he tried to strangle her and in every act that followed, she said John was behaving totally against her wishes. 'There was no way I'd ever consent to that sort of treatment from any man,' she said.

Of John's character, Sharon's assessment was that he was really in love with himself. He was 'always looking into the mirror', was vain about his appearance and was always clean and well groomed. In fact women have described John Cannan as being too pretty. She described him as a complete loner, 'very deep, with no friends at all, male or female'. He was a person who lived in a world of his own, but the things he said 'were so plausible and with a degree of truth in them'. 'I didn't know what to believe in the end,' she said despairingly. John's vanity was perhaps an outward sign of his inner emptiness and feelings of rage. His self-obsession was clearly indicated in subsequent interviews with the police.

Sharon denied having any other men friends during the time she spent with John. 'I was too scared and frightened of him to do that.'

John was always eager to go out when he was with Sharon whether he had money or not. She paid her share of the expenses and said that she never saw him with large amounts of money.

Of his moods, she claimed, 'As long as everything was going his way he was nice, and charming. He could sell sand to the Arabs, he had that much confidence. When things were against him, then he changed. The evil side of him showed through. He used to flick from one mood to another.' Sharon clearly understood John's mercurial temperament and had been subjected to a demonstration of what happened when he lost control.

John was first questioned officially about the sexual assault on Sharon some three months afterwards on 14 March 1981 while in custody at Sutton Coldfield police station in connection with a later offence. He was interviewed by Detective Sergeant Barry Butler and Detective Constable Brock Harrison. He acknowledged that he and Sharon had 'a terrible argument finishing up with us having an awful fight ... I admit that I went too far and hurt her.'

Butler told him that a letter had been found in his flat as a result of a police search. It was addressed to him by Sharon and was dated 26 February 1981. She referred to the incident on 30 December of the previous year and described John's conduct as evil, wicked, brutal and depraved. 'From enquiries we have made,' said Butler, 'we believe that you forced Sharon to have sex with you in various positions. Is that right?'

John replied, 'Well, it's not quite as simple as that. Let me explain.'

John went on to say they were having a great time in bed when Sharon brought up the subject of her other men friends, 'as if to try and upset me'. The result was that he lost his temper and hit her about the head and body. 'I just lost control and went stupid,' he said, and added, 'Looking back now I am ashamed of it and it seems that, although it was me, that it was someone else.'

This was a significant admission. At face value, it was simply a convenient way of making himself remote from the attack but perpetrators of serial violence are known to experience such feelings. (Ted Bundy, a US serial killer, talked about his victims as if he were watching a film.) DC Harrison asked John if he was saying that after losing his temper he assaulted her and forced her to have intercourse against her will and that she objected strongly. He said, 'Yes, she was shouting and hysterical. I just tried to hurt her as she's hurt me.'

DS Butler then asked, 'You are clearly admitting then that you raped her, aren't you?'

In a clear acknowledgement of his actions, he replied, 'Yes, I suppose it amounts to that; she upset me so much.'

It would be more than six years before John Cannan was questioned again about his assault on Sharon Major. After his arrest at Leamington Spa on 29 October 1987, he was taken to Bristol and held in custody there on suspicion of abducting Shirley Banks. Sharon Major made a statement to the police regarding her former boyfriend in which she said, 'I won't be happy until I know he's locked up and I'm safe forever from him and his evil ways.'

During a long series of tape-recorded interviews carried out at Filton, Bristol, John was questioned by Detective Chief Inspector Bryan Saunders of the Avon and Somerset Constabulary about the assault on Sharon. This was part of a marathon contest between John and the police following his arrest. His attitude was confrontational and certainly far from contrite. He always had an alternative explanation for events on the tip of his tongue and showed flashes of one of his strongest personality traits, which was that he thought he was never wrong about anything.

The first reference to Sharon came in John's answers to questions about his life and background. He mentioned the break-up with his wife, June, and the subsequent relationship with a lover which ended on an unhappy note. 'Is it Sharon you're talking about?' asked Saunders.

'It is Sharon,' replied John. He painted her in poor colours, calling her a 'slag' and describing her as irritable and bad-tempered. He put her moodiness down to 'an operation for her thyroid glands', adding for the benefit of the detectives, 'It is a well-established medical fact that when you have an operation for thyroid it can change your personality.'

Saunders reminded him of the allegations made by Sharon. John's reaction was to say that they were totally unfounded. 'I did not sexually assault Sharon,' he asserted. Reminded that the allegations made were not exactly run-of-the-mill, John chimed in claiming that she was prone to exaggeration and that she had merely jumped on the bandwagon after he had been arrested. 'You know what it is when somebody's arrested, anybody who's got a grudge against you – oh he's a bastard, you know the usual – it's human nature.' Somewhat aggressively, he said he was becoming a little tired of having Sharon Major constantly thrown up in his face. 'If you put something to me in a suggestive way,' he told Saunders, 'you do it with firm evidence ... you back it up, or you don't put it to me.'

Whatever his thoughts might have been at that moment, Bryan Saunders kept them to himself.

The detective asked John why Sharon hated him sufficiently to make the allegations. John referred again to 'the bloody thyroid operation' which he claimed altered her personality. He also alleged that Sharon consorted with a man who produced pornographic films and had offered her a part in one of them. 'All my friends said to me at the time, "John, what are you doing?" You know, "What are you doing? She's no good, she's rubbish." My family said that, even neighbours.' But he added that he did not listen because he was in love with her.

John's explanation was that Sharon could not substantiate the allegations of a sexual attack, which is why she did not make a formal complaint to the police at the time. 'I love people who make allegations,' he said cynically. 'It satisfies their little minds, that's fine.' He told Saunders that he had upset people in his time, including irate husbands who had chased him, and he boasted of having beaten a hasty retreat down a hotel fire-escape on one occasion. His point was that maintaining affairs with married women involved risks and frequently resulted in accusations of various kinds. The detective chief inspector acknowledged that it might be one of the hazards of such activities but John told him, 'You haven't got the point I'm making ... there are people who have a vested interest in having a go at me.' It was a theme to which he would return later.

John was asked if he had a capacity for sexual violence. Again Sharon's name came up. John said, 'We had the most amazing fight in which she was very badly injured. I do admit that to be so.' Saunders asked if it was true that he meant to kill her.

CANNAN: That is a total, total fabrication, that is not so. Wait a minute, wait a minute, wait a minute: could I have said that in, you know, anger? I'm trying to be absolutely specific and truthful, so that you don't get the wrong impression. Could I have said that in anger? But, if I did, I certainly wouldn't have meant it.

SAUNDERS: Well, again, I am reliant on what she's told my officers. What she says is that you said, 'You've hurt me so badly, I'm going to hurt you too.'

CANNAN: I thought you said that I was going to kill her – you've got your story a little bit confused.

SAUNDERS: No, there were two comments.

CANNAN: Oh, I see.

SAUNDERS: OK.

CANNAN: I see. Well, she has a remarkable recollection after eight years. The fact is I did not threaten to kill her. I did hurt her, and I've explained to you, that's to my discredit.

SAUNDERS: OK.

CANNAN: Can I ask you a question? Is Sharon still alive? Presumably she is?

SAUNDERS: Yes.

CANNAN: So, I haven't killed her?

SAUNDERS: No.

CANNAN: Thank you.

In a further interview John claimed that it was difficult for him to recount details of the incident accurately, but he promised his full cooperation provided he was furnished with copies of all the statements. Saunders ignored this request and said that he would put questions as simply as he could. 'Bryan, if I can interject,' said John. 'I think I've made my position very clear, that I am willing to answer any question that you put to me, providing, not unreasonably, that you furnish me with the statements that I have already made.'

Again, the detective ignored this request and reiterated that he would ask questions, and suggested John relied on his memory in answering them. But John refused to let go, saying that he was awaiting Saunders's response. Bryan Saunders told him that he should know enough about police interview procedures to realise that was not how the system worked.

This battle of wits continued, with John confirming his willingness to answer questions but worrying that he would not be able to answer adequately 'through lack of memory'. Saunders was adamant that no statements would be forthcoming. 'I'm going to ask you to rely on your memory,' he said, 'and, in doing that, you can exercise your right to remain silent.'

John sounded almost aggrieved at this. 'I do not wish to remain silent. I want to help you with your enquiry.' He repeated his demand to see the documents that would help him refresh his memory. 'Let's stop the tape for me to have a consultation with my solicitor,' he asked.

Saunders agreed to this but reminded him they were not talking about a routine incident: 'Don't let's smokescreen,' he said.

After John had consulted his solicitor, Jim Moriarty, in private for a few minutes, the interview was resumed. Saunders said, 'OK, I propose to continue the questioning.' John resumed his fencing with the detective, employing evasive tactics.

SAUNDERS: Have you any comment to make on Sharon's

assertion that, during agreed sexual intercourse, you put your hands around her throat and strangled her to unconsciousness?

CANNAN: There is, there exists a great difference of opinion.
SAUNDERS: Did you strangle her or didn't you?
CANNAN: There exists a massive difference of opinion.
SAUNDERS: OK. Have you any comment to make on her assertion that you beat her around the face?
CANNAN: May I refer you to my statements of 1981 and 1985?
SAUNDERS: You mean your statements to the police officers who interviewed you about it?
CANNAN: They did not interview me about it formally; they brought it up in a peripheral sense.

Bryan Saunders switched his questioning to the contents of the plastic bag, which Sharon said John had produced during the assault. John's tactical response was to refer to his previous answers.

'John, why are we going round in circles? Did you or didn't you?'

'I have made my position very clear, Bryan, that, owing to your reluctance to supply me with the witness's statements, my own, my own statements, that I've made my position perfectly clear and I regret it, I bitterly regret your attitude.'

'John, you're smiling, aren't you?' asked Saunders.

Demonstrating the patience of a saint, Bryan Saunders was after a greater prize than trivial admissions regarding the use of sexual aids. He knew that, if it was to be a process of attrition, he would win. In the meantime, he was stuck with a cocky suspect who, after a few further questions, declared, 'I'm sorry the interview is now over.' Undaunted, Saunders pressed forward and, in his own good time, referred to the statement John had made to Detective Sergeant Barry Butler on 14 March 1981. He read it to John in full, including the admission that his attack on Sharon Major amounted to rape.

John's answer to this was: 'The statement that you've read out was not my words verbatim.' He complained that the statement was inaccurate and inconsistent and that his solicitor had not been present at the time.

Saunders asked, 'Did you assault Sharon Major or not?'

'You have a statement in front of you,' answered John. 'May I refer you to the previous statements that we've made for you to draw your own conclusions.'

The detective said his conclusions were of no consequence. 'Did you assault her? Yes or no?'

'I've made my position clear,' said John. 'I am not going to discuss it any further.'

When Saunders proposed to conclude the interview, John asked, 'Did I kill her?'

'I think you're asking me silly questions now,' said the officer.

'Well, now, I mean is she still alive?' John persisted. 'Is she, has she remained unhurt since my release?'

'I think I've answered that question.'

'Well, I don't think you answered hardly anything.'

'I think then we're both in the same boat, John,' said Saunders. 'You've skated around'.

After his break-up with Sharon – whom John called 'the most gorgeous creature' one moment and a 'slag' the next

– he was distraught. 'I left my wife,' he complained, 'lived with this lover, supported her and her two kids for 12 months, paid all the bills, gas, electric, rates, mortgage, housekeeping, children's money, entertainments, clothes, food, paid my wife maintenance and for Louise, my daughter ... our relationship ends.' He loved Sharon, he said, and with greatly exaggerated emphasis claimed he was 'very, very, very, very, very, very, very upset that we'd broken up and I was also upset that I'd hit her'.

John had mixed feelings about what had happened. He missed Sharon and the children but he also blamed her for triggering his subsequent misfortunes. He felt that 'everything I had loved for years had just gone ... Believe me,' he said, 'I didn't want the birds, the booze, the clubs ... I wanted the family again.' He admitted after what he had done, 'It was too late to say sorry,' and he said he 'missed them all dreadfully'.

In a letter to the authors, and in an interview with Christopher Berry-Dee, Sharon strongly contested many of John's assertions about the time they'd lived together. She categorically denied John's assertion that he assisted her financially. 'John never gave me money,' she said. The household bills were paid by her ex-husband and she made her contribution to the welfare of her family through her own earnings. As for John's description of the time he spent with the children, Sharon's view was that he overstated it. He did buy a second-hand bicycle for her daughter at a cost of £10 and repainted it in the kitchen. But he certainly did not spend hours teaching the child to read, she stated, 'patience not being one of his strong points'.

But in John's mind, the affair with Sharon and its unfortunate outcome was pivotal to his future behaviour. 'When we broke up, I broke up,' he said. 'Suddenly, everything was a shambles. No home, no money, no job, no hope. Drink, debt and despair was all that remained. I was just losing control, I let myself go and genuinely felt I could no longer cope. Tears, shakes, depression ... it was a dreadful time. Everything it seemed had been such a waste.' What followed, he rationalised to his own misguided satisfaction, was partly Sharon's fault. She was 'the trigger', he claimed, although not 'the cause'.

John later said, 'I sobbed uncontrollably and shook and felt ill when I hadn't got a drink. Mentally I was breaking up or certainly felt as though I was.' He visited a doctor who gave him a prescription but he did not have sufficient funds to pay the £1.40 charge. He had been contemplating carrying out some kind of robbery for several weeks and had bought a lock-knife to add menace to his demands.

A few hundred yards from the guest house, past the traffic lights, lay Yenton service station. 'I thought, "Do it,"' said John. He walked across to the filling station where the two girls were working behind the counter. 'I don't know who was more scared, them or me.'

Brandishing his knife in the air he demanded cash from the till. The younger girl began to cry. 'It's all right,' he said soothingly, 'just hand over the money.' The other girl handed over about £260. 'Stand still and remain where you are, is that clear?' he ordered. Slowly he turned and made his way out through the door and across the forecourt. He kept telling himself not to attract attention by running away. 'Too bad,' he said later. 'I absolutely bolted as fast as my legs would carry me.' Minutes later he was safely back in his room at Sutton House. With funds at his disposal, he changed and went out to buy a bottle of brandy.

Looking back at this incident, John recalled that he was happy to have the money but felt awful about it. 'I remember thinking,' he said, 'how only 12 months ago I had been a smart and respectable sales exec, with a wife, a child on the way, and the prospect of a home of our own. Now ... sick, broke, living in a guest house, and a criminal.' He would admit to the petrol station robbery when he was interviewed by the police in March 1981 – 'to get it off my chest', as he succinctly put it.

In an effort to be fair to both John Cannan and Sharon Major, the authors spent much time in researching their accounts and claims of the time they spent together. A great deal of what John has written and said is untrue, although he actually believes it to be correct. Sharon Major was undoubtedly swept off her feet by John, a man who could not live up to his over-inflated ego. As their relationship developed, so did the pressure increase on John to live up to the expectations he had so romantically portrayed to his lover. Slowly, the sands of time ran out for him and this resulted in the release of pent-up frustration, culminating in a terrible sexual assault on the young woman.

John has alleged that her behaviour was a 'contributory factor' and he believes she holds herself partly responsible for the circumstances that led up to another serious sexual offence. And in a moment of vehement bitterness, he stated, 'and so in part she bloody well should!' The incident – which he conveniently externalised by saying, 'We both had to share the blame' – was his rape of a pregnant woman.

3
'JEAN'

Jean Bradford was 37 years old and married, with a 17-month-old son. She ran a ladies' knitwear shop in Sutton Coldfield. On Friday, 6 March 1981, she opened the shop as usual at 9.30am and served a trickle of customers during the morning. At 12.30pm she closed the shop and turned the 'Closed' sign round on the door. Her husband collected her and her son and they went off to lunch. They returned at about 2pm and Mr Bradford left his wife and toddler in the shop.

The premises were compact, the shop itself being a room 10 feet wide and some 15 feet deep. At the rear of the shop was a tiny office with a separate door opening on to an alleyway leading to a backyard. The rear of the premises was dimly lit, the only natural light coming from the front window and through a small skylight. Mrs Bradford found it necessary to have the fluorescent ceiling light on all the time she was open for business.

At about 2.15pm the woman from the shop next door

called in for a few minutes' chat and when she departed Jean Bradford was left alone with her son. Half an hour later, around 2.45pm, a man entered the shop. He was holding a handkerchief over his face as if to blow his nose. Just at that moment the telephone in the back office rang and Mrs Bradford made her apologies before going to answer it. She came out of the office to make sure the customer had not left the front door open, as she was afraid her young son might wander out into the street. Having satisfied herself on this point, she offered further apologies and returned to the telephone. The man mumbled something in reply but kept the handkerchief up to his nose and mouth.

With her son by her side, Jean Bradford had to hold the line while her caller was connected. She put her head round the door of the office and said, 'I'm sorry to be so long. Can I help you?' The man gave a nervous sort of laugh and walked into the office. He was holding a knife, which he pointed at her saying he would cut her up unless she kept quiet.

Then he threatened to cut the baby and, putting his finger on the telephone rest, disconnected the incoming call. Mrs Bradford picked up her son and held him to her protectively. The man instructed her to go into the corner of the office and face the wall. Still holding her son and with the intruder's knife at her ribs, she did as she was told.

His commands were emphasised by the repeated use of the expletive 'fucking'. He asked her where the cash was kept. She turned round to show him but he made her face the wall again. She explained that the cash box was behind the curtain that screened the office from the shop. Mrs Bradford's son, sensing his mother's fear, began to scream.

'Stop your little girl,' the man told her. She explained that it was a little boy and that the child was frightened and asked if she could give him a drink that was on the table in the shop. The man stood close to her, touching the knife to her face and telling her 'not to fucking move'.

He went into the shop and returned with the child's bottle, which he thrust into Jean Bradford's free hand. After having a drink, the child calmed down. The intruder located the cash box and spilled its contents on to the floor where he sorted through the change. He then asked where more money could be found, and she told him there was some in a purse on the shop table. Mrs Bradford found difficulty in articulating her words, all the while being threatened with a knife.

Suddenly, the front door of the premises opened and in walked Jean Bradford's mother who was her business partner. 'Tell them that you're closed,' the man instructed.

Jean followed his instructions but her mother only laughed and made straight for the office.

'Who's this?' the man asked.

'It's my mother,' Jean replied.

The two women stood close together while the intruder asked again about money. 'Let my daughter go with the baby,' requested the older woman.

'No,' came the reply, accompanied by the threat that he would cut her if she did not keep quiet.

Jean's mother persisted in her request and Jean could see the man was becoming increasingly nervous. She told her mother to shut up and do as she was told.

The intruder retrieved the purse from the table and brought it into the office. Jean thought it contained £20 in a brown envelope but he couldn't find it. She suggested that it might be in the writing case on the shop table but he couldn't find it there either. 'He was getting really panicky,' said Jean, 'and his voice went up a tone.'

At that moment the telephone rang. The man ordered the two women to stay in the corner. He asked who might be calling. Jean's mother said, 'It might be my husband.' Jean chipped in with 'It could be mine, it could be a customer, it could be anybody.'

The caller was Mr Bradford who was concerned when his wife did not answer his call. The intruder rendered any discussion meaningless by slashing the telephone wire. Then his mood changed. He told Jean Bradford's mother to move into another corner of the office. Then, having cut the cords used for hanging up clothes in the office, he tied her hands together behind her back. Jean could not see what was happening because she was facing the wall but she gathered from his instructions what he was doing. Having secured her feet, he made the older woman shuffle back into the corner and stand facing the wall.

He then turned his attentions to Jean and began fiddling with her dress. She asked him what he was doing and he replied, 'The best way to tie your legs is to get your tights by your feet.' So saying, he pulled her tights down to her ankles and lifting up her skirt, said, 'Beautiful.' He had already told her to put down the child and now instructed her to lower her knickers. She refused but changed her mind when he said, 'Well, you don't want your baby cut.' He then moved behind her and put his left arm around her neck while holding the knife to her face. He whispered that if she didn't want to fucking well get hurt she was to undo his trousers and give him oral sex. 'Please don't,' she begged but he became more threatening and ordered her to kneel down in front of him. He undid his trousers and told her to take out his penis. When she resisted he pointed the knife towards her child and repeated: 'You don't want the baby to get hurt.' She complied with his instructions as minimally as possible; 'I did as little as I had to,' she later told the police in her statement.

The intruder then told Jean to take off her clothes. Fearing what was to come she pleaded, 'Please don't, I'm pregnant.'

Jean's mother endorsed the plea, 'Yes, she's pregnant.'

'I don't care what you are, it doesn't matter to me.'

Again she complied with his instructions but still sought to deflect him: 'Please no, why are you being so mean?'

He said, 'You fucking do it or else.'

When she was stripped naked he told her to lie on the floor but when her son cried, she instinctively leaned across to comfort him. The man shouted, 'All right – stand up,' and, putting an arm around her neck, he raped her where she stood in the presence of her son and her mother.

After he had completed the sexual act, he told her to pull her tights up and, at that very moment, the front door of the shop rattled as someone tried to attract attention from the street. During his to-ing and fro-ing between the shop and the office, the attacker had locked the front door and put the lights out. 'Who's that?' he asked. Jean surmised it might be a customer. 'Do you know a bearded man?' Jean said it might be her husband. She was correct. The door shaking became more frantic but then stopped. Pointing to the rear door of the office, the man asked, 'How do I get out of here? Is that the way out?' He was told that it led into an alleyway. Jean found the key, which was not kept in the lock but on a ledge, and opened the door for him.

Undeterred by the noise that had returned at the front door, the man lingered to tell Jean, 'You might want to know about this, you'll realise later because I'll be dead within a fortnight.' He asked her if she was really pregnant; her mother answered for her: 'Yes.' He said, 'Well, this won't hurt you then.' When he asked for her name and address, Jean gave him the details. 'After all,' as she explained later, 'he'd looked in my purse.' He still lingered, asking where the alleyway led and, on being told it gave access to a car park, asked the two women if they had a car. Jean's mother gave him the keys to her car. He pushed Jean, still half-naked, into the alleyway and told her not to tell the police what had taken place for at least two weeks or something would happen to her little boy because he knew where they lived. He then hurried into a yard, vaulted a fence and disappeared.

After this terrifying ordeal, Jean rejoined her mother and son, then let in her husband who was still frantically hammering on the front door. They telephoned 999 and Jean later completed a statement in which she described her rapist. He was aged between 25 and 30, about 5ft 10in tall and of medium build. He had thick, dark hair which she thought was naturally curly. The man was in need of a shave and appeared to be the type of individual who needed to shave frequently. He had a pale complexion and his face had a good bone structure. He was dressed in a white-and-blue checked shirt, open at the collar with black cord trousers, black shoes and black gloves. His voice bore a slight Birmingham accent. The knife that he had used to threaten the two women was 'like a Boy Scout knife' – a small sheath knife about six inches long. A distinctive feature of the rapist's appearance that Jean had noticed was that his dark eyebrows met across the bridge of his nose.

Detective Chief Inspector Roy Bunn described the attack as 'a very nasty, diabolical crime – more horrible than I can describe'.

A large-scale manhunt was mounted and the police were reported as believing that the attacker was a local man. A photofit picture showing a man with eyebrows meeting over his nose was published in the local newspapers and was shown on television. A police telephone helpline number was widely publicised.

Exactly one week elapsed before the suspected rapist was arrested. Response to the photofit picture of the rapist had been swift and decisive, with the result that John Cannan's name was volunteered to the police. Acting on information received, as official police language put it, John was interviewed and arrested. Within a week of committing the offence, the suspected rapist found himself at Sutton Coldfield police station. Sitting in an interview room John offered an explanation for the shaved space between his eyebrows. 'I suppose you'd say it was vanity,' he told Detective Inspector Clive Mole. Pledging his cooperation, John offered no objection when Mole asked him if the police could search his room at the lodging house where he was living.

DI Mole, accompanied by two other detectives, searched the first-floor room that John rented in Ley Hill Road, Sutton Coldfield. On the top shelf of a fitted wardrobe they found a leather bullwhip and, from the shelf beneath, recovered four lengths of rope coiled together. On another shelf was an envelope addressed to John Cannan containing a letter from Sharon and a colour photograph showing them together. The letter, neatly written, was dated 26 February 1981, and it referred to John as 'evil, wicked, brutal and depraved'.

John was reminded that he had admitted being in the area at the time that Jean Bradford was raped and that he resembled the photofit picture of the rapist, particularly in respect of his eyebrows. He was told that he was being detained on suspicion of having committed that offence and he was cautioned. John said, 'Yes, I've got nothing to hide. I'm absolutely innocent,' and asked, 'What's my eyebrows got to do with it anyway?'

DI Mole told him that one of the most distinguishing features described by the rape victim was that the man's eyebrows met over the bridge of his nose. 'The photofit shows that and that's been published in the newspapers and on the television,' he said. 'The inference is obvious.'

John replied, 'I've already told you it's vanity. When I started going out with Sharon, I tried it to improve my appearance.'

It was obvious to the detective that his attention to vanity was quite recent, for there were two small cuts over Cannan's nose suggesting that he had nicked himself while shaving the area. When it was pointed out that the photograph taken of him with Sharon showed his eyebrows met in the middle, he said, 'I didn't shave them all the time.'

Asked about the letter in which Sharon described him as evil and wicked, John explained that they had had a fight and he had slapped her face a couple of times. DI Mole asked, 'Isn't it a fact that you used a vibrator and other implements on her and damaged her internally?'

John answered in his normal roundabout manner, 'I

used a vibrator, yes, and it may have moved her coil. I was dreadfully sorry afterwards.'

'What else have you used on Sharon?'

'What do you mean?'

Mole referred to the whip that had been found in John's lodgings and asked if he had used it.

'What whip? What are you talking about?'

The bullwhip was produced. 'This was in your wardrobe,' said DI Mole. 'What's it for?'

John reacted immediately. 'No way. Now that's the end of the cooperation,' he shouted. 'You know that it wasn't in my room. You've planted it there.'

'Why on earth would I do that?' said the detective.

'You're looking for somebody a bit kinky,' replied John, 'and you think that proves it.'

After John had been given a break from questioning and provided with coffee and cigarettes, the interview was resumed by DS Barry Butler and DC Brock Harrison. John asked these officers if they were senior to those who had interviewed him during the morning.

'No, we are not. What makes you ask that?' enquired Harrison.

'It doesn't matter,' said John.

The policemen told him they sought his continued cooperation and asked him to supply samples of saliva and pubic hair. 'Are you prepared to do that?'

'Not under any circumstances whatsoever,' retorted John. 'That is an invasion of my liberty and my principles would not allow me to agree to that.'

Harrison's reply was interrupted by John, who launched into a tirade about his treatment. 'Look, I'm very concerned,' he said. 'I've been here all morning, locked up for something that I haven't done. I've cooperated as much as I possibly can. I'm thinking of making a formal complaint against the inspector – is it Mole? He has been on at me all morning regarding the whip that he says was found in the wardrobe of my room. I categorically deny all knowledge of that whip – it is not mine and he has planted it. I have cooperated, but what cooperation can you expect when he's determined to fix me up?'

Harrison gave reassurances that the whip had not been planted and, in any case, did not see what it had to do with the matter in hand. John's reaction was that if the police were prepared to go to the lengths of planting evidence they might plant anything 'to convict me of something I haven't done'.

The officer dismissed this notion as rubbish and reiterated his request that John consent to giving samples of blood, saliva and pubic hair. He pointed out that this was normal procedure in offences of this kind and a way of eliminating people from suspicion as well as implicating them.

John returned to his theme. 'You have already proved,' he said, 'that you can't be trusted because you planted the whip. What about the police surgeon? He could use my body samples to suit your purposes.'

Now it was Harrison's turn to react: 'That is really an outrageous thing for you to say,' he told John.

John stuck to his line that giving body samples was an invasion of his privacy and liberty. Harrison suggested that his liberty was the reason why the samples were requested.

'For you to continue with your present attitude and refuse body samples,' said Harrison, 'can only, in our eyes, or, more to the point, in anybody else's eyes, implicate you further for being responsible for this matter.'

John answered, 'I'm sorry ... You are not having samples from me. My cooperation ended when that whip was planted.'

DS Butler decided for the time being that he would acknowledge the whip did not belong to John and that he had not seen it before, although he insisted that it had not been planted by the police. His plan was to remove an obstacle to questioning and see if he could persuade John to cooperate on other matters. It was to be an uphill struggle. The officer talked for a while about John's family background and the affair with Sharon, which ended with him committing what he agreed amounted to rape. This discussion was carried out in a conciliatory manner, calculated by the detective in the hope of calming John's anxiety to a more relaxed frame of mind. It was a basic part of police interrogation training; however, in this case it proved of little help. Having explored this avenue, Butler returned somewhat hastily to the business of giving body samples. He explained the importance of forensic results and their value in eliminating a person from an inquiry when it was clear they had no involvement. John would not budge on his refusal even when the detectives said they would ask his own doctor to take the samples if he was still worried about the police surgeon. 'No,' he said. 'I cannot forget the bullwhip being planted. I don't trust you.'

'All right,' said DC Harrison and patiently passed on to John's movements that day. 'Let's discuss your movements for Friday, 6 March.'

Let off the hook for a moment, John was willing enough to talk on this subject and launched into a detailed account including times for his activities between 8am and 5.30pm that day. He claimed to have taken a train into Birmingham during the late morning, before returning to Sutton Coldfield at about 1.30pm. He decided to take a long walk in Sutton Park and strolled down towards the shops at about 3pm. (This placed him, by his own admission, outside Mrs Bradford's shop at the time the intruder entered the premises, give or take a few minutes.) After this, he went home, before returning later to Sutton to meet a private detective called Ellis who he wanted to employ to trace Sharon's movements and whereabouts. This was a form of harassment that he would repeat when he broke up with another girlfriend in 1987.

DC Harrison, quick to follow up his initiative, pressed John closely on his precise movements between 2 and 4pm that day. John outlined his itinerary and accepted the detective's suggestion that he had probably left the park at Four Oaks Gate. 'You're right, I remember now,' he said. 'I did, but that doesn't mean to say, because I've been honest and cooperative about that, that I'm the man who raped that woman.'

With John's involvement in an earlier assault case known to them (particularly in the light of the letter from Sharon Major), John's own admission that he was in the area at the time Mrs Bradford was attacked and the photofit resemblance to John (who had recently shaved his eyebrows across the bridge of his nose), all the police needed to sew up the case was a confession from the man sitting opposite them. Harrison explained all this and that John was their prime suspect. Further, his refusal to provide intimate body samples that would eliminate him if he was innocent simply compounded their suspicions.

Like a rat in a trap, John returned to his old dodge. 'Isn't it obvious? You've planted the bullwhip and you could alter their report, couldn't you?' He was referring once again to the possible misuse of his body samples by the police surgeon and the forensic science service.

Using the well-tried 'hard-man/soft-man' technique, the detectives were obliged to explore other possibilities. Barry Butler had discussed John's family background and, being the 'nice guy', now gave John yet another cigarette. The impasse had to be broken. The officer moved on to motor cars, perhaps not fully realising this was one of John's favourite subjects. He elicited the information that 'there are very few vehicles I haven't driven' and very little else. Before returning to the cells just after 5pm, they asked him again to think about providing the body samples that they had requested. John said they were trying to trick him and he wanted time to think.

The holding cell was not exactly well furnished. He sat for a while on the red, rubber-covered mattress, staring at lime-green painted walls. Fish and chips with a cup of tea were pushed through the door but he was denied cigarettes. His shoelaces, belt and tie had been removed and, when he paced to and fro, his trousers flopped around his ankles. John Cannan had been stripped of the things he valued most – his dress sense and vanity. He had to work out a mental balancing act that would suit his needs above all else, yet retain his misguided self-imposed integrity. It was the mention of motor cars by Barry Butler that swayed his decision, for, if Butler knew about cars, he reasoned, then he couldn't be a bad copper.

The interview was resumed at John's request at 8.10pm and Butler went straight to the matter of the body samples again. He told John, 'You will be detained until we are satisfied from our own enquiries that you are eliminated from this inquiry.'

'Yes, all right,' John said. 'I seem to get on all right with you two blokes and you have been very fair with me and explained everything to me as we've gone along. I'm sorry about my attitude. It simply is a case that I feel because of the bullwhip that I can't trust any of you.'

Sensing a softening of John's attitude, the two detectives advised John to forget the bullwhip, for he was a sensible young man. As intelligent people the subject was getting them nowhere. This approach appealed to John.

'Look, you two have been very good, I must say,' John spoke in a conciliatory tone. 'What do I call you? So far it has been very impersonal. I feel that I can trust you two...' The antagonism was crumbling.

The detectives said their names were Barry Butler and Brock Harrison. Once again they returned to the 'hard-man/soft-man' routine to confuse the suspect. But they were confronted by a man who was playing them at their own game. A man who was hostile one moment and placatory the next. John Cannan liked to feel that he was in control. The detectives were nothing if not persistent. 'Isn't it about time that you agreed to supply these samples?' asked Harrison. Butler jumped in with his well-rehearsed speech about the elimination of an innocent person and added the invitation for John to attend an identification parade.

To the amazement of the two experienced detectives, John seemed to leap at this latter suggestion. 'That would be no problem at all,' he said. 'I'll go on one, but I want that done now.' The suspected rapist was still trying to keep control of his predicament.

Harrison, not wishing to rock the boat, explained that it was not possible to make the necessary arrangements so late on a Saturday night.

'Look, are you going to charge me or what?' asked John. He was back to his former evasive self.

'Not at this stage,' said Butler. 'Our enquiries are incomplete and, as we keep trying to tell you, John, we need those body samples.'

'Look, Barry and you Brock, I feel much more at ease with you two, but I am still very confused and unsure. I would like more time to think about it and then I promise you both that I will give you a definite response.' John thought he was back in the driver's seat. Weighing up the odds against him and supplied with coffee and cigarettes, he contemplated his position during a welcome respite of about 30 minutes.

When the interview was resumed, Harrison entered the fray by asking once again if the matter of the bullwhip could be put aside. Could the police surgeon make the necessary arrangements to take John's body samples?

'I've been thinking seriously about this, all right?' John replied, and he asked the detectives to sit and listen. 'Hear me out, will you?' He explained that after his split-up with Sharon he was desperately unhappy. 'I have nobody to turn to,' he said. What followed was a monologue of mitigation that culminated in his admitting that he entered Jean Bradford's shop with the intention to steal money and that rape came as an afterthought. He explained to the detectives that he took her from behind because he didn't want her looking at him during the sexual act and that he would not have harmed any of them, least of all the child. 'I'm not a violent person,' he added. He concluded with the somewhat arrogant statement that he had been more frightened than his victim.

With an admission of guilt under their belts, Butler and Harrison probed further and enquired of Cannan if he remembered the woman saying anything.

'She said that she was pregnant, but I didn't believe her, looking at her. She wasn't, was she?'

'Yes, she is pregnant.'

'Oh, God. Is she all right?'

'As we told you earlier, fortunately she is all right.'

John was asked if he had said anything unusual to the woman.

'I said that I'd be dead within a fortnight. I have seriously considered it, but I'm afraid that I haven't got the guts.' With the pressure released, John went on, 'You've no idea how much better I feel telling you two about this. It's just like me talking about another person, although I know it was me.' As he had when talking about the assault on Sharon Major, John again appeared to be distancing himself from the incident.

The detectives told him that only the man responsible for committing the offence could have described the details he had just related. Harrison asked if he was prepared to put it in writing. 'Yes, do it please, Brock. It's such a relief – do you know that for two days I wanted to come and give myself up, but I talked myself out of that.'

After making a statement that he duly signed at 10.55pm, John was returned to his cell, where he did some more soul-searching, as he demonstrated the next morning. When he greeted Butler and Harrison who were quick from their beds, he addressed them by their first names and said he wished to make a further admission. John then 'coughed' to the Yenton service station robbery. Once again in mitigation for the offence, he blamed his actions on a row with his father that had resulted in his having to leave home (not strictly true), having little money and being forced to live in an hotel room (correct). Sharon Major had apparently gone out of the window now as an excuse for this robbery.

The police had visited John's home and spoken to his now irate father. They returned with a change of clothes and shaving accessories. He was to appear before the Sutton Coldfield magistrates looking respectable. John let it be known that he was now completely happy that the police had not planted the bullwhip found in his lodgings.

Condescendingly, his explanation was that it was probably already on the wardrobe shelf when he moved into the room. 'It was there all the time without my knowing it,' he said. 'I just thought I'd mention it for what it is worth.'

He was then asked to describe the knife he had used to threaten Jean Bradford and referred to it as a 'lock-knife' with a 'chrome or something outstanding button to retract it'. Following John's admission of the rape he had told the police where he had dumped the knife. He had thrown it into a pond known as Blackroot Pool. The weapon was recovered by police frogmen and it was now produced.

'That's it. Isn't it remarkable, Barry? I would have sworn that red button was chrome, but in any event I knew it was outstanding.' He offered his congratulations to the detectives and their colleagues: 'Your lads did well to find that.'

The two detectives stopped short of thanking John for his cooperation but acknowledged his help in finding the knife.

'Well, I told you that I would be as helpful as I could be, and you've no idea how much more at peace with myself and the world I am for being straight about it.'

Looking back on the interview at Sutton Coldfield police station after the passage of several years, John was at pains in his letters to the authors to set the record straight as he sees it. He acknowledged that the statement made by Jean Bradford was '100 per cent true' and 'not exaggerated or embellished in any way'. He also wrote that his signed confession to the offence was in total agreement with her account. But he claimed that the police depositions were wholly untrue insofar as they alleged he admitted making a sexual assault on Sharon Major. Perhaps he had forgotten that he had already admitted using a vibrator on her and committing rape.

He also claimed that he repeatedly asked to have a solicitor present during the interview and was refused until after he had confessed. Mr George Pratt from Conway & Company, solicitors in Sutton Coldfield, at that time represented him.

John said he had denied the offence at first because of the incident over the whip. The whip had nothing whatever to do with the rape offence, but its discovery rankled with him. He said Detective Inspector Mole confronted him with the whip some four hours after he was arrested. The officer held it by placing the forefinger of each hand at the two ends. Holding it thus, he offered it to John to examine. 'He wanted me to touch it – I realised he wanted me to touch it.' John declined and suggested that Mole had it fingerprinted as a sure way of establishing whether or not it belonged to him. 'No need,' he alleged Mole replied. 'It doesn't form part of our case.'

John still insists that the whip was planted when officers arrested him at his lodgings and at a time when he left his room to go to the toilet. The fact that the discovery had been made in front of his landlord he dismisses as being 'totally in character with police ways of doing things'. He adds that he found out later that the whip had been kept in a locker at the police station where it had lain for 11 months after being confiscated during a police raid on a massage parlour. John claims that his informant was a uniformed officer with whom he had become friendly during his appearances at Sutton Coldfield magistrates court. He has constantly denied that he had absolved DI Mole of the allegation that he planted the whip.

While it would be extremely naive to suggest that the police have never planted evidence in an effort to secure a conviction, their reasons for planting a bullwhip among John's possessions seem obscure. After all, there was no link between it and the offence for which he was being questioned. That a uniformed officer should act as confidant to a prisoner suspected and charged with the rape of a pregnant woman, claiming that the whip came from a raid on a massage parlour, brings John's allegations into the realm of fantasy.

John subsequently rationalised his actions leading up to the rape. Where previously he had blamed his father for provoking him to violence, he now blamed Sharon Major for triggering his aggressive outburst. 'It wasn't the real John Cannan in that shop,' he said, 'but a wretched and distressed one.' As he had done previously, he sought to distance himself from the event. But he admitted choosing the knitwear shop as a target for robbery because, apart from money, he thought there might be fur coats that he could steal and sell. Since the shop retails balls of wool, cotton and knitting needles, it was far short of expert planning to think he would find mink and sable coats on the hangers. He claims he had no intention of raping anyone when he entered the shop but, when he could not find money, cash that the unfortunate Jean Bradford told him was in the shop, he felt as if nothing was going right and 'I just blew.'

His recollections of how he felt at that time in the close presence of an attractive and vulnerable woman are perhaps more important. He said he remembered standing close to her and feeling a great mixture of emotions. 'In some ways I didn't even want at heart to be there. I was scared and I was upset, but I needed money. Everything suddenly rose to the surface, all the bitterness and secret personal misery. I wanted her to feel and share my pain. I wanted to humiliate her like I had been humiliated, I wanted her to lose her innocence. I wanted to make her understand. And there was of course only one way to do it.' He raped her and later expressed his sorrow, hoping she would forgive him. 'I know how she must have felt,' he said.

John described his mental status prior to the rape of Jean Bradford as a 'breakdown'. He could neither eat nor sleep and the 'DTs were dreadful,' he said. 'I couldn't stop shaking.'

After he was arrested, Sharon Major went up to Sutton Coldfield police station to visit him but he refused to see her. He described his feelings at the time as 'humble, truthful and sorry' and he has consistently expressed his regrets over the rape.

John was remanded in custody by the Sutton Coldfield magistrates; his solicitor did not apply for bail. On 26 June

1981, he appeared at Birmingham Crown Court where he was jailed for a total of eight years by Mr Justice Stephen Brown – five years for the rape with consecutive sentences totalling three years for taking a car and stealing money. His appeal against the sentence was heard by two Appeal Court judges in London in November. In rejecting the appeal, Mr Justice Skinner commented that the psychological scars of the rape must be very great. John himself acknowledged this, describing what he had committed as 'an appalling offence'.

Prison apparently gave John Cannan further time for reflection. At Horfield prison, Bristol, where he was transferred in February 1982 following his conviction for the rape of Jean Bradford, he was housed in 'B' Wing, which was reserved for prisoners serving five years or more. It is John's inflated claim that he took pride in being considered sufficiently trustworthy to be given what he called 'the top job in the Nick', as the governor's 'red-band' (trusty). Again this provides a valuable insight into the workings of his mind. The red-band or trusty's job entails a position acting as an intermediary between the inmate population and the prison staff, similar to that of a foreman on a shop floor of a factory. The red-band has to be trusted by the 'cons' and staff alike. The nature of John's offence, the rape of a pregnant woman in front of her child, would have been made known to the prison population on his admission to Bristol prison. In reality, John asked for protective custody (Rule 43) in an attempt to save himself from the harm and assault freely administered by inmates to known sex offenders. He was labelled a 'nonce' and a 'wrong 'un' by the convicts and staff alike. More than once he was attacked on the landings and had salt tipped into his pudding, sugar thrown over his dinner and was spat at when collecting his meals. John Cannan was never a 'trusty'.

However, it was at this time that he first met Annabel Rose, who was to be an important feature in his life when he came out of prison. She was a solicitor working for a law firm in Bristol and she advised him about access rights to his daughter Louise. She was in her early thirties, slim with long blonde hair: an attractive and sophisticated professional woman. She was also married but that did not seem to be a barrier to the chemistry her visit created. John said later, 'It was obvious from then that we would have an affair at some stage if we met up again and we both had a feeling that we would.'

John claims he expressed remorse for the offence which put him in prison, and confided his feelings to one or two of the more 'sympathetic staff'. Once again, he claimed that he established a 'special rapport' with an officer at The Verne, a semi-open prison at Portland, Dorset. He was transferred there after life at Bristol became 'unbearable' and prior to release. He was moved in September 1984. 'I wanted to write desperately to the lady involved in the 1981 offence [Jean Bradford],' he said. 'to apologise for what I'd done.' No doubt this was a futile attempt to win the favours of the parole board. The matter was apparently discussed and, wisely, a senior prison officer advised him to let matters rest and to avoid opening old wounds.

Two days after he arrived at The Verne, John received a visit from his father. It would be the last time they saw each other, for Cyril Cannan was terminally ill with cancer. 'Stooping and slight, almost elfin in appearance, his visage was that of a man close to death,' said John. Father and son knew this would be their last meeting. Much bitterness had passed between them and this was an opportunity to make peace with each other. Mr Cannan passed away peacefully at his home in February 1985, soon after John embarked on his prison pre-release programme. 'Did I love him?' asked John in one of his letters. 'Yes, but we fought terribly.'

The good that prison did for John was acknowledged by him when he said, 'It did at least wean me off alcohol, albeit painfully.' For the rest, he found that all his previous ideas about the honesty and fairness of the system were overturned. As he put it, 'Never could the "public image" of our system, espoused so soothingly and plausibly by the Establishment, differ so remarkably, or to such an extent, in its esoteric reality.' Nevertheless, he found humanity in some of the staff, so it was not all bad.

One may wonder how a man facing the prospect of eight years in prison will cope with the loss of liberty and how he will use his time. No doubt John quickly came to terms with being confined: being a loner and very self-contained probably helped. With his keen brain, the world of books and debate appealed to him more than sport or craft pursuits. While these activities might occupy his intellect on a superficial level, the deeper recesses of his mind had to get to grips with his emotions, his ambitions and his sense of self-esteem.

The prison system encourages self-improvement and social rehabilitation in those who opt for it, but it also provides fertile soil for those who turn inwards to the realm of fantasy. There is little doubt that John dreamed of fame and fortune. He wanted to 'be someone' and to acquire the trappings of success – smart clothes, a stylish car and a well-appointed flat, with the lifestyle to match.

There is nothing wrong with such aspirations, which are shared by millions, but John started from a poor base in seeking to acquire them.

For one thing, although he was a bright, articulate and plausible person, the only training he had was that of a car salesman, which was not a route whereby he could achieve his ambitions quickly. For another, he tended to overrate his talents to the point where he alienated people because he always had to prove he was right; humility was not one of John's virtues.

As he emerged from his term of imprisonment, he probably realised that the only way he could savour the good life quickly was by allying his natural wit and charm with criminal means. But there was a darker side to his fantasies too. He bore feelings of resentment towards the forces that had alienated him from society. Whether he realised it or not, his emotions, while fuelling his ambitious drive, were also preparing him to retaliate. He was a man primed for both action and violence, when the opportunity arose or when he was provoked.

4

SANDRA?

Five years passed and, as the time approached for John's release from the prison system, he had to think about where he would stay. He says he refused parole because he did not want to return to live at Sutton Coldfield. That, he thought, 'would be insensitive' and he wanted to avoid having to cross the road to escape former acquaintances, and to keep explaining and making apologies. In reality, John Cannan was refused parole on the grounds that he insisted on moving back with his mother and consequently living not far from his victim, Jean Bradford. He was eventually allocated a prison pre-release hostel in London which he would use as a base to 'start life anew, with the past, whilst not forgotten, put as far as possible behind me ... I wanted in short,' he said, 'to regain my dignity, to retain my self-respect.'

He thought his best prospects for work lay in the motor trade and he hoped to resume his career as a car salesman. He wrote to Jack Barclay, the prestige car showrooms in London, to the Bristol Rotary Club and also to car auctions at Poole in Dorset. 'Despite writing from prison,' he said, 'I received replies from them all.' Not surprisingly, they were all 'no thank yous. John also had ideas, as he phrased it, of putting 'some matters right'. This included a possible reconciliation with Sharon Major who, he believed, 'was only too aware of her own part in the events that led up to the rape offence'. She had written to him in prison and this gave him encouragement to think that future contact was possible.

On 25 January 1986, John was sent to Wormwood Scrubs prison on a pre-release scheme. This lasted for six months and, while he was technically still in custody, he lived in a hostel close by, which gave him a degree of freedom and an opportunity to readjust to life outside prison. The prison hostel is seen as a means of relieving the overcrowded prison system and a way of helping low-risk offenders rehabilitate themselves in the community. The offender's daily routine and movements are still subject to control, and the hope is that, by responding to this more sympathetic regime, the offender will qualify for full release on parole under the supervision of the Probation Service. It is also the case that the pre-release system can be abused. Supervision in the hostels has been known sometimes to be fairly lax.

During this period, John worked for Superhire Limited, a firm which dealt with theatrical properties, whose premises at that time were in Telford Way, East Acton, a short distance from the prison. 'They thought the world of me,' John said. 'They didn't want me to go.'

In truth, his employers had discovered that he had gained employment with them by giving false references and that he was also a convicted rapist. He was sacked forthwith.

Although John did not have a car of his own while lodging at the prison hostel, he regained a taste for mobility by borrowing one. John confirmed this in one of his letters when he wrote, 'I also whilst on [sic] the hostel hired on a favour basis a red Ford Sierra belonging to the hostel inmate cook whose home was in London.'

The police have evidence that, on May Day Bank Holiday weekend in 1986, John was either given a lift by the hostel cook or that he borrowed his car to drive to the Bournemouth area. He went to Poole and car auctions there, presumably to follow up his application for employment which had so recently been refused. John also subsequently revealed in letters to the authors that he had once worked for a Southampton firm, University Cameras, situated in the town at Below Bargate, and that he knew the New Forest area very well indeed. He would often walk through the woods for relaxation, and used to drink at Bucklers Hard.

Perhaps more important is the claim he made to the authors that he has only ever visited Poole twice – once to a car auction in September or October 1986, and once on a trip with Gilly Paige, an ice-skater whom he had befriended a few months before abducting and murdering Shirley Banks. (Gilly appears later in this book.)

John consistently denies that he has made three (or more) visits to Poole, and specifically the trip on this Bank Holiday weekend. As we shall see in the final chapter, this 'forgetfulness' is consistent with the behaviour of a man who commits serial violence, then denies what he has done by creating conflicting stories and confusion. However, when he was arrested in 1987, the Bristol police found a pay-and-display parking ticket among his effects, which proves that John was in Poole for the whole of this particular weekend.

On 3 May, the Saturday preceding Bank Holiday Monday, a 27-year-old woman, Sandra Court, was murdered. Sandra had been working for the Abbey Life Insurance Company in Bournemouth. At the beginning of May 1986, she left her job and planned to take up a post in Spain as a nanny. She attended a farewell party at Steppes Nightclub on Friday, 2 May. She was last seen alive about 2.45am on the Saturday morning, walking barefoot in Lansdowne, a suburb of Bournemouth. She appeared to be slightly drunk. Her body was found later that day at 7pm in a water-filled ditch by the Avon Causeway near Hurn, Christchurch, several miles away. She had been strangled.

Neither robbery nor sexual assault appeared to have been a motive for the killing. No semen traces were found on the body, although they may have been washed away by the water in the ditch. Some of her belongings were discovered strewn about at scattered spots near by. A shoe, found by the side of the A31 near Picket Post, had possibly been thrown from a car heading for Southampton, so she may have been riding in someone's car. Ten days later, a letter posted in Southampton was sent to Detective Chief Inspector Rose of Dorset CID who was leading the murder inquiry. Its contents suggested that the death was an accident and that the killer was truly sorry. Examination of this note reveals that the writer, although right-handed, completed the note with a left hand in an effort to disguise the authorship.

In due course, John Cannan was interviewed about his

movements that day. He has said that the police are satisfied that he was not involved. Whatever evidence the Dorset police may have had to prompt them to interview John, at that time it fell short of anything sufficient to convict him. All unsolved homicide cases remain open and are reviewed periodically. At the time of writing, John is still a suspect.

However, the authors have carried out a cursory examination of the note sent to the police with samples of handwriting from John Cannan. Although obviously disguised by using the left hand instead of the right, there are more than 25 similarities of style, spacing and content. There appears to be a very strong link between both sets of script, style and spacing: enough to warrant a fuller investigation by the police. After we came into possession of a copy of this letter, a meeting was held at Bournemouth police station and examples of John's handwriting were handed over to Detective Inspector Stent, who said that no previous comparison had been made because they lacked the means of comparison. DI Stent gave us the information that Cannan had been in the area at the time of the killing, and officers had interviewed the hostel cook with some success. The authors have never enjoyed the courtesy of a reply from the Dorset Constabulary and, despite several requests, John Cannan's letters have not been returned.

John is adamant that he did not know Sandra Court (just as later he would be adamant he did not know Shirley Banks). He has said that he has found it 'difficult to understand what basis people are using in trying to suggest my complicity'. But the coincidence of his knowing the area well, and of being there that very weekend, then denying it, cannot be ignored.

John Cannan was released from prison and the hostel on 25 July 1986. Three days later an event occurred in West London, a tragic mystery involving the disappearance of a young woman, which commanded national press headlines for several weeks. Although John was not suspected at the time of being her abductor, a link would eventually be made to him. Once again the nature of the incident, coupled with a knowledge of his movements, drew him into the web of suspicion.

5

SUZY?

Just before lunchtime on Monday, 28 July 1986, a young female estate agent left her office in Fulham Road, West London, to meet a client. Her name was Suzy Lamplugh and her disappearance was headline news for many months. Suzy, a vivacious 25-year-old blonde, was described as a 'smashing girl'. She had worked for Sturgis, the estate agency, for 16 months and was regarded as ambitious and responsible.

When she left the office Suzy took with her the keys to a property at nearby 37 Shorrolds Road. Her office diary recorded the essential details of the appointment: '12.45 Mr Kipper – 37 Shorrolds Road o/s'. The annotation 'o/s' indicated that she planned to meet the prospective client outside the property. The office manager's expectation was that Suzy would soon be back at her desk, probably bringing a lunchtime sandwich with her.

As the hours of Monday afternoon ticked by and Suzy still had not returned, her office manager's anxiety increased.

Protracted absence without a contact telephone call was not Suzy's style. At about 5pm, the manager telephoned Suzy's mother, Diana, and explained his concern. She asked if he had been to the house in Shorrolds Road. He had, of course, made this obvious check and established that Suzy was not at the house. The occupant of a neighbouring residence recalled seeing a young couple at no. 37: he thought they were prospective buyers. He described the man as handsome, aged between 25 and 30 years, of medium height, clean shaven with dark hair and wearing a dark suit. The man attracted his attention and he had taken little account of the young woman.

Sturgis's manager did not know of a client named Mr Kipper. This was not unusual, for, in a busy estate agent's office, prospective clients constantly called in or telephoned for appointments to view properties. Suzy had followed accepted practice by recording the appointment in her desk diary. Her manager called the local hospitals to ask if an accident had been reported involving Suzy Lamplugh but he drew a blank. He telephoned Suzy's flat several times and returned to Shorrolds Road, all to no avail. His mounting concern was further heightened when he spoke again to the occupant of no. 35 who now said that the couple he had seen were arguing and he thought the man had bundled the woman into a car.

The police responded immediately. Details of Suzy's car, a white Ford Fiesta, registration number B396 GAN, were circulated and two detective officers were dispatched to 37 Shorrolds Road. A search of the house produced nothing of significance and the detectives, accompanied by Mr Paul Lamplugh, Suzy's father, moved on to her two-bedroom flat in Putney. Again, nothing was found to help their search.

The first breakthrough, but a disturbing one, was the discovery that night of Suzy's car, apparently abandoned, in Stevenage Road near Fulham football ground. Running parallel to the Thames, it is a residential road that had been made into a no through road after motorists had adopted it to by-pass busy Fulham Palace Road. Fulham Football Club's ground, various warehouses and garages lay between Stevenage Road and the river. The spot was about a mile from Shorrolds Road and there was every indication that the vehicle had been left in great haste. It was badly parked, the handbrake was off and the driver's door was unlocked; the missing girl's straw hat was on the parcel shelf behind the rear seats and her purse nestled in the driver's door pocket.

Suzy's current boyfriend, a 27-year-old insurance broker, and her male flatmate were both questioned by police. They had each spent time in the company of business associates or friends in well-corroborated accounts of their movements. Consequently, they were soon eliminated from further enquiries. By this time, the police were treating the estate agent's disappearance as a major inquiry and Detective Chief Superintendent Nicolas Carter was appointed senior investigating officer. Police dogs and their handlers began to search the area around Shorrolds Road and Stevenage Road. Drains were opened in the hope of finding the missing keys to 37 Shorrolds Road and an artist's impression was created of the man seen with Suzy outside the empty house. It was possible that this might help to identify the mysterious Mr Kipper.

The white Ford Fiesta was subjected to microscopic investigation by forensic officers at the Metropolitan Police Forensic Science Laboratory at Lambeth. While fingerprint impressions and trace evidence were being painstakingly examined, more immediate information was being gathered by officers conducting house-to-house enquiries. Then an individual telephoned the police saying that she lived in a house in Stevenage Road opposite the spot where Suzy's car had been found. Mrs Wendy Jones told the officers that she had seen a white Ford Fiesta there on Monday at about 12.45pm. The vehicle was still there a couple of hours later and, when she returned from the cinema at about 10.30 that evening, the car was surrounded by policemen.

These observations from a person judged to be a reliable witness put the cat among the pigeons. The timing was such that Suzy's car must have been driven straight to Stevenage Road immediately she left her office at 12.40; there was insufficient time to have driven first to Shorrolds Road and then to the spot opposite Wendy Jones's house. The possible permutations of Suzy's movements on that afternoon were extended somewhat when Barbara Whitfield, a partner in a flat-finding company and a friend of Suzy's, claimed she had seen the missing girl on Monday afternoon. Barbara was cycling along Fulham Palace Road towards Putney when she saw Suzy driving in the opposite direction. 'I waved but she didn't see me.' There was a man sitting next to Suzy and the time was about 2.45pm. 'I was absolutely certain it was her,' said Whitfield, who had known Suzy for five months. 'We would go and look at flats together and she was one of my best contacts.'

There were baffling contradictions in these witnesses' statements that have never been resolved. Barbara Whitfield's sighting of Suzy was especially significant because she was the only witness who actually knew the missing girl. Her evidence therefore tended to carry more weight, although it was at variance with other reports.

The police enquiry was turning into a perplexing conundrum. Unshakeable but conflicting testimony of witnesses has long been one of the nightmares of crime investigation. The Suzy Lamplugh case would prove to be totally frustrating from the investigators' standpoint.

The facts remain, however, that Suzy was seen talking to a man outside 37 Shorrolds Road; she was seen arguing and was then apparently bundled into a car. Suzy's Fiesta was subsequently discovered just a mile away and a close friend had seen her driving in Fulham accompanied by a man.

More evidence came to light when Suzy's office manager revealed that a bunch of red roses was delivered to Suzy at her office by a mystery man just days before she disappeared. Further, the owner of 35 Shorrolds Road now claimed that the man he had seen with Suzy was carrying what appeared to be a bottle of champagne. The plot was thickening.

On 4 August, the police staged a reconstruction of Suzy's last known movements. A woman police constable drove the white Ford Fiesta from Sturgis's office to Shorrolds Road. Outside no. 37 she was met by a detective sergeant posing as 'Mr Kipper'. The national newspapers carried photographs of the meeting staged at the house. Response to the reconstruction proved disappointing, not least because two workmen laying pipes in Stevenage Road within yards of the spot where the white Fiesta was found had seen and heard nothing unusual.

Two hundred police officers were engaged in the search for the missing estate agent. They combed every piece of open land and every vacant property within a mile radius of Shorrolds Road. The artist's impression of 'Mr Kipper' was published and shown on television. It bore an uncanny likeness to John Cannan. Diana and Paul Lamplugh appealed to the man whom they believed was holding their daughter to let her go. The police were flooded with calls from all over Britain from individuals who claimed to have seen Mr Kipper. It did not take long for someone to point out that, if Mr Kipper were given the first name of Dan, the words combined would be an anagram of 'Kidnapper'.

The British police faced worrying times during the hot summer of 1986. While the search for Suzy Lamplugh was at its height, there was a spate of killings across the country, in which the victims were young women. Within days of Suzy's disappearance, a 15-year-old girl, Dawn Ashworth, went missing from her Leicestershire home. The discovery of her violated body in a field precipitated a landmark in forensic investigation when her murderer, Colin Pitchfork, was convicted in 1988 (see Chapter 6).

Merseyside police were investigating the rape and murder of a 21-year-old woman in Birkenhead, and the murder of Anne Lock, a 29-year-old secretary working for London Weekend Television, made a trio of so-called 'railway murders' in the Home Counties.

For varying periods, all these women joined the official ranks of the missing, which in 1991 included over 900 women, of whom 16 per cent had been missing for more than five years. Not surprisingly, professions employing women in jobs that entailed dealing with male clients in one-to-one situations called for greater awareness. Police officers based at Fulham were therefore startled by the disappearance of Sarah Lambert less than three weeks after Suzy had gone missing.

Sarah, who was 25, worked for an employment agency in Ealing. She disappeared after arranging to meet a businessman, a Mr Simmons, who required a personal assistant. An artist's impression of this man bore a resemblance to 'Mr Kipper' so a link with Suzy Lamplugh's disappearance became inevitable. Fortunately, this was a story with a happy ending, for Sarah Lambert turned up alive and well two days after going missing and causing a nationwide search. She had spent two nights at a hotel in Woking with 'Mr Simmons', having been enticed by his offer of a well-paid job. She was unaware that the whole country was looking for her; the 'lost weekend girl' as she was called in the press was affectionately dubbed 'Noddy of the Year' by her retired father.

As the hunt for Suzy Lamplugh dragged on with no results, the focus of attention inevitably shifted to her personal life. She had trained as a beautician and worked at a Chelsea salon called Face Place. Her social aspirations probably classified her as a 'Sloane Ranger', but, after her 21st birthday, she decided to broaden her horizons by taking a job as a beautician on board the cruise liner QE2. Travel and the imagined romantic lifestyle of an attractive young woman among a ship's mainly male population led the newspapers to speculate on her supposedly active love life.

Meanwhile, further confusing evidence came from eye witnesses as the police reconstruction bore further fruit, some of which was rotten. Nicolas Boyle, an unemployed jeweller, claimed he saw Suzy on the day she disappeared standing outside no. 37 Shorrolds Road with a smartly dressed man. He was vague about the time, saying it was between noon and 4pm, but precise about describing the man. Boyle's description was of a person aged between 25 and 30 years with dark hair and wearing a charcoal-grey suit. Another witness said he saw a young woman meeting a man outside the house in Shorrolds Road. His description fitted Suzy Lamplugh and the man was thought to be aged between 26 and 32. The man was described as good-looking and exceptionally well dressed.

Once again we may draw disturbing parallels between John Cannan and 'Mr Kipper'. For, apart from the photofit likeness between the two men, other similarities include exceptional taste in dress sense – dark suits, dark hair, age, height and build. As for the red roses sent to Suzy at her office, we will soon discover that this was a romantic ploy often used by John. The bottle of champagne was another extravagant gesture of romantic intentions.

New witnesses were coming forward at a bewildering rate but their well-intended information only accentuated the fragmented story the Metropolitan Police had already compiled. There were suggestions that Suzy was set to land a large commission as a result of a property deal and that she was having a relationship with a man who lived in the West Country; it was thought possibly in Bristol. Suzy had mentioned something along these lines to friends, and John would eventually settle on Bristol and the West Country as a base for his activities.

Further diversions were created by evidence concerning cars seen in Shorrolds Road on the day in question. A businessman, who was also a motor enthusiast, drove down the road at midday and noticed a white Ford Fiesta. But what particularly attracted his attention was a dark-blue BMW. He noted that it was a mid-1970s model and logged that it was parked almost outside no. 37. He also noticed a second white Fiesta parked some distance from the BMW. With hundreds of cars parked in Shorrolds Road and many others in the surrounding streets, the police might have asked this witness why he noticed just these three vehicles, the model of each and the positions in which they were parked.

BMW cars of this period were not exactly commonplace in 1986 so the police were therefore encouraged to run a computer check. They were particularly looking for a possible link with the owner of such a car in the Bristol area. No such link emerged but there was renewed interest in the BMW angle in January 1987 when a Series 5 with metallic grey finish was found abandoned in St John's Wood, North London. When it became known that the owner was a Mr Kiper who normally lived in the Belgian city of Antwerp, new life was breathed into the police inquiry.

Unfortunately, it proved to be a red herring. Officers went to Antwerp to interview the owner, a wealthy businessman named David Rosengarten, who sometimes used his mother's maiden name of Kiper. Mr Rosengarten told detectives that his car was in a Belgian garage undergoing repairs on the day Suzy Lamplugh disappeared. The vehicle was stolen on 20 September and he had no idea that it had turned up in London. The Belgian connection was quickly ruled out as having no relevance to the Lamplugh enquiry.

The detectives returned stony-faced to London and, by February 1987, the hunt for Suzy Lamplugh was running out of momentum. Despite massive publicity and a fully resourced police investigation, there were no indications as to the fate met by the missing girl or the likely identity of her abductor. Suzy had to be presumed dead and the only hope left was the prospect of finding her body.

The police theory was that Suzy made the appointment to see Mr Kipper when a man giving that name came into the estate agent's office on Saturday, 26 July when she was working during the weekend. On Monday, 28 July she drove to Shorrolds Road to meet the prospective client as agreed and showed him round the property. When their inspection of the property was completed, Mr Kipper spoke to Suzy on the pavement outside. He used some ploy to persuade her to give him a lift to Stevenage Road. At some point en route, his charm disappeared and, when they reached Stevenage Road, he threatened her sufficiently to force her into another vehicle that was parked in the street. At this point she was spirited away and with her went the keys of 37 Shorrolds Road.

Like all such theories, it had inherent weaknesses and it did not or perhaps could not embrace all the evidence. The idea that an agile young woman could be abducted in a London street in broad daylight seemed preposterous. That such an incident could occur in a residential thoroughfare and within yards of two men working in the street seemed even more unbelievable. Moreover, there was the statement made by Barbara Whitfield that she had seen Suzy driving her car with a male passenger beside her at 2.45 that same afternoon. Nevertheless, the core of the theory, that Suzy was lured away by a man demonstrating all the normal behaviour of a potential house-purchaser whose charm turned to menace, had the sound of reality about it. Probably the same scenario was enacted with terrifying similarity in 1987 with the abduction of Shirley Banks.

After newlywed Shirley's disappearance from a busy shoppers' car park in central Bristol on 8 October 1987, the telephones and telex machines would begin to hum between the Avon and Somerset Constabulary and the Metropolitan Police. Detectives from London visited the so-called 'Bride Squad' at police headquarters in Bristol. Thus, the first links were made between the two missing women and the thought grew in the minds of the detectives that they might be looking for the same man. It could remain just a thought, but John's correspondence reveals further connections. They are aired for the first time in this book with John's permission, although he denies any involvement with either incident. The links are circumstantial in nature but they have sufficient strength to merit consideration of John as Suzy Lamplugh's abductor.

Following his sentence for the rape committed at Sutton Coldfield, John was sent to a pre-release hostel at Wormwood Scrubs in Du Cane Road, London W12. The hostel is situated about three miles from the office in which Suzy Lamplugh worked at Fulham Road, SW6. John started to look for work within a manageable radius, bearing in mind that he had no transport of his own. At this time, he was nicknamed 'Mr Kipper' by his fellow hostel inmates because of his preference for wearing kipper-style broad ties. The *Observer*, in its fifth-anniversary report of Suzy's disappearance, noted that John Cannan had borne the nickname 'Kipper' long before she made the headlines.

John was finally released from the hostel on 25 July 1986, three days before Suzy was abducted. He used to frequent two local wine bars also visited by Suzy, one being the Crocodile Tears just across the road from where she worked. While the world of the Wormwood Scrubs hostel and that of Suzy Lamplugh may seem miles apart socially, geographically they were separated only by some three miles. In John, we are dealing with an opportunist. While at the hostel, he knew that the place to find wine bars and the kind of girls he found attractive was Fulham. John's favoured lifestyle encompassed the wine bar rather than the public house. With their 'yuppie' connotations, Colonel Jasper's or the Crocodile Tears were much more his milieu than the Rose and Crown or Pig and Whistle. It is therefore quite consistent with what we know about him that he targeted the area. (As we shall see later, this is in keeping with a serial killer's desire to trawl for potential victims.)

John has always enjoyed the benefit of an excellent recollection of dates and events. Excellent, that is, until he is placed under questioning by police officers. When asked to account for his movements during the period 25 to 28 July 1986 he suffers a convenient loss of memory. John is not good with alibis. The art of proving that he was somewhere else at the material time always seems to elude him. Consequently, he resorts to the phenomenon of coincidence which has the irritating habit of placing him in the wrong place at the wrong time. The artist's drawing of a man seen in the company of Suzy Lamplugh bears an uncanny resemblance to John Cannan. Moreover, the description of the man's height, age, build, colour of hair and style of clothing link with John's characteristics. The giving of presents of red roses and champagne also has resonance with John's habits.

We know from John's record that he was both an opportunist and a schemer. He often approached young women at their place of work with spurious chat about property and talk of being a businessman. He was also perfectly capable of trawling for victims and effecting abduction as his later actions demonstrated. His easy charm was one of his most disarming characteristics. It worked with Sharon Major and other girlfriends: it could have worked with Suzy Lamplugh.

At the time of her disappearance, John was moving around the general neighbourhood in which Suzy worked. He was also mobile to the extent that he had access to a borrowed car. He may have spotted Suzy in the street and followed her to her office where he smoothly introduced himself as 'Mr Kipper', a potential house-buyer. John's *modus operandi* fitted this scenario perfectly. But the most sinister link comes later from the false number plate that he had made up and fixed to Shirley Banks's Mini car. John claims in his letters to the authors that he chose the number, SLP 386, at random. But the choice has a strange, perhaps subliminal reference to Suzy Lamplugh (SLP), third victim (3) and the year of her abduction 19(86). It is a play on letters and numbers – like Dan Kipper (kidnapper) – which John strongly denies.

John has consistently claimed that the Metropolitan Police have ruled him out as a suspect in the Lamplugh inquiry. This is not so. The Lamplugh file is still open, albeit gathering dust, and John Cannan's name remains on the suspects' list. Certainly the missing girl's mother, Diana Lamplugh, was reported as saying she believes John Cannan killed her daughter.

In a letter to the authors referring to an article in a Sunday newspaper linking him to Suzy, John acknowledged, 'Everybody is now firmly convinced I killed Lamplugh,' but added the simple denial, 'I haven't.'

He has had ample time to reflect on the matter and to set

the record straight. In all the circumstances, his blunt denial would carry some weight if he gave verifiable information of his whereabouts on 28 July 1986, the day Suzy Lamplugh was abducted. This would have the effect of eliminating him from further suspicion and would have saved a great deal of police time. But, as we will see, making straightforward statements that can be readily corroborated is not John Cannan's style. As we'll see, even the skills of a senior detective over 20 hours of questioning and incontrovertible evidence of guilt regarding the murder of Shirley Banks could not elicit an admission from him. His continuing denial of her murder is unbelievable and unacceptable, so we should not easily accept his denial over Suzy.

As his story unfolds, it becomes patently clear that John at all times seeks to manipulate people. His tactics are to make even the simplest issue obscure by throwing up as dense a smokescreen as he can. In this he might have adopted the US serial killer Ted Bundy as a role model. There are comparisons between the two men that give a chilling perspective to the Lamplugh affair.

Finally, John has told the authors that he is withholding certain information about a number of unresolved issues. His reason for doing so is in order that he can remain in control: 'information is power' is the way he puts it.

6

'DONNA'

John Cannan said he spent the first two months after his release from prison on 25 July 1986 with his mother at Sutton Coldfield. Then he decided to try his luck in Bristol where he thought he might find peace in what he regarded as a clean city and an attractive environment. 'So I came down with my suitcase,' he said, knowing nowhere to stay. 'I found pleasant lodgings at Chatsworth Guest House in Winsley Road where the landlady was prepared to accept unemployed people funded by the DHSS.' He did not have a car at this time but quickly set about finding a job in the trade he knew best and one that would provide him with a set of wheels.

He looked up several motor dealers in *Yellow Pages* and telephoned them enquiring about job prospects. Although broke and with no contacts in Bristol, the silver-tongued Casanova was determined to re-establish himself, fully aware that his record of five years in prison would take some 'explaining away'. He resolved not to resort to crime but was prepared to use a little guile to achieve his purpose.

He succeeded in securing an interview with Holders, a firm of motor dealers in Congresbury (about ten miles away), which was complicated by their request for references. This was where Cannan made use of native cunning. 'So I went to Prontoprint ... and the rest is history,' he said, referring to the way photocopying can now be so easily abused. 'They got their references and I got the job.'

He transferred his bank account to Lloyds at nearby Yatton, where the assistant manager Mr Dimmock welcomed his promising new customer, but, although he was on the payroll, he had to wait a month for his first pay cheque. Consequently, the first few weeks were rather miserable, although he was provided with a company car. He drove home each evening to his lodgings with no television to watch and no funds for socialising.

Holders was a family firm whose members held senior positions in the company. There was little scope for outsiders to break into this close-knit management circle and John felt very much out in the cold. He badly wanted to buy new clothes but was so impoverished that on some days he could not afford the 10p for the coffee vending machine at the car showrooms. But he was determined not to indulge in self-pity. 'I wasn't going to scrounge off the DHSS,' he said. 'I wasn't going to rely or depend or be a burden upon anybody.'

Instead, he decided a little more guile was required. John wanted to be self-employed and was always on the lookout for opportunities that would help him achieve that goal. Consequently, he established a rapport with an independent motor dealer who regularly traded with Holders. He introduced this dealer to a contact in Exeter and acted as agent to oversee a deal between them involving a Ford Cortina. John received a commission of £50 for making the introduction, a sum that was worth a fortune to him at that particular time.

A week or so later, the same dealer asked John to act for him over another car deal. He agreed to call at the man's house to inspect the vehicle, which he did the next day. When he returned to Holders, he was summoned into the office and informed by his employer that his extra-mural sales activities had been discovered with the cooperation of the dealer concerned. His telephone call to the dealer had been recorded and he had been followed on his visit to inspect the car. John argued that the vehicle did not belong to Holders and maintained that he was doing nothing unethical. He said he had been set up by the car dealer, who was trying to ingratiate himself with Holders. 'The upshot was Holders sacked me,' said John. Deprived of his company car, he had to rely on the junior salesman to drive him home.

But John, with his special talents, claims he had the last laugh on the car dealer who shopped him. The dealer employed a particularly attractive young woman on whom, according to John, he had designs. But she left the dealer's employment and appeared one day at Holders with her husband shopping for a car. John sold the couple a second-hand Vauxhall Cavalier and, as he recalled later, 'One thing led to another,' and he and the girl became lovers. Not surprisingly, the lustful car dealer was irked that John succeeded where he had failed. In a magnanimous gesture, John parted company with his new conquest because he did not wish to compromise her marriage: 'I did what I thought was right to save her from disappointment. I said goodbye to her.' The truth paints a different picture. The woman is a figment of John Cannan's romantic imagination.

John had rented bedsit accommodation at 6 Richmond Hill, Clifton, Bristol, on 10 September and was already installed when he lost his job at Holders. 'It was back on to DHSS.'

While waiting for his Giro cheque to arrive one Friday, he was out of food and down to his last 21p. Saturday came and went with no improvement in his finances and on Sunday he decided to blow his money on a Mars bar. He left his bedsit and found himself walking along with people headed for the local church to take part in the evening service. On the spur of the moment, he decided to join them.

He found himself in the friendly interior of a small church and became absorbed in the service. In due course, the person sat next to him passed him the collection plate: 'Goodbye went my 21p,' he said later. 'If there is such a place as heaven,' he added, 'and if, in the most unlikely event, I ever went there, I hope that St Peter remembers to allocate my 21p in the credit section of his account.'

On Monday, 6 October 1986, at about 1pm, an attempt was made to abduct a young woman in Whiteladies Road, Bristol. This offence took place a few minutes' walk from Leigh Woods where John Cannan eventually took up residence. (This attempted abduction occurred a year to the day before a similar attempt to abduct Julia Holman – see Chapter 8.) The victim, who was not named by the police, reported the attempted abduction and made a statement including a photofit description. The photofit bore a remarkable likeness to John Cannan. A suspect was rapidly arrested, interviewed and then released. This man was not John Cannan. But John's bank statements reveal that at 1.31pm that day he withdrew £25 from a cashpoint dispenser at Lloyds Bank in Clifton. This transaction placed him close to the scene of the offence and within 30 minutes of its occurrence. We have no information as to whether John was one of those interviewed by the police – all we can ask is, was it him?

Later that same day, a rape occurred in the Berkshire town of Reading. Donna Tucker had been watching a video recording of Jeffrey Archer's *First Among Equals* with a neighbour at her home on the outskirts of Reading. At about 10.30pm, she retired to bed, but an argument ensued with her husband, the reasons for which were so trivial that the couple could hardly remember them later. But the consequences were far-reaching and could have resulted in death.

Donna and Gerry had recently returned from a holiday in Egypt where they had picked up a gastric infection. As a result they were both tired and the argument concerned Gerry's decision to retire to bed earlier than usual. Donna slipped into bed but could not settle down. The argument smouldered on. Eventually, 30-year-old Donna decided to get up. She dressed in a yellow jumper and blue skirt, then went out of the house to calm down.

It was a cool night and Donna reflected that she and Gerry had been married four years. Although their relationship was a good one, they occasionally had tiffs, for which their antidote was that one of them went out to cool off. On this particular occasion, Donna took a book with her and went for a drive in the family's Vauxhall Cavalier. She drove down Langley Hill along the A4 and turned into Chantry Green off the Sava Centre roundabout. After parking under a street lamp, she turned off the engine and listened to the radio while reading her book. She recalled hearing the midnight news on BBC Radio 2 and afterwards heard approaching footsteps.

Looking in the rear-view mirror, Donna noticed a man walking along the footpath on the opposite side of the road. He walked past the car. About two or three minutes later, she saw the man again walking towards the Sava Centre roundabout. She went back to her book and looked up again when she was aware of someone approaching the car.

Her driver's side window was open. The man spoke to her. 'Excuse me,' he said. 'Can you tell me where Balfour Drive is?'

Donna replied, 'I'm sorry, I'm afraid I don't...'

'It's supposed to be around here somewhere. I've been walking around here for quite a while.' They conversed briefly about Balfour Drive with the man looking up and down the road.

'Have you got an *A–Z* in the car?' he asked.

Donna glanced over her shoulder into the back of the Cavalier and, as she did so, was aware that he was reaching for the door handle. He opened the door and said, 'Don't make a fucking move, or noise. See this knife? If you don't do as you're told, you'll get this in your gut.' He was holding a knife with a blade four inches long.

Donna was terrified, but she had worked in a building society where staff were advised always to give in to any demand rather than risk violence. She had also worked for the Red Cross in Uganda where threats of violence were commonplace. She said, 'What do you want?' thinking the man was after money or her jewellery.

'I just want sex,' he replied. 'Get in the back of the car. Get down on the fucking floor.'

She did as she was ordered as slowly as possible in the hope that a passer-by might appear whose attention she could possibly attract. She clambered into the back of the vehicle with some difficulty due to her heavy build and the position of the passenger seat, which was set as far back as it would go. The man climbed into the driver's seat and started the car. She noted that he was carrying a carrier bag, and had pulled a blue-knitted balaclava over his head. He asked where the headlamp switch was located, then, after making a U-turn in Chantry Green, drove towards the A4. He repeated that she would not get hurt if she did as she was told.

As they drove away, the attacker asked Donna what her name was. She replied, 'Jane', but then thought better of it, for she realised he would discover the truth if he rifled her handbag. 'No, I'm sorry,' she said, 'I lied to you: it's Donna.'

He asked her, 'What are you doing sitting there alone?' and she explained that she had argued with her husband.

When they reached the A4, he asked, 'Where's the fucking countryside?' She asked what kind of countryside and he replied, 'Somewhere dark and quiet.'

'Just carry on along this road.' She asked him what his name was and he replied, 'Don't be silly,' and then said, 'No, OK. Well, you can call me Horse.'

When they reached junction 12 on the M4 motorway Donna directed him towards Theale. They turned off into the Theale Industrial Park and stopped next to a rubbish skip. There were a few security lights around the factory premises adjacent to a car park where they stopped. The car was in partial darkness and it set the scene for a terrifying rape.

The attacker instructed Donna to remove her knickers

and he climbed over the front seats to join her in the back of the car. Lifting his balaclava, he kissed her several times on the mouth and then ordered her to perform oral sex. She attempted to masturbate him first in the hope of relieving his sexual tension. He told her to stop fooling around and then attempted sexual intercourse with her lying awkwardly in the back seat. This failed, so he forced Donna to move into the front passenger seat, which was now racked down into a reclining position. Straddling her, he said, 'You've not been raped yet.' Then he entered her, groaning and calling her by name. 'Now you've been raped,' he panted.

When he had finished, he sat back in the driver's seat. He told her not to look at him: she was so distressed she could not close her eyes and, to comply with his wishes, put her hand over her eyes. While she rearranged her clothing, she asked him what he was going to do. He said he would take her back to the place where he had found her, adding, 'But we're not finished here yet.'

From the carrier bag he produced a pair of white gloves. Donna recalled that they were too large for his hands. He wiped the steering wheel and the window winders and door pulls on the driver's and passenger side of the car.

He then asked, 'Has your husband ever fucked you up the arse?' Donna said, 'No,' to which he replied, 'Well, I'm going to with lubricant so I won't hurt you,' adding, 'I haven't got AIDS.' He produced a tube and explained that it was KY jelly. He applied it to her anus and told her she would have to 'guide him in'. Having enquired if he was 'on target', he buggered her, groaning in excitement before he ejaculated.

When he finished, he gave her some tissue to wipe

herself and fumbled around on the floor of the car looking for the cap of the KY jelly tube. Donna lit up a cigarette and offered him one. Then he started the car and began to drive back towards Reading. At some point in their conversation, he mentioned that his wife had died two and a half years previously.

'I'm sorry about that,' said Donna. 'Have you any children?'

'I had,' he replied. He seemed anxious to talk and kept asking Donna if she was all right. For her part, she was keen to keep the conversation going in the hope of finding out more about her rapist. But there was no reply to her question whether he came from the locality.

As they approached Reading town centre, Donna asked him where he wanted to go, suggesting the railway station or perhaps the bus station. He said he knew where he was, explaining that he had come to Reading to see someone and had parked his car in the town. He drove on to the inner distribution road and turned left into Abattoir Road just before the railway bridge. Abattoir Road is a dead-end running parallel to the railway line. He stopped the car a little way down the road and instructed Donna to get out and brush down the seats. She did as she was told while he once again wiped the steering wheel with his gloves. Kissing his rape victim on the lips, he said, 'Goodbye, Donna, take care and be good, and, if you can't be good, be careful.' With that, he strolled off into the night clutching his carrier bag.

Gerry Tucker had dozed off after Donna left the house but woke up at about 1.25am when the family dog started to bark. Donna had returned. He stood on the landing as she mounted the stairs calling out to him, 'I've been raped.' She was terribly distressed, although coherent, and told him in detail what had happened. Before contacting the police, Gerry looked inside the car. He noticed that the towel normally kept on the rear seat for the dog to sit on had been screwed up in a corner. Realising there might be important evidence in the vehicle, he decided not to use it to drive Donna to the police station. He went to the telephone and reported the incident.

In her statement to the Thames Valley police, Donna described the rapist as a white male in his late twenties or early thirties. He was of average height and slim build. He had collar-length dark hair and a dark 'five o'clock shadow' around his face. His eyes were dark and his eyebrows 'met in the middle'. He was wearing a dark, two-piece business suit with a light-coloured shirt that was open at the neck as he had loosened the knot on his striped tie. The plastic carrier bag in which he kept the KY jelly and the white gloves was plain white. Donna said he was well spoken and, although she could not place his accent, the way he said 'Somethink' or 'Nothink' made her think of a northerner.

Within five hours of the rape, Donna and her husband accompanied WPC Angela Balcombe to the KUKA factory car park at Theale Industrial Park and pointed out the location where she had been raped. Later that day, detective officers visited the scene and conducted a search of the area in which Donna's car had been parked. Scenes of Crime officers collected a number of cigarette ends and two used tissues.

At Reading police station in Castle Street, Donna Tucker was asked to hand over the clothing which she had worn when she was assaulted. The yellow jumper, blue skirt, slip, shoes, bra and pants were sealed into clear plastic crime bags. Her panties, a pair of M&S white knickers, was labelled exhibit AJB/6 and destined to become a crucial item of evidence. Donna also handed detectives another tissue, which she had used to wipe her vagina. This too was sealed in a bag and labelled AJB/7.

Next, Donna was examined by the police surgeon, Dr Mandhar Lal Swami, at his surgery in Russell Street. WPC Balcombe was present during the examination. The doctor recorded no injuries or bruises either on her body or around the genital area. Specimens taken for forensic purposes included saliva, vaginal and anal swabs, blood, head and pubic hair, and fingernail scrapings.

The Tuckers' Vauxhall Cavalier was taken to the Home Office Forensic Science Laboratory at Aldermaston where it was minutely searched for trace evidence. No semen was found but tapings of loose debris on the car seats were taken and retained for future reference. All the samples collected at the scene of the crime, together with Donna's clothes and the specimens she had provided, were examined by John Bark, one of the laboratory's forensic scientists. He discovered traces of semen on both the vaginal and anal swabs and semen staining on the slip, skirt and knickers. Tests showed the presence of type A blood group substance in the semen traces.

Three weeks after the rape, DC Brian Higgins and two other Thames Valley police officers from Reading paid a visit to the Caversham home of a local taxi driver. Anthony Carter had picked up a fare on the night of 6/7 October. He was shown a number of photographs and paid particular attention to one, which he thought resembled in most respects the man he had picked up, except for the hair colour. The photograph was of John Cannan. Carter also said that his fare had mentioned living in Acton. DC Terry Caine took special notice of the reference to Acton and contacted the local police collator. Seventeen names of sex offenders had been raised in an internal police memorandum – among them was that of John Cannan.

On 6 November, DC Higgins drove down to see Donna Tucker, who was staying with a friend in Kent. She was asked to look through a selection of 'mug shots' and it was explained that the man who raped her might or might not be featured in the folder. She felt drawn to a photograph of a man on the second card because 'he looked just like the man who raped me'.

Donna was concerned about the eyes, which she thought were lighter than those of the rapist. 'I was tempted to identify that photograph,' she said, but, having been warned not to make an identification unless she was a hundred per cent sure, she did not do so. She told the detectives, 'It could be him but he had darker eyes.' The photograph Donna Tucker referred to was that of John Cannan.

After leaving his employment at Holders, John paid a visit to the Citizen's Advice Bureau in Bristol where a helpful assistant liaised on his behalf with the DHSS to provide much-needed funds. Then it was back to scrutinising the 'Situations Vacant' columns of the *Bristol Evening Post*. He found a position for a sales executive advertised by the Marsh Barton Motor Company at Exeter. He attended an interview and was given the job. Working at Exeter involved a 140-mile round trip but he was given a car and

free petrol, which eased the expense. 'It was a job and that
was all that counted,' he said.

But it was a job that only lasted a week. In the middle of
the afternoon on Friday, 14 November 1986, DC Brian
Higgins and another detective from the Thames Valley
Police strolled into the showroom of the Marsh Barton
Motor Company. They asked for John Cannan and said
they were making enquiries regarding a rape that had
occurred in Reading on 6 October. John was taken
completely by surprise. He told the policemen that he had
never been to Reading and during the first week of
October had been staying with his mother at Sutton
Coldfield. As usual, he pledged his full cooperation and
agreed to take part in an identity parade, to permit a
search of his room at Richmond Hill and to give blood and
saliva samples.

'Embarrassed by their approach in front of my
colleagues,' said John, 'I accompanied them back to Bristol.'

At the central police station, he again denied being in
Reading and explained that, since his release from prison
in July, he had been dependent on public transport and
travelled to and from Sutton Coldfield by coach. Dr
Reginald Bunting, the police surgeon, took blood and
saliva samples. John said that he saw no reason to ask for
a solicitor 'since, being an ex-offender, I thought it was
just routine'. The two detectives searched his room. 'They
didn't find anything, of course,' he said. 'I hadn't done it.'
He made them a cup of tea and when they left he sat
down to contemplate his future prospects.

He recalled the looks of his work colleagues as he was
escorted out of the showroom. 'I just thought, "You've tried,
you've had a go, you've got jobs, you haven't committed an

offence, you've done things by the book, by the rules, you've lost, you've failed."'

Annabel, the solicitor he had met while in Horfield prison, had sent him a Christmas card but there had been no further communication until September 1986, 'the twenty something', as John recollected, when they bumped into each other outside the Mauretania Wine Bar in Clifton. This was soon after John had been sacked from Holders. 'We both knew what was going to happen,' he said, 'and, as I asked her out for a drink and she accepted, our eyes met, both of us aware and understanding that the inevitable was going to happen.' He said that he was not really ready for an affair bearing in mind that he was on the dole, as he put it, and only had a one-room bedsit.

Their 'remarkable affair', as John liked to describe it, was to last 11 months. 'I think that if somebody put it in a romantic novel it would be a bestseller in many ways. It would beat Mills & Boon.' The irony of the ex-con seducing the solicitor appealed to him but he also admired her intelligence. 'Absolutely brilliant,' he claimed, 'wipe the floor with me any day.' John described their relationship as 'very sexual' but spoke of the caution they had to observe in order to keep their liaison discreet.

On their second date, they went to Colonel Jasper's for a lunchtime drink. After a few glasses of wine, according to John's account, he asked her if she would go to bed with him and she answered, after a few moments' reflection, 'I'd have thought that I had made that pretty obvious.' Within an hour, the affair started in earnest in John's room. Once again, his charm had worked like a dream.

Now he dreaded Annabel coming round that evening. 'I had, it seemed, another false start to report.' He told her everything that had happened and, when she left, he sat on the bed and thought things through. He realised that his employers were now aware of his criminal record, so the following morning he telephoned them and gave in his resignation. Marsh Barton Motors collected their car and John watched from the window as they drove it away. That night he swallowed 68 paracetamol tablets. The attempted suicide bid failed and the next morning feeling extremely ill he admitted himself to Bristol Royal Infirmary. He was placed on a saline drip and his blood was tested every two hours.

Subsequently, he was visited by the hospital psychiatrist who had John admitted as a psychiatric patient. While under observation, John tried to think through his future. Then his depression lifted and 'suddenly everything became clear ... why not return to crime?' he asked himself. 'Why not have a nice home, a nice car, some excitement and plenty of money?' He recalled later hobbling down the corridor outside the ward towards the smoking area with the patient who occupied the next bed to his. 'Our pyjamas didn't fit,' said John, 'and Eric had forgotten his false teeth.' His toothless companion lit up a Woodbine and, drawing deeply on his cigarette, said he felt better. Looking at him, John remarked, 'So do I, Eric, so do I.'

He checked himself out of hospital, having convinced himself that he was not afraid of death. 'My life is not ruled by fear,' he said. 'Death is the most final of all things; once you are not afraid to die, you are not afraid of anything.' This dramatic turn of events occurred two weeks after John met Annabel Rose.

Without the benefit of a firm identification of her attacker by Donna Tucker, the Thames Valley police were at a disadvantage. It would be left to the forensic scientists to solve the Reading rape case.

On 17 November, Thames Valley officers took John's body samples to Aldermaston, where they were dealt with by John Bark. The three items crucial to the forensic investigation of the rape were Donna Tucker's knickers (AJB/6), her bloodstain (MLS/15) and John Cannan's blood samples (RAB/1). Each of these was sent separately to the Metropolitan Police Forensic Science Laboratory at Lambeth: MLS/15 on 23 October, followed by AJB/6 on 13 November and RAB/1 on 26 November. Dr Graham Divall examined Cannan's blood and the stain on the knickers and grouped the stains as both GL02-1. In his statement dated 29 December 1986, John Bark at Aldermaston noted that 'Grouping tests indicate that the semen on the slip (AJB/3) and knickers (AJB/6) could have originated from John Cannan.' (Dr Divall reported that he had not obtained a result with AJB/3.) This fell far short of the confirmation for which the police had hoped, and there the matter rested until March of the following year when DNA profiling was carried out.

This was an exciting period in the world of forensic science with developments being made in DNA profiling, popularly called 'genetic fingerprinting'. Dr Alec Jeffreys of Leicester University made the discovery in the early 1980s that an individual could be identified by means of his or her unique set of genes. A test was developed using human tissue or body fluids to determine a person's genetic profile or 'fingerprint'. The importance of this discovery from the standpoint of forensic science was recognised at the outset by staff at Aldermaston, including Dr David Werrett and Dr Peter Gill who worked closely with Dr Jeffreys.

DNA profiling was first successfully used in court in November 1987 in a rape case and a year later in a murder case. In January 1988 Colin Pitchfork, a Leicestershire man, was convicted of sexually assaulting and strangling two 15-year-old girls. His identification as the murderer was made by means of DNA profiling, after the police carried out a massive screening programme involving the testing of some 5,000 men. The account of this dramatic use of DNA profiling was told by Joseph Wambaugh in his book *The Blooding*. The screening programme began in January 1987 and, by May, more than 3,000 men had given blood samples. Most of these blood samples were tested at Aldermaston. The forensic staff were swamped. Kept in cold storage, because a murder case had priority over rape samples, was John Cannan's sample RAB/1. Meanwhile, John went on his way, having lost his job at Marsh Barton Motors and given up his bedsit at 6 Richmond Hill. On 30 November 1986, he returned to Sutton Coldfield to live with his mother.

On 23 January 1987, John Bark, the Aldermaston forensic scientist, passed a number of items to his colleague Dr David Werrett at the Central Research Establishment, Aldermaston. These were the knickers (AJB/6), Donna's blood sample (MLS/15) and John Cannan's blood sample (RAB/1). Dr Peter Gill examined the knickers and recovered a small amount of DNA material from the semen stain on them. He reported on 12 March 1987 that 'the profile obtained was consistent with the spermatozoa having originated from John Cannan'. Dr Werrett confirmed those findings and elaborated further. He said, 'There are five bands present in the partial profile obtained from the DNA ... these five bands match a corresponding five bands in the profile obtained from the blood sample of John Cannan (RAB/1).' He noted that the theoretical possibility of this happening by chance 'can be calculated as once in 2,000 times'.

These odds would be lengthened in due course but, for the time being, John continued to enjoy his freedom. On 1 May 1987, he was asked to attend an identification parade at Reading police station. Donna Tucker was accompanied by WPC Angela Balcombe and it was obvious to everyone that the rape victim was very nervous. Inspector Philip Gulliford, who conducted the ID parade, described her demeanour as 'one of fear and shock'. Donna did not identify any individual in the line-up of nine men while she was in the room but, on leaving, she turned to one of the police officers and blurted out, 'It was number eight, wasn't it?' She then broke down. Asked by one of the officers why she had not properly identified the man (now known to be John), she said that she was not certain.

'I can remember looking at this man and thinking I would like to identify him as being the man who raped me,' she said, 'but I was told that I must be one hundred per cent sure.' As she had been with the photographs, Donna was uncertain about the man's eyes, which she did not think were dark enough. 'I spent some time looking at the man,' she said feeling unsure of herself and aware that she was under pressure. She still equivocated and wanted to say, 'Yes, that's the man if he had darker eyes.'

Inspector Gulliford asked again if she could make a positive identification. Her hesitation was seized upon by the suspect's solicitor, who remarked, 'I think we can take it that this is not a positive identification.'

Gulliford concluded that a positive ID had not been

made, although her hesitation over no. 8, John Cannan, was noted. A possible explanation for her hesitation was that a person's eyes appear darker in dim light because the pupils expand, whereas in brighter light, when the pupils contract, more of the iris is visible. The rape took place in a darkened industrial park, while John's 'mugshot' had been taken place in a brightly lit room, as had the ID parade.

In his letters to the authors, John claimed the ID parade was 'an absolute disgrace'. He said that Donna Tucker had been primed by being shown his photograph beforehand. 'At no time,' he says, 'did she ever give any indication that her assailant was on the parade.' This was not the only allegation that he would make against the police. When he was arrested in Leamington Spa on 29 October 1987, there was renewed interest in the DNA evidence. In the intervening months, great advances had taken place in DNA profiling techniques and, in March 1988, John Bark was able to say that the semen on (AJB/6) was of a type originating from 'only approximately 1 in 14,000 of the UK male population' and that the semen could have originated from John Cannan.

But the net closed tighter around John when one of Bark's colleagues, Michael Sayce at the Home Office Forensic Science Laboratory at Chepstow, looked at this evidence in a statistical light. Taking account of Donna Tucker's description of her assailant as 'a white male of about late twenties to early thirties in age', he determined from the 1981 Population Census figures for Great Britain that 3.6 million individuals came into that category. Of these men, approximately 1 in 14,000 would be expected to have the same blood-group type as the semen found on

Donna Tucker's undergarment. Hence, only 250 men in the entire country had those same characteristics, and John Cannan was one of them.

It came as something of a surprise to the authors when John did not really dispute that the semen was his. 'Apparently my sperm appeared upon a pair of white M&S knickers. The DNA said it was mine!' What he questioned was that the knickers had ever been worn by Donna Tucker. And, of course, he had a breathtaking explanation of the way in which he believed evidence had been incorrectly used against him. He maintained that, as a consequence of raping Jean Bradford in 1981, an offence that he reluctantly admitted, his sperm was found on her knickers. But, after the rape, she changed her pants and, as a result of vaginal drainage, this second pair also bore traces of semen. 'Both pairs bore my seminal presence,' was the way he explained it.

'One pair of plain white Marks and Spencer's knickers is indistinguishable from another pair,' he argued, and claimed that, 'acting in perfectly good faith, the scientists conducted their tests believing that the knickers (AJB/6) were in fact those worn by Mrs Tucker when in fact they weren't.'

Crucial to John's argument is that a pair of knickers carrying traces of his semen which were an exhibit in the rape case five years previously were substituted for those worn by Donna Tucker. The whereabouts of the knickers she wore on the night of 6 October 1986 thus becomes very important if we are to be fair to John Cannan. In her statement made on 13 June 1988, long after the event, Donna said, 'Shortly after I was raped, my clothes were taken from me by the police. Many months later they were returned to me, but I cannot exactly remember when. I remember that I threw the knickers (AJB/6) into the bin.'

John contended that the police deliberately obscured what happened to the knickers by muddling the documentation. Indeed, it was later confirmed that the label had become detached from (AJB/6) at one point, and that one of the scientists involved had been misled into signing the label confirming that he had taken possession of the garment when in reality he had not. There were also discrepancies with the exhibits' register over this item. Perhaps his criticism was justified on these points, but who would believe John Cannan's story?

John steadfastly maintained his innocence over the rape of Donna Tucker. He told DC Brian Higgins that he had not been to Reading and said that at that time he did not have a car and travelled only by coach and train. He claimed that, during the first week of October between Thursday 2nd and Wednesday 8th, he was staying at Sutton Coldfield with his mother. This proved to be a lie. John's banking records showed that he had used his cashpoint card at 1.31pm on 6 October to draw £25 from the Lloyds cash dispenser in Clifton, Bristol, and, later on the same day, at 9.21pm he had used another Lloyds cash dispenser at York Road, London SE1, withdrawing £20. So on 6 October he had travelled from Bristol to London. The following day, we find him back in Clifton, where he withdrew a further £5 from the machine.

Two things are confirmed by this. The first is that, after a possible attempted abduction in Bristol, he distanced himself from the offence by travelling to London. From there he travelled to Reading where he raped Donna Tucker and then returned to Clifton. The second issue is that he was not staying with his mother at Sutton Coldfield as he insisted.

By his own admission, John was using coach or rail

transport at this time and his means of travelling from Bristol to London was most likely via the Inter-City route which passes through Reading. The journey time from Paddington to Reading is 25 minutes so he had ample time to board a train for Reading after using his cashpoint card in York Road and be in the town well before midnight – the time Donna Tucker was approached by the man who raped her. Significantly, after the rape, she was driven to Abattoir Road, which is a mere two to three minutes' walking distance from Reading station. The rapist abandoned her at that point and disappeared into the night. The time according to Donna Tucker's estimate was about 1.20am. The first Inter-City express from Paddington to Bristol calls in at Reading at 7.10am, arriving at Bristol Temple Meads station at 8.42am.

Despite all his denials, there can be no doubt that John was the Reading rapist. The DNA provides an indelible indication of his presence. But what triggered off this violent act? Probably he was still smarting from the humiliation of losing his job at Holders. It would certainly fit the pattern of his previous violent acts for this incident to have triggered off his rage and the urge to seek his revenge by hurting another person. It was Sharon Major's rejection which drove him first to abuse her and then to rape Jean Bradford.

His presence late at night on the fringe of Reading may have been because he was trawling for a likely victim; a woman returning home on her own perhaps. That he came across Donna Tucker sitting alone in her car, her thoughts concentrated on a recent domestic tiff, made her easy prey.

7
ANNABEL

As John's affair with Annabel Rose developed, he began to press her to leave her husband. He believed her barrister husband was a dull professional man and that when she escaped into John's company he made her laugh with his jokes and cry with the tales he told her about his life. He supposed Annabel found him a romantic rebel who 'loved life passionately and nearly always allowed his impetuosity to triumph over reserve and caution'.

He felt that she was too bound up with money, status and privilege to appreciate romantic values – that is, until she met him. But he wanted her total commitment. 'For months,' he said, 'she'd kept on about the money her husband had, yet on the other [hand] she hadn't a good word for him.'

As he had done with Sharon Major, John started to put on the pressure. He admitted this: 'I pleaded with her, I threatened her, I did everything I could to sort matters out properly. The pressure I put her under was horrific, she had the chance...' These words were written many months after the event when John had the benefit of hindsight. Having a love affair with Annabel Rose was one thing, but trying to manipulate her life was another. As John acknowledged, she had a powerful intellect and he claimed that, while he loved her, he was never emotionally dependent on her as he was on Sharon.

John gave up his bedsit at Richmond Hill and, on 30 November 1986, returned to Sutton Coldfield, where he stayed with his mother. In April 1987, he had a telephone call from his solicitor, Jim Moriarty, asking him to drop in at the office. He was told that the Reading CID wished to see him again. After speaking to DC Higgins, he agreed to travel down to Reading with Moriarty on 30 April. 'We drove down, arriving at lunchtime,' said John. 'Police aggressive and arrest me on suspicion. I get angry and uptight.' Acting Inspector Stephen Kirkpatrick interviewed John and asked him to take part in an identity parade.

'Next day, ID parade clear! I'm released ... Kirkpatrick and me at loggerheads. I TOLD HIM I HADN'T DONE IT! HE KNEW I HADN'T DONE IT ... I moan to Annabel Rose!'

To continue his affair with Annabel, John made frequent trips to Bristol where he lodged in various hotels. During this period he financed his lifestyle with the occasional building-society robbery. According to his account, he and Annabel even made love out of doors in Ashton Park, lying on his mackintosh – a claim vigorously denied by Rose. John started talking about setting up a management consultancy. For a person who could not manage his own life, attempting to organise the affairs of others was a pretty silly thought. Nevertheless, he made plans, 'albeit only a shell,' he said, 'and for reasons which in the end, wouldn't have been legal.' He had seen an old shop in Clifton Village that had taken his fancy; 'as a prestigious and seemingly respectable front, it would have been ideal'.

Further trips to Bristol were financed by a gift of £5,000 from a distant relative, John Perks, who had been the chairman of a successful engineering company in Sutton Coldfield. In addition, when his father died, John inherited £2,000, which had been set aside to help him get back on his feet again.

Despite these windfalls, John had no compunctions about his resolve to make money illegally. He claimed to have learned from pillow talk after lovemaking sessions with Annabel that, without mentioning any names, she had represented clients who were suspected of dealing in drugs. This was hardly a secret, but perhaps he saw a way of using this information to his advantage.

He claimed that his return to Bristol was largely due to Annabel. She offered him the prospect of some work that involved setting up financial investment channels. This, according to John, was due to begin in December 1987.

One of John's favourite haunts in Bristol before he took the flat at Foye House was the Avon Gorge Hotel. It was there on 14 June that he met Gilly Paige, an attractive, 24-year-old showgirl. She was a former Olympic ice-skater and was taking time off from the *Holiday on Ice* show. John had met Annabel Rose earlier that day and, after she had returned home, he left his room and went down to the restaurant for dinner where he spotted Gilly.

As she put it later, he 'kept making eye contact with me'. According to John, the restaurant staff were aware of the signals and the waiters were taking bets on whether or not he would seduce her. 'It's a well-remembered incident,' he said.

He sent her a bottle of champagne with a note giving his room number and saying, 'I'd love to see you. Don't disappoint me.'

Gilly thought, 'What the heck,' and decided to accept the invitation. She said later, 'I have never met anybody so charming. He had this way of making a woman feel very special.' She remarked on his good looks and 'amazing eyes'.

John liked the Avon Gorge Hotel because it was the only hotel in the area that offered a suite with a Jacuzzi. 'It was in the Jacuzzi that I first made love to the ice-skater,' he claimed.

The following day John gave Gilly a lift to Birmingham in his hired Ford Escort. They chatted during the journey and touched on some rather odd subjects. He talked about the police searching for bodies in woods and rivers, but gave it as his opinion that the best way to get rid of a body was to put it in concrete on a construction site. John ventured to say that that was probably what had happened to Suzy Lamplugh. John also allegedly asked her if she knew the name to describe people who had sex with dead bodies and talked about bondage and anal intercourse. He volunteered the information that he enjoyed sex with other people looking on.

When they pulled off the motorway and drove into a service station, they sat talking in the car and, at one point, John put his hands round Gilly's neck and said, 'You know I'll never hurt you, you're much too nice to hurt.' 'Maybe this is the way Suzy died,' he said.

At some point during the trip, they drove off the

motorway into country lanes and Gilly was questioned as to whether anyone knew where she was. Despite being scared, she was sufficiently entranced by John to meet him again, which they did twice in Bristol and also in Poole. John said later that she rang him one night and he said, 'Look, stay where you are and I'll come down.' They stayed at a hotel near Poole old docks. When asked during a police interview if he had the ice-skater's autograph, he replied, 'I don't need that, I got everything.'

Their relationship was brought to an abrupt end by Gilly's skating commitments, which required her to return to the *Holiday on Ice* show. They parted on good terms and John spoke of the interlude as 'another brief flirtation', adding, 'It was ego I suppose, she was a very, very, very attractive girl.' He also explained his dalliance in terms of not being willing to sit around tapping his fingers waiting for Annabel Rose to leave her husband.

Gilly wrote to John from France six weeks later, inviting him to fly out to see her in Grenoble. He declined because he was again short of money and was planning trips to India and the West Indies. John said that she kept telephoning him from abroad but by the end of July he was busy moving into his new flat at Foye House.

The day after John was convicted at his trial at Exeter Crown Court in April 1989, the *Sun* newspaper carried an interview with Gilly Paige, whom the paper described as an 'ice show beauty'. She talked about her encounter with John and of her nightmares in which she was haunted by his hypnotic eyes. She told a reporter that, during her car ride to Birmingham with John, he spoke about his interest in buying property and his insistence on being shown around by a woman. He mentioned an estate agent who had disappeared and said the police were searching for someone called Mr Kipper. His opinion was that Mr Kipper had got rid of the body by putting it in concrete. Gilly was reported as saying, 'It gave me the creeps.'

John completely denied the remarks attributed to him and called Gilly 'a liar and an opportunist'. Never short of a theory, he later told the police that 'she was a bit of a moody girl' and put this down to her unhappy upbringing.

John kept fairly mobile during the summer months of 1987, and early July found him in Paignton, which adjoins Torquay. The visit was memorable for two reasons: he had a nostalgic attraction for the place in which he had spent his honeymoon with June, and he picked up a parking ticket. He recalled staying at the Commodore Hotel, although he could not remember if he had a companion on that occasion. After he was arrested, he was questioned about a number of keys found in his car and the locks to which they belonged. One key proved to be a room key for a hotel in Paignton where John had stayed, as he put it, for a 'dirty weekend'. When pressed for the name of his companion, he told detectives, 'Mind your own business.' The lady in question was Gilly Paige.

John had the company of other conquests, including Liz, a successful businesswoman in the West Midlands whom he described as a 'gem'. There were also many one-night stands – girls he picked up at Racks, a wine bar at the Avon Gorge Hotel. 'You know,' he said, 'occasionally, you talk to somebody, and occasionally, you know, these things happen.' Rationalising his amorous inclinations, he said, 'And why not? I wasn't married nor engaged to be, and was always hot and cold on forming a permanent future with Annabel anyway.'

In June 1987 John rented the flat with a garage at Foye House, Bridge Road, Leigh Woods and thereby set himself up with a base in Bristol. Foye House is a block of spacious flats and John's had two bedrooms. He furnished it tastefully with a blue cottage suite, expensive dining table and chairs. The walls he covered with good-quality watercolours and prints. It had all the trappings of a young executive and eligible bachelor. All this lifestyle was financed from his uncle's legacy and through the proceeds of robbery. Through a finance house he purchased a black BMW from Roger Head Motors Ltd in Gloucester, which he parked outside the flats as it was a tight fit in the garage. John was very busy and his emotional and business affairs became inextricably entwined.

At about this time he made the acquaintance of Christine Fortune, who ran a plant and pottery shop in Clifton called Rainbow. John paid £40 for plants that he was buying for the new flat and asked for them to be delivered to Flat 2, Foye House. A few days later, Christine and her husband, Andrew, delivered the plants and John invited them in for coffee. 'I got the impression from looking about that he was just moving in,' said Christine in a police statement. The Fortunes admired the view of the gardens and woods from a large picture window in the flat while John talked, mostly about himself.

He said that he felt a bit lonely and mentioned that he was estranged from his wife who had custody of his daughter. He showed the couple a number of recipe books and talked about getting some advice on interior decorating. While they were chatting, a blonde woman in her late twenties or early thirties arrived at the flat. She was carrying a bottle of wine; John introduced her as

Annabel. The visitor immediately commented on the view from the window, perhaps indicating that she had not been to the flat before. Annabel was dressed in a smart navy-blue suit and 'looked like a professional woman', Christine said later. She and her husband used Annabel's arrival as their cue to leave after John had extended an invitation to them for dinner and drinks at some future date.

The occupant of Flat 5, Foye House was Valerie Humphreys, a 31-year-old widow who worked as a secretary. She had lived at Foye House since Christmas 1985 and first noticed her new neighbour in Flat 2 in June 1987 when she saw him at a residents' meeting, although they did not speak to each other. Val next encountered John at the entrance to the flats around 5pm on 11 August when they chatted about the telephones which were not functioning in the flats that day. True to form and with a parting shot, John asked her if she would go out with him for a meal that evening. Valerie accepted graciously.

She spent the early evening washing her hair and sorting through her wardrobe for something special to wear. John knocked on her door at 8pm. He escorted her to his BMW and opened her door. They drove into Clifton where he parked in Queen's Avenue and they made their way to the Berni Restaurant at Dingle's Store. They walked straight through the bar and into the restaurant. 'John was a bit familiar with the waitress,' recalled Val, and during the meal he acknowledged other members of the staff, giving the impression that he had been there before. While they were enjoying the meal, John's conversation turned to economics and Val remembered him making a reference to 'gross material product' which was 'a term used in economics'.

John paid the bill by cheque and invited Valerie back to his flat for coffee. He explained that he had bought the sofa and plants in Clifton and talked about making a feature of a painting on an easel in the lounge. They chatted for some time, ranging through topics including writers, perhaps prompted by a Harold Robbins novel that was on the coffee table. Val accepted a small cognac after drinking her coffee and she sipped it sitting on the sofa facing the window while John relaxed on the floor.

After a short while, he joined her on the sofa and they kissed. 'I can't remember the sequence of events,' said Val, 'but we eventually went to bed together.' She was not a promiscuous person but felt she 'was expected and coerced by John to have sex with him', although she did not feel in any way threatened. 'Once in bed together there was a general awkwardness,' she said, 'and it transpired that no intercourse took place.' She got out of bed and dressed while John made a cup of tea. She returned to her own flat during the early hours of the morning.

The following morning, Val posted a cheque for £10 through John's letterbox as her contribution to the cost of the previous evening's meal. She saw him several times after that, once to celebrate her birthday. Their conversation on various occasions covered everything from philosophy to travel. 'I do remember him discussing Bertrand Russell,' said Val, and 'we have had some lengthy and deep conversations on a number of issues.'

Understandably, Annabel Rose has refused to cooperate in the writing of this book. John, however, has become somewhat obsessed about her and this is echoed in his letters. He described August 1987 as a time when 'a lot was happening and a lot was discussed'. She was normally defensive but very occasionally she opened up – 'that usually happened after we had made love'. But their relationship was starting to cool and John said he was beginning to feel 'as though I was being used and put at risk'. He alleged he had information damaging to her reputation and threatened to go to the police.

Annabel allegedly pre-empted his intervention by making contact with her own solicitor who would inform the police about a 'troublesome client complaint'.

John's thoughts at this time when their 11-month relationship ended on or about 18 August 1987 are illuminating. 'I felt that she had pre-empted the end,' said John. 'She'd ended it too early. I didn't want it to end.' They had a blazing row, which precipitated a parting of the ways.

John later telephoned Annabel at home later asking if they could talk.

She said, 'As far as I am concerned, John, the relationship is over'.

He answered, 'Look, don't be so silly, for God's sake. Just come round, we'll have a talk. We'll meet for lunch and have a talk.'

She replied, 'No, no, I don't think I will ... the relationship is over.'

In recent letters to the authors, John Cannan's thoughts are clearly confused. He says of his feelings for Annabel, 'I loved her to a point but funnily enough never liked her.' He was determined that she would not hurt him as he believed Sharon Majors had and he told her as much. By retaining his independence, he believed 'it made Annabel Rose want me more'. When the break-up came though, he professed to being 'not upset, just a little miffed. ... I didn't feel any great sadness. I mean, yes, sadness, but yes I mean I wasn't deeply, emotionally churned up and upset with Annabel. I was sad, it wasn't Sharon Major though.'

A few months later, when asked by the police if Annabel had not been quite a catch for him, John replied dismissively, 'I've had far better.' And on that sour note the affair was apparently ended, although certainly not forgotten.

Subsequent events showed that John pursued Annabel with the same tenacity as he had previously dogged Sharon Major. His struggle to discredit the young solicitor clouded his judgement and ultimately ended in disaster for him.

John did indeed make good his threat to contact the police. On 22 August 1987, he telephoned the central police station at Bristol. Using the name Jessop, he spoke to Detective Sergeant Reeves and made extraordinary allegations against Annabel Rose. On the same evening he also called the Birmingham Law Society, claiming that he was being legally compromised by a solicitor.

When DS Reeves went on leave, John telephoned Woman Detective Constable (WDC) Sandra Burnett at Bradbury Road police station. Their first conversation took place on 28 August and John subsequently called at frequent intervals, often talking for 45 minutes at a time. He tried to persuade WDC Burnett that his allegations were true, but not unreasonably WDC Burnett asked him to substantiate his claims. 'Sandra wanted more evidence,' he told the authors. 'In a nutshell, I didn't have it,' and, according to John, the police continued to accuse him of malice. He therefore resolved to employ a private detective to help him pursue his own enquiries. Once again John Cannan returned to the Walter Mitty world of hiring a private eye to track down the movements of a former lover, just as he had done with Sharon Major.

There was no Mike Hammer listed in the telephone directory, so he searched through *Yellow Pages* where he came across Tom Eyles, Legal Services, whose address was in Fishponds, Bristol.

What John hoped to achieve with this move, beyond harassing Annabel Rose, is unclear. Having used the name of Jessop in his conversations with the police, he now called himself John Peterson and introduced himself as such when he telephoned Tom Eyles on 24 September 1987. He told the private detective that he wanted to talk about a surveillance job he wished to carry out immediately. They arranged to meet at Eyles's home at 11am the following day. John did not turn up at the appointed time. After waiting until 2.30pm, Eyles left in order to fulfil other engagements. He returned home at about 8pm to find that Peterson had telephoned while he was out and had arranged to meet his wife Janet at Colonel Jasper's wine bar in Clifton village.

Tom Eyles had left the police force six years previously and Janet assisted her husband, helping him to build up his enquiry business. They enjoyed excellent relations with the local constabulary and with numerous law firms and finance companies. The couple duly drove into Clifton and, while Tom parked the car, Janet sought out Mr Peterson in Colonel Jasper's. John's eyes lit up when he spotted a tall very attractive woman walk in and look around the bar. He spoke to her, introducing himself as John Peterson and offering to buy her a drink. He was somewhat miffed when Janet asked for a pint of lager for her husband who came in behind her. In an interview with the authors later, Janet said that, from the outset, Peterson made her feel distinctly uneasy. 'It was the way he sized me up,' she said. 'He really thought himself a ladies man.'

Dressed in a navy-blue pin-stripe suit with a matching blue tie and breast-pocket handkerchief, Peterson stood out from the other customers who were mostly casually dressed young people. The three sat down and John explained what he wanted. 'In order to clarify certain matters,' he wrote later, 'it was absolutely essential for me to identify and discount a person allegedly said to be the father of Annabel Rose.' He told Tom Eyles that he wanted a photograph of John Brian Rose and his wife who lived at an address in Hallem Road, Clevedon.

'He wanted me to enquire into the personal and business details,' said Eyles. When he asked about the reason behind Peterson's request he was told that it concerned the recovery of some important documents relating to his father's business which may have been given to Mr Rose by a disaffected former employee.

Eyles was given detailed instructions including a diagram showing the location of the house to be placed under surveillance. John handed over £25 on the understanding that the balance would be paid on completion of the enquiry. The private investigator's first attempt at photography was not entirely successful as he reported when John telephoned him from the Midlands. Eyles was asked to try again and on 28 September he repeated his surveillance at Hallem Road. That evening John called in person and was given a set of colour photographs. He paid Tom Eyles £30 in cash and left, saying he would be in touch. Eyles noticed that his client had parked his car out of sight, so he followed him discreetly in the darkness. He watched from behind a privet hedge as John drove off in a black BMW, registration number A936 FJU. He did not see John again.

'In all of my limited dealings with Peterson,' said Eyles, 'he never gave me his address, but he told my wife that he lived in a flat in Leigh Woods.' Tom Eyles pursued a businesslike approach with his clients and had prepared notes on the surveillance enquiry he had carried out for Peterson. John asked for them when he called at the investigator's home, but Eyles was reluctant to part with them 'because they were not up to standard'. He had recently broken his right arm, which was still in plaster, and the notes were thus very untidy and somewhat scribbled. But John was keen to have them as they were, even though Eyles offered to get his wife to type them out. They agreed that a photocopy should be made and John left with this in his pocket. This document, subsequently found in his flat, was to play a crucial role in John's subsequent troubles.

It seemed that the photographic surveillance was at least partly intended to satisfy John's suspicion that Annabel had been seeing another man. When he questioned her about this, he claimed she told him the man he saw her with was her father. Tom Eyles's brief was to take photographs at Hallem Road so that John could identify this man.

It emerged that, prior to hiring Eyles, John had spoken to the vicar of Almondsbury church asking permission to view the baptism records. The notes that he made on that occasion as part of his own private enquiry were later found in John's briefcase. He had also taken photographs of the house in Hallem Road as 'a point of reference' to brief

Eyles. Yet, the roll of film remained undeveloped until after John was arrested. The prints proved to be of poor quality in any case, and John's response was, 'I'm pretty useless with cameras' – a ripe excuse for someone who had worked for a while in a camera shop.

John believed the photographs taken by Eyles confirmed that the man he had seen with Annabel was not her father but a person affiliated to the legal profession. This was part of his plan to furnish the police with evidence of wrongdoing on the part of Annabel Rose. It reeked of harassment and backfired badly.

Eyles's surveillance resulted in the notes, which contained references to three vehicle registration numbers. John disregarded this information and thought the notes were useless. His explanation was that Eyles had exceeded his brief. 'I didn't ask him to do that ... I think he was trying to substantiate his fee, which was about eighty quid.'

John summarily dismissed the surveillance document: 'It's worthless,' he said later. Nevertheless he kept it, placing it in the monk's chest in his flat, where it was subsequently found with deeply incriminating consequences.

John said he telephoned WDC Sandra Burnett nearly every day, sometimes twice a day, up to 9 October 1987. But he did not tell her he had employed Tom Eyles and he never gave his real name. WDC Burnett knew him as Mr Jessop or Peter and, according to John, their conversation over the telephone led other detectives at the police station to think they were having an affair. Yet when he had an appointment to meet her as arranged on 13 October 1987 he failed to honour it. His reason was that he was not in Bristol that day and, in any case, he maintained that he would only meet her when she had checked the information he had given her. There was a suggestion that John simply backed off when he realised that Sandra would be accompanied by a male officer. When questioned about his allegations after he had been arrested, John said, 'I went to the police.' It was pointed out that he had not disclosed his identity. 'But I would have done at the end of the day,' he said.

These activities showed John exercising his powers of manipulation. He liked to think of himself as always one step ahead of everyone else and boasted that he knew more than the police. He wanted to use the power of information (and disinformation) as a means of exerting control. His willingness to engage the police in dialogue, albeit at a safe distance and using a false name, was his way of achieving supremacy. It is another characteristic that he shares with men known to be serial killers.

During the long series of tape-recorded interviews with Detective Chief Inspector Bryan Saunders, which took place after he was arrested on 29 October 1987, John talked about his relationship with Annabel Rose. His account was recorded in three interviews lasting over three and a half hours. Early on, Bryan Saunders established that the young woman was aware of John's rape conviction. 'Yes, she knew everything,' he said. He explained that he had once thought a lot of her but not any longer. 'The opposite of love,' he said, 'is not hatred. The opposite of love is indifference.' He reiterated that their relationship was 'a remarkable affair'.

Bryan Saunders disclosed that Annabel Rose had said that John threatened her.

'With what?'

'With disclosing your relationship to her husband in the first instance?'

'That is correct.'

'And also threatening her with physical violence.' The detective explained that he was interested to know the way John's relationship with Annabel finished and how he felt about it.

'I know what you're getting at,' said John. 'Was I so dramatically upset that it's thrown me off my balance?'

'Yes.'

'Let me state quite categorically, that is not the case.'

The officer suggested it was one thing to split up with a woman and something else to hire a private detective to find out things about her to assist the police. 'It's unique to me,' Saunders said. He again put his point that, when the relationship ended, John became very angry and threatened Annabel with violence.

'With what?'

'Threatened to hit her.'

'What an amazing thing,' retorted John angrily. He went on to explain that he had seen her many times since they broke up, 'so, if I had wanted to hit her, beat her up or whatever ... I would have had so many opportunities'. He furthered this by asking, 'If this allegation is correct, (a) why have I not hit her and (b) why did she not, at the time when the threat was supposed to be issued, complain formally to the police?'

Bryan Saunders suggested that John was so annoyed by the break-up that he offered 'mild violence' and threatened to create embarrassment.

'And have I done that?' John asked.

'Well, you employed a private detective.'

John went on the defensive, saying, 'I went to the police; did she?' adding, 'I can't win, can I?' He recounted how he had contacted the police, made his allegations to Sandra Burnett, and how he had undertaken to obtain evidence to support them by hiring the services of Tom Eyles, the private investigator. Saunders thought it was 'an amazing story'.

'Oh well, I don't quite know, amazing is a most amazing adjective,' retorted John.

Referring to Tom Eyles, Saunders asked, 'What was his brief, John?'

'Ah!'

'What was his brief?'

'Well, that is all part and parcel of what I was trying to do. This conversation is getting us nowhere.'

The detective wondered why John did not give his correct name or present himself in person to the police when he made his enquiries. John said he would have done so at a point in the inquiry when his information had been proved correct. Saunders implied it was odd that, having hired a private detective and after making telephone calls to the police, he neither identified himself properly nor made a formal complaint.

'I think we have firmly established beyond any reasonable doubt,' declared John, 'that, far from partaking in any illegal act, I have in fact tried conscientiously to do things the right and proper way by contacting members of the Avon and Somerset Constabulary.'

'You didn't give your name, John.'

'Right, can I come on to that?' John argued that, as he had not hurt anyone and gone about things in the correct way, it did not matter that he had not given his name.

'Don't let's fall out about this, John,' said Saunders, 'but I am dealing with a man, a man scorned by his lover, who then undertook to basically make her life difficult.'

John denied he was a man scorned and he repeated that he had never threatened to hurt Annabel Rose. 'Let me make that absolutely certain,' he said.

'What were you in fear of?' asked Saunders.

'Well, I don't know at this stage. I don't know, but she had access to my records.'

'So it was some uncertain thing that she might allege?'

'Yes, yes, there was a big axe falling on my head, the likes of which I don't know ... She did have access to my criminal records.'

'Yes, John, I got access to your criminal records.'

'Everybody seems to, including the *News of the World*,' John retorted sarcastically.

Bryan Saunders failed to see how knowledge of John's conviction for rape and robbery could be used to blackmail him. 'It is public, it was in the newspapers.'

'She knows about everything,' said John. 'She knows about Sharon Major.'

'But, yes, what is she going to do to you, John?'

'Well, I don't know. Well, she hasn't done it, so I don't know.'

'What did you fear she was going to do?'

'Nothing, I don't know...'

Saunders asked him if he had not threatened Annabel.

'That is not true, Bryan, that is not true.'

John acknowledged they had had an angry row – 'rhetoric on both sides' was the way he described it – and, of his affair with her, John concluded, 'I wish I had told her nothing. I wish I had never met her...' But he was not sufficiently upset 'to go and hurt anybody, no, no, certainly not'.

On 11 September 1987, John was in Coventry. He went into Beatties Store intending to buy a pair of shoes and was served by Marija Vilcins. The particular footwear he wanted was not in stock so the helpful manageress telephoned Lewis's in Birmingham to order a pair. 'We chatted for about 40 minutes,' said Marija, adding, 'I think it was then that he told me he was a management consultant.'

Later that afternoon John telephoned the shop and asked Marija if she would have dinner with him.

It was the classic John Cannan charm offensive. 'He seemed extremely courteous and plausible,' said 28-year-old Marija.

He arranged to pick her up from her home where she lived with her widowed mother, and on Sunday evening, 13 September, John arrived at 7pm in his black 1.6 series 3 BMW bearing gifts of chocolates and flowers. They drove to the Chateau Impney Hotel in Worcester where they dined and walked afterwards in the gardens. He took Marija home at about midnight but did not go into the house. The next day John called into the shoe shop to take Marija to lunch. They continued to see each other in the following weeks. Marija met John's mother at her home and the young woman got the impression that John was 'a well-off gentleman, with good manners, attentive towards me, well dressed on all occasions and generous'.

At the end of September John went on holiday to Crete. During the first week of October and still glowing with his Mediterranean suntan, he paid an evening visit to the Suitor Dating Agency in Park Street, Bristol. The agency, which was run by 28-year-old Caroline Francis, a former member of Britain's Olympic synchronised-swimming team, specialised in video-dating. Prospective suitors appeared in a five-minute video costing £95, in which they talked about themselves and the sort of companion they were seeking.

John, who gave his name as John Peterson, was later described by Caroline Francis as 'very jumpy and wild-eyed. He was worked up, almost animal-like. His eyes constantly flitted around the room.' She was apprehensive and pleased that her husband was on hand. Tim Francis invited their visitor to put the bag he was carrying on a chair but he declined. 'Mr Peterson' paid the requisite fee and appeared smiling before the camera to make his film.

One of the authors was allowed to watch the video at Bristol police headquarters. John Cannan cut a good image on screen in his dark business suit, white shirt and striped tie, and confidently answered the dating agency's questions. 'If you were stranded on a desert island, what sort of person would you like to take with you?'

'Physically someone like Stephanie Beacham,' he answered, adding, 'But no, joking apart, someone natural, nice, pleasant, somebody with character.' Asked if there were any particular female characteristics which he disliked, he replied, 'Yes, I have a dislike of inflated egos. People who are "Look at me, I'm great" type. I don't like that at all. I just like normal average people.'

The interviewer asked him what he looked for in a person of the opposite sex when they first met. 'Apart from the physical side, I think somebody who is pleasant, who is natural, who is relaxed, somebody who is calm,' was his comprehensive answer. Are there any famous people you admire? 'Yes, a few. People like Gandhi, philosophers like Bertrand Russell, present-day people like Prince Charles, who is socially aware, to people like Bob Geldof,' John said, adding, 'but I admire them – I don't idolise them. I think there is a subtle difference.'

Do you have any ambitions for the future or do you feel

that you have achieved them? 'I've achieved them,' said 'Mr Peterson'. 'Financially, I have achieved them.' It was an assured performance in front of the camera that later won mocking admiration from the police.

While talking to Caroline Francis and completing his dating-agency enrolment form, he described the type of girl he was looking for. She must be aged between 25 and 35 and be in excellent physical shape with stunning good looks. He ruled out redheaded women and stipulated that he only wanted to meet 'clean-living girls'. He made reference to his business and also to his new BMW car and flat. Politically, he described himself as 'one of those dreadful SDP types'. Asked what period of history he would have liked to have lived in, he replied unhesitatingly, 'The Elizabethan.' He explained that he thought a ruff would have suited him, along with the tights and sword. 'I can see me on some bridge of some galleon being a pirate,' he said.

John portrayed himself as a romantic, cultured figure, combining the enjoyment of holidays abroad with motor-racing and theatre-going. He said that he spent his evenings reading books on Aristotle and Adler. Of his appearance, he claimed that he was often mistaken for Sacha Distel, the French singer, and Trevor Francis, the football star.

John wrote to the authors claiming he was inundated with telephone calls from women as a result of his video. But Caroline and Tim Francis were so concerned about their client's intentions that they took his name off their dating list and did not show it. 'We felt there was something very strange about him,' they said later.

The video-dating incident came up in the tape-recorded

interviews with DCI Bryan Saunders that took place after John was arrested. Their exchanges provided some of the lighter moments of these long interview sessions. The detective showed John a photocopy of his enrolment form for the Suitor Dating Agency.

'They are extremely complimentary about you,' he said.

'Are they? Can I have a look?' John explained that he had only enrolled at the agency 'for a bit of fun. Yes. Only a bit of fun … I felt it was time I got married. No! No! Actually, don't laugh, please don't laugh … please don't laugh. I mean – there are girls and there are girls, and I felt that it's time that I pack everything in and perhaps look for somebody and get married. And there are many people who wish to sort of get married just for companionship and I, you know, I did – crossed my mind – that perhaps … but I did nothing about it. She [Caroline Francis, the dating agency owner] will tell you that I was the worst client she had ever had, because she kept putting these girls to me, right – "Will you come in because they want to meet you, sir?" – and I never did. I never went. It was just a silly thing.'

Reading the application form and the section which noted John's preferences as a suitor, Saunders remarked, 'Excellent physical shape, stunning good looks.'

'Well, there you go, you see,' answered John.

'No redheads.'

'No.'

'Why, don't you like redheads?'

'I don't like redheads,' John confirmed, adding, 'Anybody with red hair, I shy away from.'

Saunders went on: 'Good character, tolerant of children, take each person on their merit.'

'Of course.'

'A born romantic.'

'Oh yes, maybe.'

'I'm interested in this where it says hobbies and interests,' commented the detective. 'Just to try and establish if we've missed anything that will tie in with your movements. Plays tennis.. I wonder if this is some poetic licence?'

'No, I used to play tennis,' said John. 'I have an interest...'

'Motor racing?'

'Yes, I'm an avid motor-racing watcher.'

'Walking? Enjoy the theatre?'

'Yes, which ties up with what I said about Leamington,'

Saunders continued to muse his way through the application form, reading out John's entries. 'Wine bars.'

'Yes.'

'Eating out.'

'Yes.'

'Weekends abroad.'

'Yes.'

'Enjoys reading.'

'Yes, of course.'

'And this is the SDP manifesto?'

'Yes, well that is where my political leanings lie.'

'Harold Robbins ... You're interested in Eastern philosophy?' Assuring John that he was not taking the rise out of him, Saunders asked, 'Is that a fact, though?'

'Yes,' came the firm answer. 'It's my raison d'être of life if you like.'

Observing his chief's bemused reaction, DI Terry Jones said, 'That's buggered you now then.'

'The silence is stunning,' said Saunders.

'That is my main interest in life,' continued John.

'Philosophy; and I am associated with a Buddhist monk, one of the most famous in the West, Kimodamo...'

'Can you repeat that?'

'His name is Kimodamo and he lectures at Warwick University in Buddhist psychology ... It was going through my mind and perhaps I might have had that option open to me had I chosen to study for a degree.'

Continuing the discussion of John's intellectual pursuits, Saunders enquired, 'Any other philosophy?'

'Yes, Freud, well, psychology and philosophy. I have read Freud, Adler, Jung. I have studied Russell, Kant, Plato, Aristotle – most of the famous philosophers, both traditional and contemporary. That is what I do most nights, actually.'

'Is it really – reading?'

'Yes.'

'Alone?'

'Well, yes, mostly.'

'There's a book in your flat,' said Saunders, 'it caught my eye...'

'Shall I tell you what it is?' offered John.

'Yes.'

'It refers to death.'

'That's right, John.'

'I was wondering when you'd mention that. Yes, there is a book in my flat and it's ... the topic is death ... whether one can justify death or killing. For example, if one is a purist and believes that killing is wrong, totally wrong under any circumstances, would you then have not killed Adolf Hitler? If it would have meant saving lives of six million Jews? Would killing have been wrong then? It also deals with topics such as abortion, that a foetus can be terminated at 24 weeks which is perfectly permissible under law and yet is that really morally permissible when children have been born at 22 weeks and have gone on to live and thrive? So it calls into question various moral issues and, as life is important to us all, so is death.'

Warming to his theme, John continued, 'And, before you can understand what life is, you also have to have some sort of appreciation of what death is. So it is important that, if you read about life on one hand, you have an appreciation of what death is on the other. That is why I read.'

'OK, thank you for that,' interrupted Saunders. 'I've been enlightened there I think.'

Next he moved on to questions about the possibility of John taking a university course.

John said he believed he would have been accepted as a full-time mature student but that was only one option open to him at what he described as a 'cross-roads in life'.

'Have you ever had any of your girlfriends at university?' enquired the officer.

John sought clarification. 'Had them in a sexual sense?' he asked.

'No, I'll rephrase that. Any of your girlfriends currently at university?'

'No.'

Throughout his life John had amply demonstrated that he had a facility for charming the opposite sex and acquiring girlfriends with ease. Why then should he want to approach a dating agency? People prone to serial violence trawl for potential victims and there can be little doubt that, after three rape attacks, John was in the grip of powerful urges. It was perhaps a glimpse of that intensity which so unnerved Caroline Francis. John explained the incident as an aberration. 'I DID NOT AT ANY time have the slightest intention of actually meeting any of the young ladies whose videos I had been shown,' he said.

Why then did he do it? He said it was for fun but clearly he was excited by the possibilities – 'psyched-up' might be an appropriate description of his mood. Perhaps he was aware that he had made too great an impact. As a means of finding a companion, video-dating was too public, too well documented. His marauding instincts told him there were other ways that involved less risk.

8

JULIA

Julia Holman had been working in Bristol for less than a month. She was employed as a recruitment administrator by Arthur Andersen & Co, whose offices were in Broad Quay House. When she finished work at 5.30pm on Wednesday, 7 October 1987, she went with three office colleagues to the Colonial Bar at the Watershed in central Bristol. She stayed, drinking and chatting to her friends, until 6.50pm when she decided to leave.

Julia had left her car that morning at Canon's Marsh car park, not far from the Watershed. She walked alongside the harbour for a short distance and then used an alleyway to reach Canon's Road. Using a gap in the fence, she entered the open-air car park and strolled towards her blue Ford Fiesta. She took the keys out of her handbag as she approached it, then unlocked the door, slid into the driver's seat and pulled the door shut.

As she put the key into the ignition, her driver's door was wrenched open and she found herself looking at a man

131

who was a total stranger. He produced what she took to be a handgun with a barrel about six inches long. Bending his head into the car and thrusting the gun against her side, he said, 'If you do what I say, you won't get hurt.' He pushed her as if he wanted her to move across into the front passenger seat while continuing to point the gun at her.

With great presence of mind, Julia Holman swung her legs round to the right and kicked out at him, at the same time pushing him off-balance with her hands. She also shouted at him and let out a loud scream. As the man straightened up, she slammed the car door shut, started the car and rapidly drove out of the car park. She noticed that he casually walked off in the direction of the city centre.

Julia then drove to the Colonial Bar, from where she called the police. She told detectives that she did not notice anyone following her while she made her way to her car. She described the man as aged about 30 to 35 years of age and about 5ft 8in to 5ft 10in tall. He had a dark complexion which she described as Latin or Italian, clean shaven but with sideburns level with the bottom of his ears. His hair was black, collar-length but tidy. He was wearing an unbuttoned grey or beige mackintosh with epaulettes, under which she saw a dark-coloured business suit, a light-coloured shirt and a dark tie.

When John was subsequently questioned about this incident, he described Julia Holman's account as a 'highly original little statement'. He said he did not know where Canon's Marsh car park was. When DCI Saunders pointed out its location on a map of Bristol, John, in one of his characteristic attempts to pre-empt the police, asked, 'And are you going to say, "Where were you at 7 o'clock on that day?"'

'Well, I am ultimately,' replied Saunders.

'I'm having everything thrown at me, aren't I?' was John's rejoinder.

Referring to the imitation handgun found in John's car when he was arrested, the detective asked, 'Can you tell me the purpose that you've got that gun?'

Once again John went off on a diversion, wanting to know if he was being arrested for committing the offence or for suspicion of the offence.

Patiently, Bryan Saunders said that the woman in question had been confronted by a man with a gun.

John interrupted. 'Did the man say anything about abducting her?'

'No.'

'So, we're not talking about the abduction of a person. We are talking about an approach on to a person by an unknown person, with a gun for whatever purposes could have been in mind?'

Quick to seize the opening, Saunders asked, 'Well, put it this way, was it you?'

'No, it wasn't.'

'Right ... Let's try and place you on Wednesday...'

'You had enough trouble trying to place me on Thursday,' laughed John, 'let alone Wednesday.'

'Let's ask the simple question. You say it wasn't you. Why have you got an imitation gun in your car?'

John's reply was to maintain that it was clearly an imitation weapon.

Saunders countered with the view that what was important was the reaction of a person at whom such a gun was pointed. The upshot of all this questioning clarified that John had purchased the imitation firearm in Weston-super-Mare eight to ten weeks previously, well before the attempted abduction of Julia Holman and the disappearance of Shirley Banks. John went on to add that it was his habit to lock the gun away in his flat.

He then launched into a discussion about defining abduction and disagreed that the incident at Canon's Marsh car park could be described as attempted abduction. 'All I'm asking,' said John, 'is that you do not attach emotive, emotive adjectives to something which you cannot support by fact.'

The detective suggested they stuck to the facts: 'The question is ... where were you at 7 o'clock? Unless someone else was using your telephone,' Saunders told John, 'you were in your flat at 7.46. This "attempted abduction" – they're my words – occurred at around 7pm. The man described by the victim had a suntan and was wearing a trench coat.'

'Apropos the trench coat,' John enquired of Saunders. 'Ever watched Maigret?' John continued by asking what the light level would have been like at 7pm on an evening in early October. The two detectives agreed that it would be twilight. John's point was that it would not be possible to identify a person in those conditions.

Julia Holman was an attractive young woman whose quick thinking had plucked her from danger. 'I did not receive any injury or discomfort in this incident,' she confirmed to detectives. Late on the night of her attempted abduction, she was shown a photofit picture of a man known as Mr Kipper. She could not say that this was the same man who had accosted her but his appearance was very similar.

Later, on 5 November, when John was in custody on a

more serious charge, he was asked to attend an identity parade at Bristol central police station. His request that all those taking part should wear white boiler suits to match the forensic suit he had been made to wear was agreed. The ID parade was held in the police station's main report-writing room on the ground floor. Inspector David Harper reported that 'Eight other persons of similar age, height and general appearance as the defendant were assembled in a line.' John's solicitor's clerk, Terry Moore, was present and the witness, Julia Holman, stood behind a one-way mirror that permitted her to see without being seen. Her eyes took in a row of figures looking like 'Hovis' flour men.

At Terry Moore's request, two participants in the line-up were asked to remove their spectacles and those wearing ties were asked to loosen or remove them. Inspector Harper then asked John to take up any position he liked in the line-up – he stood in the third position from the left: number three in police parlance. Julia immediately identified number three as the man who had threatened her with a gun. Inspector Harper asked her to repeat it, which she did. In her statement she said that from her position behind the screen she saw 'straight away a man ... at number three who I recognised as the man who had attempted to abduct me'. She followed the procedure explained to her, by waiting until she had looked at all the men on the parade before making her identification. 'I was still in no doubt that that's the man at number three, my attacker.'

Asked if he had any comments to make on the conduct of the ID parade, John replied, 'None whatsoever.'

In his subsequent letters John denied any involvement

with the attempted abduction. 'No, I was NOT in that car park,' he stated. 'I genuinely was at home that evening.'

Nevertheless, following Julia Holman's positive identification John was formally charged with attempted kidnap.

The day after Julia's attempted abduction, Thursday, 8 October, Shirley Banks disappeared from the centre of Bristol. What the police did not put together when interviewing Julia Holman was that a similar attempted abduction had taken place a year to the day in 1986 in Whiteladies Road – less than a mile from Canon's Marsh car park.

9
SHIRLEY

Christine Fortune and her husband had been invited by John Cannan to have dinner with him at his flat at Foye House that coming weekend. She had to cancel the arrangement so she tried desperately to contact him by telephone. On 7 and 8 October 1987, she telephoned several times. She rang Cannan again between 6.30 and 9pm from her home. 'I cannot recall exactly how many times I telephoned,' she said, 'but there was no reply.'

Later, when he was asked to recall his movements on Wednesday, 7 October, John said, 'I went and had a piss-up with Val Humphreys [his neighbour].' He thought he saw her at her flat at about 7.30pm and 'turned into bed tired and mellow at about 11.30pm'.

When he was reminded that he made a telephone call to his mother that evening at 7.46pm, John agreed that he saw Val afterwards, which, bearing in mind the call lasted seven minutes, made the time of their meeting nearer 8pm. Then he thought he'd gone up to Val's flat before calling his mother. He remembered that he had left a joint of lamb in the oven to roast and he had to go back down to his flat to attend to it: 'It's quite likely that I made that phone call while I was there.'

Val Humphreys could not corroborate this claim, although she said John had been to her flat on two or three occasions. On one of these he had to return to his own kitchen to tend the oven in which he was cooking a joint of lamb. She could not recall when this happened.

It would be rather odd if this incident had occurred on Wednesday, because Val would surely have related it to meeting John the following day. For on Thursday afternoon at about 2pm, John took her to her hairdresser in Park Street, Bristol. She had an injured foot and was not very mobile. He dropped her off at Geoffrey Stewart's salon and collected her at about 4pm. They drove straight back to Foye House which took around 15 minutes. He dropped her at the entrance and she saw John drive out of the car park towards Clifton.

John answered the telephone on Friday morning sometime between 9 and 9.30am. A voice said, 'Hello, John, it's Chrissie Fortune.' He replied hesitantly, as if befuddled with sleep, and could not at first place the caller. 'Chrissie Fortune from Rainbow Pottery, the plant shop,' she offered by way of identification.

'Oh, yes, hello,' answered John.

'I'm sorry, have I woken you up?'

He said something about it taking him a while to get going.

'I'm sorry but we aren't going to make it tomorrow,' Chrissie told him. 'Sorry it's such short notice, but I did try to contact you yesterday.'

'No problem,' said John. 'I'll be in the shop anyway sometime.'

John admitted later that he had forgotten her name – 'I thought, "Chrissie who?"' He claimed, however, that she had called not on Friday morning but on Thursday.

At about 1pm on Friday, John called on Val Humphreys in Flat 5 again and asked if he could borrow her vacuum cleaner because his machine was broken. She lent him her cleaner and asked him to return it later in the day as she needed it herself. He brought it back that evening at around 7.30pm and stayed chatting to Val and her boyfriend who was visiting till late that evening.

Sometime that afternoon there had been a fire of sorts in Leigh Woods near Foye House. It was then that Amelia Hart witnessed what she took to be a violent incident when she and her husband drove past. Later they linked what they had seen with the disappearance of Shirley Banks.

Shirley Anne Banks (nee Reynolds) was born in Edinburgh on 4 August 1958. She had moved with her parents to Liverpool and later to the West Country, where she attended Yeovil High School. Shirley was a bright pupil and left school with nine 'O' level qualifications and 'A' level passes in English and History. She was fond of music and played both the piano and violin. The possibility of a university place was open to her but she chose instead to study for a diploma in business management at Bristol Polytechnic.

Slim, blonde and attractive, Shirley was the eldest of three girls; two years separated her from Gillian and five from Alison. In 1980, Shirley decided to go off to live in Corfu for a few months and, soon after she returned, Gillian introduced her to Richard Banks. 'It was mutual attraction between us right from the word go,' he said later.

Shirley went to work for Hourmont Travel Ltd in Bristol and Richard moved in to share her room at Gillian's flat. They stayed there for about six weeks before moving into a place of their own. After a few months, they were in a position to buy a house and raised a mortgage on a property in Coldharbour Road, Redland, Bristol.

In June 1984, Shirley answered an advertisement in the local newspaper and found employment with Alexandra Workwear Ltd at the company's headquarters in Britannia Road, Bristol. The firm designs and manufactures clothing for the work environment and operates a number of retail outlets in the United Kingdom. Shirley settled in quickly and made new friends including Karen Pearce, a 24-year-old design assistant, with whom she shared confidences. Before Shirley had a car of her own, Karen gave her a lift into work and, at the end of the day, the two women sometimes called into the Cambridge Arms for a drink. On occasions, they were joined by Richard Banks and it was no secret that he and Shirley were living together.

Around Christmas 1986, Shirley bought a car from a colleague at Alexandra Workwear. The vehicle was an orange-coloured Mini, registration number HWL 507N, which her boss described as tatty and in a very run-down condition. There was a great deal of rust on the car, particularly at the bottom of the doors and in the sills. Some of these rust patches had been treated with grey primer. The driver's door did not function properly and Shirley used the door on the passenger side to get in and out of the car. She told her colleagues that she only intended using the Mini to drive from A to B and would not rely on it to travel any distance.

Apart from driving to and from work, Karen Pearce believed that the furthest Shirley went in her car was to the riding stables at Churchill on Saturday mornings. Riding and squash were among Shirley's favourite leisure activities and her black riding hat and leather crop were habitually kept on the back window shelf of the Mini.

Richard Banks was a year older than Shirley and, when they first met, worked as a salesman for Pitney Bowes plc. He and Shirley decided to get married in the autumn of 1987 and set the date for 22 August. Her boss at Alexandra Workwear recalled that, leading up to the wedding, Shirley went on a diet, losing several pounds, and also took up smoking, a habit that she had not previously indulged in. The couple had moved upmarket on the housing front a few months earlier and taken out a joint mortgage on a house in Clifton valued at £53,000. They were married at Yeovil Registry Office and held a reception for family and friends at the home of Shirley's parents in Crewkerne.

Richard and Shirley spent their first night as a married couple at a Somerset hotel, before returning to Bristol the next day to hold a party in the afternoon for their friends. Afterwards, they drove down to Devon to visit Richard's grandmother and an elderly aunt, neither of whom was well enough to attend the wedding. They stayed Sunday night at a small guest house in Paignton after enjoying a fish and chip supper and a game of bingo on the pier. The next week was spent in Cornwall, where they rented a holiday cottage.

This was not quite the conventional start to a honeymoon but Richard and Shirley had been living together for several years and the few days in Devon and Cornwall were a prelude to something special. For his attainments as his company's top salesman, Richard had won a holiday for two, staying in a first-class hotel on the Isle of Capri for five days. So, at the beginning of September, they flew to the Mediterranean with the prospect of a holiday in the sun and in the knowledge that Richard would return to a better job at the end of the month.

He had taken a position with Prime Office Developments in Bristol for a higher salary and better commission. He would also be able to exchange his 'C' registration Ford Escort for a BMW that went with the new job.

Their friends observed no particular strains in Richard and Shirley's relationship. It was noticed, however, that, whereas Richard had bought a number of suits and shirts, Shirley seemed to have only a limited selection of clothes. Indeed, her boss described her appearance as not very good. She hardly ever wore make-up and he thought her a generally untidy person whose desk was always a mess. A female colleague remarked that Shirley's wardrobe was limited whereas Richard's was quite extensive. She had also heard Shirley complain that her husband was sometimes frivolous with money. Nevertheless, everyone thought they were a happy couple; they had a number of good friends and often met them for dinner and drinks at the Avon Gorge Hotel.

The question of buying new clothes was on Shirley's mind on Thursday, 8 October 1987 when she woke up to go to work. She took Richard a cup of tea in bed at about 7.55am and told him she wanted the chequebook to go shopping that evening to buy a dress. He needed the chequebook himself but promised he would call back at the house and leave it for her to pick up later. Shirley kissed her husband goodbye and left the house with a workmate, Sally Wilkins, whose car was off the road and who had asked Shirley to give her a lift. In keeping with her image as a dull dresser, Shirley was wearing a well-worn ankle-length black skirt that had a slit at the back.

Richard arose at about 8.10am and when he went downstairs found a note from Shirley in the front room reminding him about the chequebook: 'DON'T FORGET CHEQUEBOOK, OR ELSE!' she had written playfully. He had various appointments throughout the day in and around Bristol but remembered his promise about the chequebook. He secured his first order for his new company and had it in mind to take Shirley out for a celebratory drink that evening.

When Shirley arrived at work, she told some of her friends about her plans to go shopping in Broadmead that evening. It was pay day for Alexandra Workwear employees and Shirley asked Karen Pearce if she would go into town with her for an evening shopping trip. The two women had been out before but on this occasion Karen declined. Shirley told Jeanne Duvivier that she was thinking of buying a dress at Debenhams department store. She also mentioned that she had a lot to do that evening for, apart from her planned shopping excursion, she was supposed to attend a meeting of the firm's social club and also intended to get someone to look at her car. She indicated to Jeanne that she might have to forget the car but could use it as an excuse to leave the social club early. Jeanne said she also planned to go shopping that evening and might therefore see Shirley later in Broadmead.

Shirley left her office at about 5pm, heading for the social club meeting. She then returned home where she changed into close-fitting yellow slacks and a cream-coloured top; she also picked up the chequebook. At about 6.15pm, she telephoned Karen Pearce to see if she would change her mind about going shopping. Karen said she couldn't afford to go but the two women made a date for the following evening to meet at the Avon Gorge Hotel with two other colleagues. Karen asked Shirley to call in on her when she had finished shopping so she could see what her friend had bought. Shirley said she might but would not promise.

After leaving the office at about 5.15pm, Jeanne Duvivier collected her 17-year-old daughter from her workplace and drove back to central Bristol. It was drizzling and they enjoyed a snack in a Wimpy Bar before going into Debenhams store in Broadmead. It was almost 7pm when mother and daughter approached one of the escalators. They saw Shirley walking towards them and they stopped and chatted. Jeanne introduced her daughter and Shirley, pointing to her slacks, said, 'As you can see, I've changed into my shopping gear.' She said she was going up to the first floor where the ladies' department was located. Jeanne said she would probably see her there later as she intended looking round the department herself.

The next time the shoppers encountered each other was in the ladies' section on the first floor. Shirley was carrying a full-length navy and white dress that she held up against herself and asked Jeanne what she thought of it. Jeanne was complimentary about the dress and Shirley said she was intent on buying it; the price seemed reasonable at

£24.99. They stood and chatted for a while and Shirley mentioned she wanted black high-heeled shoes and a cardigan to go with it, although she would wait until Saturday before buying them. By now it was nearly 7.30pm and Jeanne and her daughter went off to a cubicle to try on some clothes. Shirley walked off towards the check-out saying, 'See you tomorrow.' She never did.

Seventeen-year-old Nicola Wiltshire worked part-time at Debenhams store in Broadmead on Thursday evenings and all day Saturdays. On Thursday, 8 October 1987, she was at her station in the store's Top Shop section from 5 until 8pm and worked at the cash register no. 42 because the store was busy. She served Shirley Banks and recorded her purchase of a navy-blue and white dress. The transaction amounted to £24.99 and Shirley paid by cheque drawn on the joint National Westminster Bank account of Mr R. Banks and Mrs S. A. Banks. In accordance with company practice, the shop assistant wrote her employee number on the back of the cheque, a cheque guarantee card number, the till transaction number and the code of the item purchased. The till roll recording transaction number 1053 was time-stamped at 19.26 hrs. The customer's receipt was placed with the dress into a Debenhams (Top Shop) bag which, due to a shortage of bags of the size normally used for dresses, was of a larger size.

A slim vivacious blonde, Shirley Banks probably turned many men's heads that evening. We know she turned one for sure – that of John Cannan. We cannot be certain of his movements, but, following his previous pattern of behaviour, he had probably been wandering through the store, driven by an overwhelming desire to seek out a female victim. Then his blue eyes would have settled on

Shirley while she browsed innocently through the clothes' rails in search of a dress. In an effort to remain inconspicuous in the ladies' department he would seemingly have interested himself with a possible gift for a girlfriend. However, his eyes would have been furtively following Shirley's every move. Now he would be stalking his prey, waiting patiently for the chance to pounce. As she walked to her car, he would have been but a few steps behind her.

If we follow the pattern of his attempt to abduct Julia Holman, he probably approached his victim with menace, and got into her car beside her.

Richard Banks finished work that day at about 6pm. He went back to the office, which was closed, but, feeling elated about his success at securing his first order, he wanted to share his news with friends. He sought out acquaintances at a couple of public houses but could not find anyone he knew, so he headed for the Avon Gorge Hotel where he encountered some friends from his previous firm. Owing to exceptionally heavy traffic in the Bristol area, it was 6.40pm before he reached the hotel. At about 8pm, he telephoned home to speak to Shirley but there was no reply. He stayed for another drink with one of his companions and remarked that he wanted to take Shirley out that evening for a meal.

According to statements he later made to the police, he arrived home at about 8.30pm. Shirley was not back and there was no note indicating where she might be. Richard was not unduly concerned and he reasoned that she had probably met up with a friend while shopping and gone for a drink afterwards. He stayed in the house until just before 10pm when he called in at his local, The Port of Call public house, expecting that he might find Shirley there. He spoke to several people he knew and returned home at about 10.40pm.

By this time, he was growing concerned about his wife's whereabouts but was unsure what to do. He decided the best thing to do was to wait so, as, he explained later, 'I cracked a bottle of Scotch, had a couple of drinks and went to bed.' He woke up during the small hours but still Shirley had not returned. 'I sat in bed waiting and wondering,' he said. Feelings of fear and panic were beginning to churn his stomach. He knew his wife very well. She was faithful and only had eyes for him. He reasoned she could not be with another man. But, if she was with a girlfriend, why did she not phone him if only to put his troubled mind at rest? Something was terribly wrong...

Richard arose on Friday morning at about 7.30am. The telephone rang just before 8am and he rushed to it, thinking at last Shirley had made contact. But it was her friend Sally Wilkins wanting to know if Shirley would give her a lift to work. Richard explained that Shirley had not come home and asked if Sally had seen her. He received a negative reply. By 8.30am he was driving through Bristol on his way to the office. He went into the building in Victoria Street and waited until 9am before telephoning Alexandra Workwear. He spoke to his wife's boss, Paul Wilcox, who told him that Shirley had telephoned a little while earlier reporting sick. She had not talked directly to Wilcox or to a person in her own department, which would have been normal practice, but to someone in the wages office.

At about 9am that morning, Jennifer Watkins, a clerk in

Alexandra Workwear's wages office, answered the telephone. The caller, whom she immediately recognised as Shirley Banks, said, 'Jenny?'

'Hello, Shirley,' replied Watkins.

'The lines to the division are engaged,' explained Shirley. 'Can you give them a message? I've been up all night with an upset tummy. I won't be in today.'

'Fine, Shirley. I'll let them know,' replied Jenny. (Later Jenny was to say that she detected nothing strange in Shirley's manner.)

Paul Wilcox was duly given the message and shortly afterwards received a telephone call from Richard Banks.

'I was now extremely concerned for Shirley's safety,' said Banks, but he did not immediately report his wife missing to the police. He telephoned the part-time mechanic who occasionally worked on Shirley's Mini to see if he could shed some light on her whereabouts. Colin Brown said that at Shirley's request he had arranged to look at her car on Thursday evening but she had telephoned during the afternoon saying she planned to go late-night shopping and asked if he would see the car for her at the weekend. Richard also called Karen Pearce at Alexandra Workwear; she had no information to offer but shared his concern.

Richard carried on with his work as best he could, discussing a contract with his boss and arranging for a quotation to be typed. At some stage in the morning, he went home to check if Shirley had returned. She had not. He bought some chips at lunchtime and sat in his new red BMW eating them and reading a newspaper. He was in and out of the office several times and telephoned the switchboard to enquire if there were any messages for him. He also went home a couple more times but there was no information or indication of any kind to relieve his deepening anxiety.

Following a late-afternoon appointment with a client he returned home. The time was 5.45pm – there was still no sign of Shirley. At about 6pm Karen Pearce telephoned to say that she had rung several times during the day to see if Shirley was at home but to no avail. She told Richard that she had made an arrangement with Shirley to meet that evening at the Avon Gorge Hotel. Karen went to the hotel to see if Shirley had turned up but telephoned Richard at about 6.15pm with the news that she was not there.

Karen went to Richard and Shirley's home to discuss the situation. They went through the names of all the friends and family members they had contacted between them and Karen believed that the time had come to call the police. For some reason known only to himself, Richard was reluctant to do this. They telephoned the local hospitals and Karen called the police to enquire if Shirley's car had been involved in an accident. There were no reports of any incident involving her car. Finally, in desperation, Karen drove to Redland police station where she reported that Shirley Banks was missing. A policewoman accompanied Karen back to the house. Shirley had been absent for just about 24 hours.

As the days stretched into weeks, the police took statements from Shirley's friends and contacts looking for possible reasons why a young, recently married woman might wish to absent herself from her home and work. All the missing woman's friends agreed that such behaviour was completely out of character. Her boss at Alexandra

Workwear said, 'Shirley Banks was, I believe, quite happy with her work, which was well within her abilities. She appeared content with her home life and had a strong interest in her cats, and I can think of no reason why she should have disappeared.'

Jeanne Duvivier, who was probably the last known acquaintance to see Shirley before she disappeared, said that during the day she was quite normal and happy: 'She seemed the same when I saw her at Debenhams store. I can think of no reason why she should go missing.'

The last spoken word from Shirley to be heard by any of her regular contacts was the telephone call taken on Friday morning by Jenny Watkins. The only slight mystery about the call was that it was placed to Jenny in the first place, for, although she knew Shirley, she was not a close friend like Karen Pearce. The ostensible reason for her taking the call was that the lines to Shirley's own department were engaged. Later enquiries cast doubt on this. Paul Wilcox said that he had been in the office since 8.30am and not one of the four telephones had been in use. 'I cannot see why a call could not have been made to our office,' he said.

There was no shadow of doubt in Jenny Watkins's mind that the caller was Shirley. 'I know her voice very well,' she said to the police. 'I often speak to Shirley and thus I know her voice well on the telephone.' She remained certain of her opinion even after learning that Shirley had a sister with a similar voice. 'I have never spoken to Shirley's sister to the best of my knowledge, and indeed I didn't know she had a sister,' said Jenny. 'I still remain positive that the voice was that of Shirley Banks.'

The Avon and Somerset Constabulary set up their enquiry team, nicknamed 'The Bride Squad', in

Kingsweston House, Bristol. They mounted one of their most comprehensive hunts ever for a missing person. Police frogmen searched Bristol docks and a 20ft-deep pool in Leigh Woods. Aerial reconnaissance photographs were taken by a Royal Air Force Canberra jet equipped with thermal-imaging cameras seeking out a possible grave.

Richard Banks suffered his private hell in the days following Shirley's disappearance. He was sustained by friends and neighbours and, understandably, found it difficult to concentrate on the new job at which he had made such an outstanding start. He spent a great deal of time on the telephone talking to friends. 'They let me rant and rave for hours,' he told a reporter from the *Western Daily Press*. 'It is an outlet for the unbearable pressure.' Equally disconsolate in their own way were Shirley's two cats, Sooty and William, who sat around moping.

Shirley's parents, George and Liz Reynolds, eased their anguish by mounting their own search – they set about looking for their daughter's orange Mini which she drove on the night she disappeared. 'We found 15,' said Mrs Reynolds, 'but of course none of them was Shirley's.'

On Saturday, 10 October, two days after Shirley Banks had disappeared, Marija Vilcins drove down to Bristol to see John as planned. They met at Gordano Services at 6.15pm and drove in convoy to Foye House. John parked his BMW in the driveway next to the flats and Marija pulled her Fiesta up behind; neither car was put in John's garage. This was Marija's first visit to the flat, which she described as expensively decorated and furnished. He explained that the two friends he had invited to dinner had cried off because their children were ill. He also said he had drawn out £90 to buy ingredients for the meal, which he was preparing himself.

They went for a short walk to see Clifton Suspension Bridge before dinner and then ate the meal in an atmosphere that Marija said was 'very romantic'. For £90 it should have been. John mentioned a divorcee in one of the nearby flats who sometimes 'bothered' him and they talked about themselves. John said he accused Marija of 'being scarlet' on account of her other boyfriend, 'and pulled her leg unmercifully'. They kissed and cuddled on the settee but, when they retired for the night, used separate bedrooms. 'I did not have sexual intercourse with him,' explained Marija, 'as I had a period.'

As John put it, 'My big weekend of sex, seduction, souffles and soft music with Marija had been well and truly "thwarted".'

On Sunday morning, they were up by 8.45am to watch the hot-air balloons taking off from Ashton Court in Bristol's annual balloon festival. John went out to buy some newspapers and they spent most of the morning reading them. At about 11am, they drove in the BMW through Ashton Court and then on to the picturesque village of Castle Combe in Wiltshire. After some sightseeing they returned to Bristol at about 4pm and decided to buy a takeaway meal before Marija left for home. They bought the meal in Clifton and went back to the flat to eat it. John mentioned he was running short of money so Marija paid for her own meal.

Around 7pm, they packed their belongings and set off in separate cars to Gordano Services. John bought petrol for Marija and they began their journey north along the M5, she making for Coventry and he for his mother's home at

Sutton Coldfield. When she reached home, Marija telephoned John to say she had arrived safely. He had been complaining of feeling unwell and having a sore throat. In due course, it became apparent that he had a dental abscess.

On Tuesday, 13 October, John took his mother back with him to Bristol and she brought her dog Ben. John was still complaining of being unwell with toothache and sat about reading and watching television. The next day he paid a visit to his dentist, Derek Crayton, at his surgery in Victoria Square, Clifton. John had been a patient since October 1986 when he was living in Richmond Hill. He was given treatment and a prescription for antibiotics and a further appointment for 10am on 16 October. John cancelled a third appointment made for 19 October but completed his treatment on a visit to the surgery on 21 October. Mr Crayton's bill for treatment of £27.72 was not paid.

Mrs Cannan stayed longer than she intended because John was 'poorly'. But on Saturday, 17 October, she decided to return home to Sutton Coldfield and John drove her back. When Marija finished work that day, she called upon John at his mother's home and they spent the weekend together at the nearby Moxhull Hall Hotel at Wishaw. He had booked a double room and a table for two in the elegant restaurant and Marija recalled that the receptionist recognised John. They slept together but did not make love because John was still feeling unwell with his abscess.

They returned to Marija's house on Sunday and spent a lazy day reading the newspapers. John enjoyed a meal with Marija and her mother in the evening, then said goodbye at about 8.30pm. He stayed with his mother until Tuesday, 20 October, when he returned to Bristol in order to keep his final dental appointment. He explained to Marija that he had a business appointment in London, although he did not give her any details. They had arranged to meet each other on Saturday, 24 October, but on the Friday he telephoned to tell her it was off. 'He would not tell me why,' said Marija, 'only to say that he was being picked up. He was very evasive.' He rang again on Sunday to apologise for cancelling their date and to say he wanted to take her out on 3 November, her birthday.

It was an appointment he was destined not to fulfil. On 29 October, he was arrested in Leamington Spa and spent his girlfriend's birthday in police custody.

10
CARMEL

On Thursday, 29 October 1987, three weeks to the day since Shirley went missing, a man entered a boutique known as Ginger in Leamington Spa. It was about 3.55pm and the owner, 40-year-old Carmel Cleary, was arranging clothes on the rails while her manageress, Jane Child, sat at a desk in the front of the shop. They were the only people in the premises which was situated at 20a Regent Street. The man who was wearing black trousers and a grey, zip-up bomber jacket had a silver-grey crash helmet on his head with the visor raised. His jacket was bulging as if there was something bulky in it and a pair of blue-grey gloves poked out of the top left-hand pocket.

The man stood beside one of the clothes rails and said, 'I'm looking for some gift ideas.' Carmel Cleary walked over to where he was standing and produced some jumpers. He said, 'She's a size 38.'

Carmel drew his attention to one of the garments and

explained, 'This is a medium, this will fit her.' 'I could tell,' she said later, 'that he was not interested in the jumpers.'

The man said he wanted something brighter and walked over to the display rails near the desk. 'She's only 24,' he said and paused to look at some of the items displayed.

Sensing that the man did not appear genuine in his enquiries, Carmel Cleary moved over to the desk and casually spoke to Jane Child. She asked her to phone 'Room Service', a nearby shop, on the pretext of settling an account. This was a ploy to bring someone else into the shop. Suddenly, the man was standing next to the two women. He held an orange-handled knife with a serrated blade in his left hand with which he threatened Mrs Cleary. Holding the weapon close to her stomach and speaking to Jane Child, he said, 'Turn out the lights, lock the door and, if you scream, I'll knife her.'

Mrs Cleary picked up the shop keys from the desk and Jane Child walked to the corner of the boutique where the light switches were located. The intruder said, 'What are you doing?' and, still brandishing his knife, walked over to her.

At this point, using great presence of mind, Carmel Cleary dashed across to the front door of her shop and ran out into the street screaming, 'Help! Help! There's a man in the shop with a knife!'

Her desperate screams attracted the immediate attention of Andrew Riley, a builder, who had just entered Regent Street from Portland Street. He ran towards her, asking, 'What's up?'

The shop owner gasped out, 'He's got a knife.'

As they spoke, the man rushed out of Ginger, turned left and ran down into Portland Street. 'I decided to chase him,' said Riley later. 'Almost immediately I was joined by another man [Robert Filer] ... the two of us ran down Portland Street towards Portland Place.'

The fleeing individual, still wearing his crash helmet, was seen to run along Augusta Place, a turning off Portland Street. His pursuers momentarily lost sight of their quarry at this point, but Riley raced towards the entrance of a car park and saw his man cut through to Bedford Street. 'We pursued him into Bedford Street,' said Riley later to the police, 'but by this time I was out of breath.' Reasoning that the man did not have sufficient time to make it to the end of the road, Riley stood out in the middle of the street opposite a minor thoroughfare leading to the back of St Peter's Church. Building work was in progress in the vicinity and construction site hoardings blocked off some of the usual access points from Portland Place and Augusta Place.

While the pursuers were catching their breath and watching for a sight of their man, a motorist driving a Jaguar pulled up. His car was equipped with a telephone and Riley asked the driver to use it to alert the police. Riley then spotted a man, walking between two cars. He was dressed in a black sweater with a white shirt collar appearing above it and black trousers. There was no crash helmet. Despite the different clothing – loss of bomber jacket and helmet – Riley was convinced 'within myself', as he put it later, that this man was the same person he had been chasing. Another difference was that he was clutching a blue plastic bag. Riley continued to observe him from a discreet distance as the man walked calmly towards the rear entrance of St Peter's Church. 'I saw him lift the rear left-hand side of his jumper up,' said Riley. 'I saw what appeared to be a bright orange "stick" protruding from his waistband.' Shouting to his fellow pursuer, Riley cried out, 'That's him! I'll go and cut him off.'

Riley now ran to the bottom of Bedford Street where it joined Dorner Place. Looking towards the church, he saw the man emerge from the entrance of the building and cross over to the Pump Room Gardens. Riley was slightly vexed at this stage, for the man, while still dressed the same, was no longer carrying the blue plastic bag.

Looking round, he saw two police officers in a patrol car talking to the driver of the Jaguar. Riley joined them and pointed out the man, who was now walking towards Adelaide Road. Riley rode in the police vehicle with PC George Sears and PC Robert Calvert and they drew level with the man who was striding purposefully along. The fact that the man was not carrying a plastic bag worried Riley: he was now convinced they had come too far and were not pursuing the person he had seen earlier.

PC Sears now drove back towards St Peter's Church and the two policemen, aided by the determined Riley, began to search the vicinity. It was Riley who discovered a pile of plastic bags, which he took to be fertiliser sacks, at the side entrance of the church. Underneath these, he pointed out a blue bag to PC Calvert. It contained a crash helmet and a light-grey bomber jacket with a zip front, in the pocket of which was a pair of gloves. The jacket had fresh blood on it and there was also blood on the bag. A search amongst the rubbish and debris in an alcove close by turned up a black scabbard holding an orange-handled knife. 'Part of that knife was orange,' said Riley. 'It struck me that this is what I had seen sticking out of the man's waistband.'

A police dog-handler arrived at the scene and the German

Shepherd's nose was drawn to blood on the pavement across the road from the church. This exercise was to prove rather academic as suddenly a shout went up, 'He's hiding round the corner!' Everyone ran in the direction of the Regal Cinema and, as PC Sears noted laconically in his subsequent report, 'I saw a male person walk from my left near to Smithfield Garage towards the cinema ... The male person answered the description of a man we had been given previously.' This individual was walking quickly with his head lowered and with his left hand thrust deep into his trouser pocket. Sears and Calvert stopped him in front of the cinema. 'It was immediately obvious to us,' said Sears, 'that he had cut his left hand with blood dripping from it on to the footpath.'

The two officers took the man around the side of the cinema in order to question him away from the curious gaze of bystanders who had begun to gather.

'Where have you come from?' asked Calvert.

'I have been in the parts department of the garage,' he said, indicating Smithfield Garage.

'How did you cut your hand?'

'What have I done? I only came over here shopping.'

Calvert's reply was, 'I am arresting you on suspicion of attempted robbery.'

'I haven't done anything,' the man answered cockily.

With that he was put into a police car and conveyed to Leamington police station. During the short journey, Sears asked him, 'How did you get to Leamington Spa today?'

'I am not saying anything until I have spoken to my solicitor,' he replied.

On arrival at the police station, the man with the cut hand was identified as John David Guise Cannan, whose address was Flat 2, Foye House, Bridge Road, Leigh Woods, Bristol. While in the charge room he asked PC Calvert, 'Can you get me some cigarettes please?'

'Where's your cigarettes?' the policeman said.

'I lost them in the struggle,' replied Cannan.

'What struggle?'

'Can I see my solicitor please?'

John Cannan was put in a cell. PC Sears returned to Dorner Place and the area in which John Cannan had been arrested. During the course of his scrutiny he noticed a black BMW parked in Portland Street. The unattended vehicle, licence number A936 FJU, was parked about 50 yards from Ginger boutique. A PNC (Police National Computer) check of the number by personal radio showed that the registered keeper was John Cannan. The owner was Mercantile Credit, a finance house who were selling the vehicle on a hire purchase agreement to Cannan.

Sears continued his search and paid a visit to the premises of Smithfield Garage, located in Dorner Place close to its junction with Augusta Place. The constable entered the gents' toilet adjacent to the workshop where he saw fresh blood on the floor and also in one of the WC cubicles. The cistern in the cubicle bore traces of blood and, when the policeman lifted the lid, he was surprised to discover four pieces of white nylon washing-line in the water.

Stephen Weller, the spare-parts supervisor at the garage, recalled an incident that had occurred during that afternoon. Between 3pm and 3.30pm – he could not give a precise time – he left his department and went to use the toilet located in the service-bay area. The toilets were intended for use by customers and staff and there was access by means of a sliding door to the street. As he entered the toilet, Weller saw a man bent over the solitary hand washbasin, sluicing water over his face with both hands. The man did not look up when Weller entered and, only being able to see his face in profile, the parts supervisor assumed he was a customer. As Weller approached one of the urinals, he saw the door close on the WC cubicle nearest the washbasin. He only had a fleeting look at the man but noticed he had thick, black, wavy hair of collar length and appeared to be well groomed. In a subsequent police interview, Weller claimed it was difficult to judge the man's height, for he was bent over the washbasin, but Weller could say that the man was wearing black trousers and a dark, long-sleeved sweater. What struck Weller as rather odd was that the man washed before apparently using the WC cubicle.

Carmel Cleary and Jane Child provided essentially similar descriptions of the man who had threatened them. He was approximately 5ft 6in tall with black hair and wearing neither beard nor moustache. He was aged somewhere in the mid- to late-twenties bracket and was wearing a grey bomber jacket, black trousers and black footwear. He was not carrying anything, but his jacket bulged as though he had something tucked inside. The crash helmet that obscured the best part of his face was silver grey with a smoked visor in the raised position. On Thursday evening, Carmel Cleary was shown the crash helmet and orange-handled knife which had been recovered during the search around St Peter's Church. She positively identified both items as having been in the possession of the man who had been in her boutique earlier that afternoon.

The black BMW that had been parked close to the

boutique, and now known to be registered to John Cannan, was driven to a garage in the basement of Leamington Spa police station. Inspector Robert Kitchen briefly searched the vehicle and found a replica .38 Smith and Wesson revolver in the glove box. Meanwhile, Detective Constable Alan Fletcher, a Scenes of Crime officer, was conducting a close examination of the gents' toilet at Smithfield Garage. He took a number of photographs of blood spots outside one of the cubicles and on the toilet cistern. He also collected samples of bloodstains for later forensic examination, and recovered the four pieces of nylon washing-line from inside the cistern.

Soon after 7pm, John Cannan was interviewed at Warwick police station by Detective Constable Steven Rawson and Detective Sergeant Adrian Stone. His rights were explained to him in the context of the Police and Criminal Evidence Act, 1984 (PACE) and he was cautioned. What follows gives a remarkable insight into his behaviour shortly after his arrest. It is the mind of a sexual psychopath and sociopath. The account is taken from official police documents and papers held under a Section 511 extended closure order.

DS Stone opened by saying, 'You were arrested shortly after an incident in premises known as Ginger ... From enquiries made, I have reason to believe you entered the premises. Once inside you brandished a knife and made certain suggestions to two female members of staff.'

'First of all,' replied John, 'would you explain to me why I am here? You say that you are led to believe that I was involved. What basis do you have for believing this is so? Furthermore, on what basis was I unceremoniously dragged off the street?'

This question was answered with another: 'Do you own a BMW motor car?'

'Yes, I do.'

'What is the registration number?'

'A936 FJU.'

'Did you come to Leamington Spa today in that motor vehicle?'

'Yes.'

'From Bristol?'

'No, from Sutton Coldfield.'

'And your purpose in visiting Leamington?'

'Purely for shopping. I also was hoping to find a decent theatre, since theatre is one of my passions.'

At this point, DS Stone abandoned the skirmishing and went on the offensive. 'Is there anything in the vehicle of a contentious nature? For example, when a cursory search was made, a weapon was found.'

'Nothing contentious,' replied John.

'What about an imitation pistol?'

'No pistol or anything of an ominous nature should have been found in my car. A fact which I'm sure you are well aware.'

DC Rawson then told him, 'Mr Cannan, you are undoubtedly well aware that there was an imitation firearm in your motor car and that we have now recovered it into our possession.'

'It looks as though we are getting nowhere,' retorted John, 'and that I find myself...'

He was stopped in mid-sentence by the arrival of Detective Chief Inspector French. The interview was suspended for about half an hour and tea was brought in.

Questioning was resumed at about 8.40pm by DS Stone.

He asked Cannan, 'Do you own a BMW car?'

'I do.'

'Do you own a crash helmet?'

'As I have said before, I would appreciate access to a solicitor – to my solicitor.'

'As I said before, do you own a crash helmet?'

'I do not and reiterate yet again that I wish to speak to a solicitor.'

'You agree you came to Leamington to shop. Did you enter a ladies' dress shop at any time?'

'I did not go into a ladies' dress shop as far as I can remember.'

'Did you at any time enter a garage salesroom premises or workshop and there make use of the toilet facilities?'

'No comment.'

From this point in the interview, John became less cooperative, offering a string of 'no comments' in answer to perfectly reasonable questions or saying that he would reply but only to the satisfaction of a judge and jury. Suddenly he admitted that the blood found in the washroom at Smithfield Garage was his, although he refused to allow a blood sample to be taken from him. He declined to answer a question about the lengths of nylon washing-line found in the toilet cistern and denied owning an imitation firearm. DC Rawson confronted him with the fact that such an imitation firearm had been discovered in his BMW and informed him that his denial of ownership implied that it was in his car without his knowledge.

'The firearm is not mine,' said John. 'I have no knowledge of it.'

'Have you at any time loaned your vehicle to any person?'

'No.'

'Has your vehicle at any time been stolen?'

'No.'

'Unlawfully entered?'

'No, not that I am aware.'

'When did you last look in the glove compartment?'

'Two days ago, I think.'

'For what purpose?'

'To look for my bridge card [for paying the Clifton Suspension Bridge toll].'

'I assume,' said Rawson, 'that you saw no imitation firearm in your glove compartment at that time?'

'Hardly,' replied John.

The interview session finished at 9.48pm and John read through the notes containing the questions and answers but refused to sign them.

The following morning, DC Fletcher made a further examination of John's BMW and removed a black briefcase from the front passenger seat. When Peter Ablett, a forensic scientist who had been summoned to Leamington, arrived, the two men donned protective anti-contamination suits and began a systematic examination of the BMW inside and out. Most people's cars become an extension of their homes and contain a clutter of miscellaneous items. John's car was no exception and proved to be a repository for all manner of articles including clothing, toiletries and personal documents. In the car boot and interior were found a blazer, a man's jacket and overcoat, a pair of trousers and a pair of jeans, two ties, a shirt, a pair of socks, a pair of slippers and a pink blanket. There were three coat-hangers and, for a rainy day, two umbrellas, one a ladies', the other a gent's. The documents included a Woolwich Building Society account book and a Lloyd's Bank chequebook personalised to J. D. G. Cannan. Among the bric-a-brac were a bottle of Paco Rabanne aftershave lotion, a can of air-freshener, disposable razor, chewing gum, sundry parking tickets, a number of newspapers, a brochure featuring kitchen units and a solitary champagne cork.

There were also a number of plastic shopping bags from Woolworths, House of Fraser and Debenhams (Top Shop) stores, together with a length of rope (white nylon washing-line) found in the glove box and further washing-line (still in its packet with a price label affixed) in the door pocket on the driver's side. The most unusual discovery was a pair of handcuffs in the jack well in the boot. All these items and many more trivial artefacts of daily routine were duly logged by DC Fletcher.

Peter Ablett took tapings from all the interior surfaces of the car, including the boot, together with debris collected by vacuum from the floor areas, glove compartment and door pockets. His screening tests for blood and semen revealed no staining inside the car.

While forensic examination was taking place, the contents of John's briefcase were being itemised at Warwick police station by Detective Constable Raymond Allen. Among the motley collection of bills, receipts and cheque stubs were a number of personal documents, including a registration document for the BMW, an MOT certificate, Mercantile Credit hire purchase papers, a British visitor's passport in the name of John David Guise Cannan and a driving licence in the same name. Two of the items logged by DC Allen would subsequently acquire special significance. These were a business card in the name of Tom Eyles, Legal Services, and a vehicle excise licence disc in respect of an Austin vehicle, registration number HWL 507N, which did not belong to John Cannan.

Just after 3pm on Friday, 30 October 1987, the interview with Cannan was resumed at Warwick police station. On this occasion, Mr Terry Moore, a solicitor from the firm of Blackham, Maycock and Hayward, 20 High Street, Sutton Coldfield, was present. DS Stone reminded Cannan that he was still under caution and told him that he wished to ask further questions relating to his arrest the previous day. 'Did you enter the premises known as Ginger, a ladies' clothing shop situated in Regent Street, Leamington Spa? Having entered the premises, did you brandish a knife and make certain threats to the female staff?'

John replied that he had pledged his full cooperation in a court of law and concluded, 'This has become something of a nightmare ... I feel it's best to place myself in the hands of my solicitor.'

Stone said he appreciated his need for consultation but still wished to put questions to him. 'Did you or did you not enter the ladies' clothing shop?'

'No comment,' came the answer.

'You live in Bristol?'

'I do.'

'When did you last sleep in your own flat?'

'No comment.'

'Is it correct that on Wednesday night you stayed with your mother?'

'No comment.'

'But you agree, bearing in mind you were arrested in Leamington Spa, that at some time you travelled into this area?'

'No comment.'

Clearly aware that this procedure was leading them nowhere, DS Stone asked John if he had been advised by his solicitor to answer 'No comment'.

'Owing to the disquieting nature of your question,' said John, 'and to some matters which I am not very happy about, please be advised that anything discussed between my solicitor and myself is confidential and therefore my answer must be no comment.'

DS Stone persisted by suggesting that, if he had a legitimate reason for being in Leamington Spa, surely it would be in his best interests to give an explanation.

'As to what?' John retorted.

'That you did enter premises, brandish a knife and threaten two women.'

'How can I offer a full explanation when you pre-empted that explanation by going to great pains telling me that you wouldn't believe it and, in so doing, instead of being fair and objective, you have behaved as your own judge and jury before I have even been given a chance to explain. It is now too late; you've shown your colours.'

DC Rawson now cut in with: 'Are you prepared to stand on an identity parade should it be requested, or not?'

'I positively insist.'

'That you do, or do not?'

'That I do,' replied John.

The fencing session continued when DS Stone asked John if he stood by the answers he had given previously.

'I reiterate what I said,' was the uncompromising reply.

Stone pressed him to indicate whether he wanted to alter or add to the notes of the previous day's interview.

'Without reading them through and refreshing my memory as to their context, I honestly wouldn't know.'

'But surely you know if you have at any time lied?' asked Rawson.

'As far as I am concerned, I stand by what I have answered and made clear.'

'Do you want to refresh your memory?'

'No.'

DC Rawson next asked a series of questions about the ownership of the knife, the crash helmet, the lengths of washing-line and the replica firearm. In each instance he received the reply, 'No comment.'

John was then reminded that his explanation of his most recent visit was to look for a theatre. 'I am sure my memory serves me well,' Rawson said, 'when I say that yesterday we did not discuss specific theatres you may or may not have intended to visit. Leamington is not renowned for entertainment of that nature and it surprises me if you came to Leamington for that purpose and cannot name the theatre.'

This question inspired John to deliver something more than his previous sparse replies.

'If you remember,' he said, 'you asked me quite reasonably why I was in Leamington. Let me remind you that I stated, quite clearly and truthfully, that I came primarily to window-shop and, secondly, to see if there were any good theatres or entertainments which I could visit and enjoy in the future. What is unreasonable about that?'

'Do I understand that you did not intend to visit such an establishment yesterday?'

'I went to Rackhams yesterday,' replied John, 'and will describe in detail if you wish the layout of the store.'

'If I may interrupt,' said Rawson, 'I refer more to the theatre.'

'To go to the theatre yesterday?' asked Cannan, apparently seeking confirmation of the obvious question.

'Yes,' said Rawson.

'Oh no,' came the answer.

DS Stone took over the questioning once again at this point and asked John, 'How long were you in Leamington?'

'Approximately an hour and a half.'

'Having done whatever you were going to do, you were going home to where?'

'Sutton Coldfield to my mother's for tea.'

'Was your mother expecting you?'

'I can't remember if I said to her.'

'When were you to return to Bristol?'

'I hadn't decided.'

'So, you weren't working this week?'

'My arrangements are, I feel, my own affair, and are not directly related to why I am here anyway.'

'Your reason for being in Leamington was to carry out the purpose for which you were arrested. Is that true?'

'May I refer to my previous comments?'

This unrewarding question-and-answer session ended with an unexpected piece of cooperation.

'Are you prepared to give an intimate sample which will prove or disprove your involvement?' asked DS Stone.

'I am fully prepared to help the forensic science laboratory in any way I can,' replied John.

The interview concluded at about 4.30pm, but John refused to sign the interview notes. Later that evening, following a private consultation with his solicitor, he gave his oral and written approval for body samples to be taken. These were taken in the medical room at Warwick police station by Dr Sullivan and consisted of blood, saliva and both cut and pulled head hair. Shortly before 8pm, he also provided fingerprint impressions at the request of DS Stone. During this procedure, the two men chatted and John apologised for not telling the detective everything he wanted to hear. 'But you have to agree,' he said, 'I have a lot to lose.'

Stone quite properly reminded Cannan that he was still under caution and said that he would have to put on record any conversation that passed between them.

John told him, 'What is important is that whatever happens you must give me certain credit, look at my history. Have I ever inflicted any form of violence?' He went on, 'I have committed offences of robbery and rape but you will find no one has ever been injured – was anyone injured yesterday?'

'What are you implying?' DS Stone asked.

'I am saying that no one was injured yesterday.'

To Stone's retort, 'Is that first-hand knowledge?' John replied, 'Let's not play any more games – of course I know. I gave you the indication yesterday. If I admit to the knife and the blood, was it not obvious it was me?'

'Of course it was,' the policeman said. 'That was why you were arrested and why we persisted in questioning you along those lines.'

'Well, there you are then,' said John. 'I went into the shop for cash, not as your top man said to carry out a rape. Always remember that,' he admonished. 'Never prejudge an issue.'

It was a pity that John did not heed his own advice, for the reference to committing rape was entirely his own creation. He had been asked if he had 'made certain suggestions' to the two women in Ginger. The word 'rape' was not mentioned and the fact that he volunteered it perhaps showed something of his state of mind.

Stone asked him why, after two lengthy interviews, in which he had not been direct in his replies, he had chosen to speak now.

'Everything I do is measured,' John told the detective. 'I calculate events. I do it all the time.' He went on, 'Just tell me on a one-to-one issue – forget all about the West Midlands and all those other so-called offences you are prejudging – what will I get?'

Stone declined to be drawn on this question and John answered himself. 'I reckon two and a half to three years, yes?'

'Now *you* are prejudging,' said Stone with a wry smile.

'I will have this one and no other,' declared John. 'This was the first time since way back.'

After five sets of fingerprints had been taken, John was returned to the custody cell. Half an hour later, the custody sergeant told Stone that John had asked to see him and a further conversation took place in the medical room.

'I have again measured the facts and what I want to do is to tell you everything,' John said. 'I am prepared to make a statement about yesterday's events and admitting my part, but I must ask a question.'

'Go on,' said Stone.

'If, for example, other persons from other places wanted me for, say, robbery, if I tell you, do I stay here?'

The detective sergeant had no authority to answer such a question and confined his reply to stating that his own interest lay in the incident at Leamington.

'You must agree,' John went on, 'although I say it myself, I am not naive, I am reasonably educated and I have again measured the events. There is every possibility that I may have been seen from far-off places and I do not want this.'

'Far-off places?' queried Stone.

'For example, West Midlands one and, two, Bristol,' answered John.

'You expect these forces to visit you?'

'I'm pretty damn sure.'

In letters exclusive to the authors of this book, John Cannan told the real reason for his visit to Leamington Spa that fateful day. He had sat in the coffee lounge at Rackhams store in the town on that afternoon of 29 October, contemplating an act of robbery. He was down to his last £6 and, among other things, needed money to pay Tom Eyles, his private detective. His intention was to rob the National Provincial Building Society office in the High Street. From his reconnaissance, he knew that this was a comparatively small sub-branch with a partitioned counter running down the left-hand side of the office to a smaller office at the rear of the premises. There were no glass security screens and the staff were all female: two young counter assistants and an older woman he took to be the manageress. He had targeted the place weeks before, regarding it as 'a possible'. 'It was a little public for comfort,' he wrote, 'and this was about my only fear.'

But while he was looking for a place to park on 29 October he noticed Ginger, 'an extremely expensive and opulent-looking shop, a view further reinforced by the cut of two of its customers who were leaving'. In the event, he decided upon Ginger for a quick cash haul. On his way to Leamington, he had realised he had left his length of washing-line behind and purchased more from a hardware store in Kenilworth, about six miles from Leamington. John also added that robbery was his only motive when he entered Ginger. 'There was absolutely no question at all of sex, in fact it was the last thing on my mind at that time – money was.'

This incident had echoes of the 1981 robbery at Sutton Coldfield and the rape that followed. Only the alertness of the two women in Ginger forestalled a more violent outcome. It is difficult to believe that the lengths of cord were intended for any purpose other than that of restraint as a prelude to a violent act.

Indeed, in his letters to the authors reflecting on the circumstances which led to his arrest, John regretted that he had not tied up the two women. If he had, they would have been prevented from raising the alarm. 'I should have tied them up straight away,' he wrote, 'and been more aggressive, but I didn't and I wasn't and the result was, I was caught.'

11

'I AM IN CONTROL'

John Cannan's forecast of intense police interest in him and his activities proved correct. As a result of the incident at Leamington Spa, he was found to be in possession of a car tax disc for a vehicle other than the one he was driving.

The tax disc – an excise licence for an Austin car with the registration number HWL 507N – was for Shirley Banks's Mini, for which police throughout the country had been searching for three weeks. John knew, and detectives were soon to find out, that it was standing in his garage at Foye House in Bristol.

Following his arrest in Leamington Spa and the confirmation of his links with the West Country, a telephone call was made to Kingsweston House, Bristol. This was the centre of operations for the police investigation of Shirley Banks's disappearance and Detective Chief Inspector Bryan Saunders and Detective Inspector Terry Jones of the Avon and Somerset

Constabulary duly travelled to the Midlands. At 11.15pm on Friday, 30 October, Terry Jones confronted John Cannan in the charge office at Warwick police station and arrested him 'for the abduction of Shirley Anne Banks in Bristol on 8 October this year'. The prisoner was cautioned and asked if he understood. 'I do,' replied John. The initial formalities completed, he was put in a police car and driven to Bristol.

As they travelled along the motorway in the small hours of Saturday morning, Saunders cautioned John again before asking him, 'Can you help us with the present whereabouts of Shirley Banks? Is she alive or dead?'

'No, I can't,' John answered, 'and I don't wish to discuss the matter until I see my solicitor'.

When they arrived at Filton police station, John was put in the cells for the rest of the night. He was destined to see a great deal of DCI Saunders and DI Jones during the following days. Even before John began his journey to Bristol, Scenes of Crimes officers were at his flat in Foye House. In the garage allocated to Flat 2, detectives found a blue Mini car, registration number SLP 386S. After the vehicle had been dusted for fingerprints, it was hoisted on to a low-loader and taken to the Home Office Forensic Laboratory at Chepstow. There DC Clive Peters removed the front number plate, which was made of yellow plastic and adhesive backing. This proved to be false. Underneath was a metal index number plate bearing the number HWL 507N – matching the disc found in John's briefcase when he was arrested.

'That first week at Filton,' said John, 'was a week of absolute horror, a week I will, or can, never forget.' His clothes were taken from him and he was dressed in a white disposable forensic suit. 'I either sweated or was bitterly cold,' he complained in a letter to the authors. 'My cell was 8 feet by 6 feet and was like a box ... it wasn't big enough to swing a cat.'

Because of his earlier attempted suicide, John was placed under 24-hour supervision. He became friendly with the police officers assigned to watch over him, 'all of whom I came to like and respect,' he said. John was permitted to buy food from his own funds and recalled how he had cheekily asked the duty sergeant to use his personal radio to order him an Indian takeaway. 'Imagine my surprise when I saw him pick up a radio and, with a mischievous grin, do precisely that.'

'Without doubt, that first Saturday at Filton was a busy time for everyone,' said John, 'police included.'

Indeed it was. Detectives had interviewed Marija Vilcins at Sutton Coldfield on the previous evening and taken a statement from Val Humphreys on Saturday afternoon. Scenes of Crime officers spent the weekend combing through John's flat, and his solicitor, Jim Moriarty, was vigorously engaged in rescheduling his appointments. He travelled down to Filton and arrived just before midday to ensure that his client had legal representation.

John said later, 'I needed time to sit quietly with either Jim or Terry [Moore] and go into great detail, everything that had occurred. It would have taken me literally hours – I needed hours, so that they understood every difficulty and facet of the case.' In the event, the first police interview began just before 1.30 that afternoon. DCI Bryan Saunders – a tall, slim, bearded man with the air of a business executive rather than the stereotypical policeman – began the tape-recorded session with due regard for all the formalities. Besides himself, John Cannan and Jim Moriarty, there was DI Terry Jones.

During the next seven weeks, John would be questioned over a wide range of his activities. During this first interview, Saunders restricted his questions mainly to generalities. He established that John worked from his flat at Foye House, buying and selling cars and that he did not keep any records of these transactions. There was a sting in the tail, though, and an early indication of the cat-and-mouse game that the detective and suspect would play during the many hours of interviews.

'You are aware that we have searched your home?' asked Saunders.

'Yes, I understand you did, yes.'

'In the garage we found a Mini. Can you tell me the origin of that Mini?'

'Under legal advice, my solicitor has advised me not to comment on that.'

After John consulted Jim Moriarty in private, the interview resumed. Saunders went straight to the issue of the blue Mini car and John said, 'I admit freely that the Mini was in my possession and that it was found in my garage.' It was a fact he could hardly have denied. He went on to claim that he had bought the car from a man called Hodgeson, whom he had met at a car auction in Bristol. This was the first plank in an elaborate conspiracy theory that John endeavoured to construct during the police interviews and later in correspondence with the authors.

Asked why he did not report the purchase of the car when he realised through the newspapers that it belonged to the woman who had gone missing, he replied that he didn't think he would be believed. He knew then that he would have to dispose of the vehicle, but it was too risky just to drive it away. 'If I'd moved it during the day, in orange paintwork, then I'd have been fucked so I thought I'll paint the car...' He painted it blue and fitted it with new number plates, putting himself to a great deal of trouble for an old banger that had cost him, by his own misguided account, a mere £125.

John recalled that Jim Moriarty was wearing a disturbed look when he visited John at Filton on Sunday. The solicitor reported that an article had appeared in that day's *News of the World* newspaper that had disclosed John's previous criminal record and resulted in press reporters laying siege to his mother's home. 'I went absolutely mad,' said John, and with every justification. As a result of the newspaper's disclosure and follow-up by the tabloid press, he was placed in a highly prejudiced position. He spoke bitterly of the articles 'which left little to the imagination and massively undermined my legal position at a time when interviews and enquiries were taking place'.

As a result of his complaint, the Solicitor-General initiated proceedings against the *News of the World* which, in due course, was fined £15,000.

'Never in my life had I felt so dismayed and upset,' said John. 'Never had I been so frightened. Suddenly I had become the focus of the most horrific and damaging national media attention. My thoughts turned to my mum and whether she was coping.'

Not surprisingly, John's anger and bitterness spilled over into his interviews with DCI Bryan Saunders. His demands to be allowed to read what the papers were saying about him were refused. Saunders expressed his regrets but said it would serve no purpose if he allowed the possibility that John's answers to his questions were coloured, no matter how inadvertently, by his knowledge of the stories appearing in the press.

John went on to argue that he was more concerned about the effect of the press reports on his family rather than himself. He said he would compromise on anything but that, adding he was willing to be truthful and honest. 'Fairness both ways, not just one way,' he told the detectives in a bid to assert himself. 'The ball's in your court, gentlemen – that's entirely up to you.'

That first weekend at Filton was tough. John did not know who was leaking information to the press – he suspected what he called a 'police-press axis' – and he knew that many former associates and girlfriends were being questioned. 'On tablets I tried to sleep, but couldn't. It was awful.' To round off his misery, Bryan Saunders charged him at midday on Sunday, 1 November with 'the theft of a motor vehicle' (Shirley Banks's Mini). Later the same day he was charged with 'an offence of assault with intent to rob' (the incident at Leamington Spa). Asked if he wished to make any reply, John answered, 'None whatsoever.'

As DCI Bryan Saunders later commented to Christopher Berry-Dee at Kingsweston House, 'These early charges were simply a holding tactic so we could press further into the abduction of Shirley Banks.'

While John sat it out at Filton, Scenes of Crime officers were relentlessly turning over the minutiae of his daily existence at the Foye House flat. Photographs of the interior showed tastefully furnished accommodation for a person not long out of prison and without a permanent job. But then John had made no bones that his money was being made illegally. 'It was nice to have money, it was nice to have a beautiful home, a BMW motor car and all the trappings of wealth,' he said, but he found it difficult to answer when people asked him what he did for a living. 'It was awful not being in a position to tell them the truth.'

DC Michael Rutty made a meticulous search of the flat. Numerous documents and other articles, including dirty washing and cigarette butts from the ashtray in the lounge, were taken away for examination. All likely fingerprint-bearing surfaces were dusted and a number of finger- and palm-prints were lifted with adhesive tape. The contents of the sink traps in the waste outlets of both the bath and hand washbasin in the bathroom were collected along with the towels, floor cloth and bathrobe. Blankets from the bedrooms and the covers from the two settees in the lounge were removed for detailed examination. Even the contents of Val Humphreys's vacuum cleaner were retrieved in the knowledge that John had borrowed it for use in his flat on 9 October.

Books and papers were garnered from drawers, cabinets, shelves and tables throughout the flat – everything from copies of the *Daily Mirror* to a receipt from Woolworths. The procedure was well tested and very efficient. One officer selected an article and stated to his colleague where it was found. The items were logged room by room. There could be no mistakes.

Every item was allocated a number and logged as a possible exhibit. To this steadily mounting collection were added the contents of John's briefcase and his BMW and items found in the Mini parked in his garage. Among DC Rutty's long list of exhibits was the seemingly innocuous entry: 'MR4/A. Documents from wooden chest, lounge area, Flat 2, Foye House.' One of these documents, a photocopied report, would provide the police with the only confirmation they would have of Shirley Banks's presence in the flat.

On Monday, 2 November 1987, John appeared before Bristol magistrates as he would on several occasions, to be remanded in custody while the police pursued their enquiries. In between court appearances, John sat through numerous tape-recorded interviews with DCI Bryan Saunders. 'It was like the mongoose and the snake,' wrote John, 'both of us trying to work out what the other was up to.'

Saunders was understandably keen to find out the circumstances behind John's acquisition of Shirley Banks's car. But John had only acknowledged that he came into possession of the car after the weekend visit to his flat of his girlfriend, Marija Vilcins, on 10/11 October.

The appearance of the Sunday-newspaper article still rankled with John, and he very much wanted to read at first hand what was being said about him. But that was only his first point. 'Point two,' he declared, 'I have been in police custody for some 60 hours in which time I have been alone, most of the time confronted by a series of detectives with questions fired at me day and night with little sleep and with little regard to other matters.' This was a reference to his mother's wellbeing. With rising indignation, John told DCI Saunders, 'I wish to help you with your enquiries. I wish to answer any further questions you put to me.' His price for continuing was to be assured that he could speak to his mother and be allowed to read the newspapers. 'Unless those two criteria are satisfied,' he demanded, 'there will be no further discussions on any subject or any matter with any person at any time, at anywhere whatsoever. And I hope that by saying that I make myself perfectly clear.' This was John at his most assertive, attempting to wrest control of the situation from the practised hands of the police.

An attempt had been made earlier to contact Mrs

Cannan by telephone but she was not answering. She had left her home in Sutton Coldfield to escape the attentions of the press and was staying with a family friend. Saunders assured John he would arrange for him to speak to her as soon as she was tracked down. On the other sticking point, the detective patiently explained that knowledge of what was in the newspaper reports about him would not serve his cause: 'I honestly feel that it's in everybody's interests that you try to draw on your memory to give the truth as to what happened.'

The suggestion that John's knowledge of the newspaper reports might influence his answers, albeit inadvertently, brought on another tirade. 'That is, that is, that is for me to decide,' he argued. 'You are automatically assuming that I (a) have lied, or (b) could lie. That one is therefore guilty before one starts. You are prejudging.'

With the patience of Job, Bryan Saunders's response was to offer to accumulate the newspapers and make them available to John after he had answered questions about his movements. The detective made it quite plain that he did not intend to allow his questioning to be influenced in any way by reports in the media.

'That is totally hypothetical,' raged John. 'The point ... that is totally hypothetical. You are saying ifs, and, buts, could bes, mights...'

At this juncture, Saunders gently exercised his authority, telling John that he was raising a smokescreen as an excuse not to answer questions.

'I am offended, I am offended,' exclaimed John. He went on to point out that material prejudicial to his case had appeared in the press which made it impossible for a fair trial to take place.

During a break, John spoke in private to his mother and expressed his appreciation to Bryan Saunders when the interview resumed. It was agreed that he would be allowed daily newspapers subject to the deletion of any reference to his case. That settled, the detective came back to the question of John's possession of Shirley Banks's car and his attendance at motor auctions.

'When you met the fellow that said he had a Mini for sale,' asked Saunders, 'was that ... during the day or at night?'

'During the day.'

'Do you know what time of day it was, morning or afternoon?'

'I can't remember.'

Saunders reminded him that the car auctions at St Philips, Bristol, were held on Tuesday and Thursday evenings. John thought that he had met his contact at midweek and it might have been Tuesday or Thursday evening. He had already acknowledged that this occurred after his weekend with Marija Vilcins, which meant the dates in question were 13 or 15 October. John was certainly in Bristol on 13 October, for that was the day he brought his mother to stay with him. It was also the day he failed to keep an appointment with WDC Sandra Burnett. He was troubled with toothache at about this time and was at his flat in Leigh Woods on 15 October with his mother.

John claimed that he met his contact outside the auction, fully aware that transactions made in this manner might involve stolen vehicles.

'This chap just came up and introduced himself, did he?' asked Saunders.

'No,' replied John. 'You look around, you just generally meet people.' He said that, although he had been to many different car auctions, he had only been to the Bristol auction once before. 'It's a very poor auction,' he explained.

There was a large question mark over John's knowledge of the St Philips car auction. When he was asked to describe the location his memory failed him again and he replied with one of his multiple answers: 'Not accurately, not accurately, not accurately.' It transpired that he could not remember anything at all about the auction, least of all the rostrum area where the deals were hammered down.

Bryan Saunders then asked John if he had spoken to a police constable when he was taken into custody and enquired where the main car auction was in Bristol. John acknowledged that there had been some conversation about buying cars. The detective thought it strange that he should ask such a question when he had already stated that he had bought a car from a man at the car auction. John said that he had visited the auction at St Philips, but there were two others. 'I don't know where the main auction is in London,' he said.

'But you told me that you met the man that you bought the Mini off...' said Saunders.

'At the car auction,' interjected John.

'At the car auction?'

'But that doesn't mean to say it's the main car auction.'

'Well...'

'Do you know which is the main car auction in Birmingham?'

'Forget Birmingham.'

'No, well, it's an interesting point,' John argued.

'No, it's not. Don't go off in a tangent, John, when we've hit a nerve.'

'You're not hitting a nerve.'

'We're hitting a nerve, John.'

When John was asked what he did for a living, he answered, 'I am a businessman,' adding that he had other interests besides motor trading. Asked by DI Terry Jones how much cash he carried with him when he went to a car auction, John answered flatly, 'Twenty-five quid.'

'Twenty-five quid!' repeated Jones incredulously.

John explained that just a few pounds' deposit was sufficient, although the level of deposit varied from auction to auction. Saunders homed in straight away on the subject of car deals, in the knowledge that John was not even registered for VAT. He wanted to know the names of people John had traded with, so the police could talk to them.

'It doesn't work that way,' said John. 'Now look, you'd better go to a motor auction.'

'I know all about motor auctions.'

'No, I don't think you do.'

'I do.'

'I don't, sir, think you do.'

'Don't call me sir. Go on.'

'All right, Bryan.' Again John was trying to gain the ascendancy. 'I would ask respectfully that nobody tries to tell me about how to trade motor cars.'

'Now I don't give a shit who I buy a car off,' John went on, 'and I don't give a toss who I sell it to ... he could be God, he could be the Queen, Prince Charles's brother, he could be anyone, I don't care.'

If his patience was being tried, Bryan Saunders didn't show it. 'OK,' the detective said, 'can we go back to Shirley's car?' The officer referred to John's alleged meeting with the man outside the auction.

John thought his first name was Philip and his surname

either Hodgkinson or Hodgeson adding, 'something like that'. He went on to give a vague description of a man whom he had never seen before but thought he might recognise if he saw him again.

Summarising John's encounter with the car vendor, Bryan Saunders said, 'So it's meeting the fellow one night outside the "ring" and he said he might have something that you're interested in. He got your address jotted down on a fag packet, I think you said, he called round the next night, it was dark, and, with a quick look at the car, I think you said you tested it and drove up the road.'

'Well, only a cursory...'

'Yes.'

'It didn't have a very good reverse gear. Then the car was put in the garage at Foye House.'

The detectives leaped on this admission because John had said earlier that he seldom put his BMW in the garage at Foye House because there was little room to manoeuvre. Obviously the Mini was smaller and he claimed he garaged it out of consideration for his neighbours and the general problem of congestion around the flats. DI Jones thought this was inconsistent with the fact that, when Marija Vilcins visited, both her car and John's BMW were left outside. The implication was that the Mini was already in the garage at that time, a suggestion that John emphatically denied.

John paid cash for the Mini and accepted the seller's assurances that he would send the log-book and MOT certificate later.

'Weren't you accepting a bit of a risk there?' asked DI Jones.

'Yes,' said John. 'I can explain that.' He accepted that the 'purist view' was never to buy a car without its documentation but, in the real world of motor trading, 'You judge people, and if the guy says, "Look, I haven't got it with me but you'll have it," and he did seem all right.'

On 5 November, while John was attending the identity parade in connection with the attempted kidnap of Julia Holman, detectives were interviewing Sharon Major. She mentioned that John had telephoned her, a year earlier, on 6 November 1986, from Bristol. She was concerned because she thought he was still in prison, although he was at pains to stress that she was in no danger from him. In answer to her question about how he had found out where she was living, John said he had traced her with the help of a solicitor friend whom he was thinking of marrying. 'I obviously made it very clear I didn't want to see him,' said Sharon. He told her to be happy and a few days later he sent her a letter.

The telephone call worried Sharon at the time and she reported it to the police at Sutton Coldfield. A few days later, she learned that John had been arrested about a rape committed in Reading. When Detective Constable Brian Higgins called to interview her regarding her relationship with John, Sharon said, 'I told him of my feeling about John and the Suzy Lamplugh inquiry in London. I felt that John was particularly dangerous towards women because he is so charming and no one would find out his evil side until it was too late.'

She went on to say that, when Shirley Banks's photograph was published in the newspapers and shown on television, several persons who knew her said how much she resembled the missing woman. 'In fact, when I was going out with John, my hair and appearance was very similar and I can see the likeness between me and Shirley Banks.' When it was made public that a man was being held in custody at Bristol in connection with Shirley's disappearance, Sharon said she 'felt without doubt it would be John Cannan'.

John ridiculed a comment allegedly made by Sharon to DC Higgins likening him to the Mr Kipper picture in the Lamplugh case. He claimed she could have said no such thing. 'Had she done so,' he said, 'the police would have been round to see me very quickly given my supposed resemblance' and 'me with a previous rape conviction'. He maintained that press speculation about the disappearance of Suzy Lamplugh began during the week Sharon made her statement and therefore the details were in her mind. In reality, the Lamplugh affair had already been in the news for over three months.

At the next interview session, Bryan Saunders showed John a knife and asked him if he had seen it before.

'I've seen it before, yes.'

'When?'

'I saw it when it was produced in Leamington.'

'Is it your knife?'

'I think again I refer to the statements I made in Leamington Spa...'

'Were you in the shop?'

'I refer to the statements made in Leamington.'

'You refused to sign the written interview notes, is that correct?'

'I have refused to sign any notes.' John said he had found disquieting errors in the police procedures at Leamington and had therefore refused to sign the notes of the interview.

Saunders said it was alleged that John had been in the shop in the town and produced a knife. He wanted to know if he had been present and, if so, was it his intention to steal or was his motive a sexual one?

'I am not going to lie,' answered John, 'and therefore my reply to your question is no comment.'

The detective told John that the evidence available suggested he was the man in the shop at Leamington Spa. 'I'll ask you again,' he said. 'Were you in there to commit robbery?'

'No comment,' answered John calmly.

Undaunted, Saunders moved on to the clothes-line that was found in the toilet cistern at Leamington which was similar to that discovered in John's BMW. 'What was the rope doing in your car?'

'Is being in possession of a clothes-line an ominous affair?'

'Well...'

'Is it illegal to own a washing-line?' John parried sarcastically.

'It depends in what circumstances...'

'Yes.'

'Why did you have the washing-line in your car? And I ask you in the context of the man – who placed the stuff in the cistern. You see what I mean, that's the context I need to ask you.'

'You're, you're making, you're implicating me by possession of rope.'

'No, I'm asking you...'

'The answer to your question is no comment.'

Reminded that the clothes-line found in his car had a receipt attached to it dated 5 October 1987, John was asked if he could remember where he had bought it. He said he had no idea and went on to explain at great length about his temperamental washing-machine and the need for a washing-line on which to dry his pullovers. 'But you know,' he said, 'under the circumstances that is now becoming dreadfully ominous.'

'No, well, it's not ominous if that's your explanation,' said Saunders.

But John couldn't leave it at that. Not John Cannan. 'I also around 5 October went for a Chinese takeaway. No doubt there will be some sort of insinuation made about going for a Chinese takeaway,' he said dryly.

'I note that comment, John,' said the detective.

Attention was then drawn to the fact that John had a washing-line in his BMW and also in his flat. 'Did you intend to incapacitate somebody...?'

'No comment.'

'Was the rope to tie people up?'

'No comment.'

Saunders went on to question John about his reasons for visiting Leamington Spa and drew a number of vague, mundane answers in return. He reminded John that the purpose of the questioning was to find Shirley Banks. He also referred to John's rape of Jean Bradford in June 1981 when he had tied her up in her shop. 'You tied somebody up when you committed that last rape?'

'Loosely.'

'Loosely?'

'Yes, loosely, very loosely.' John's irritation became evident at this line of continual questioning and he vehemently rejected the idea that, because he had a previous conviction for rape, he was implicated in the abduction of Shirley Banks. He denied knowing her and denied she had ever been a girlfriend.

Saunders's patience was now wearing a little thin. 'Right,' he said. 'You've got her car, and you happen to be arrested in circumstances that indicate to me that you were about to commit an offence where somebody was going to be tied up. OK?'

'That is the conclusion that you have drawn.'

'They're facts, John, aren't they?'

John's answer was to tell the detective he was 'entitled to the luxury of inference'.

After a while, Saunders got John to acknowledge that he was capable of rape and robbery. 'Are you still capable of it?' he asked.

'That is for a court to decide.'

When Saunders suggested that John was a charming individual, attractive to women, but might be a person who snapped when something went wrong in a relationship, he provoked the reply, 'Well, sir, now you're entering into the realms of metaphysics.'

Saunders harked back to the violence, but was again interrupted with the remark, 'The *Titanic* only sank once.'

'Well, OK,' said Saunders, 'but it didn't come back up again and go to Leamington Spa, did it?'

John's weaving and dodging was a tactic to give him thinking time. He knew he had a great deal to explain and he knew that Bryan Saunders would keep coming at him with questions; his answers had to dovetail. John thought the tone of questioning was transparent. 'They weren't trying to eliminate me,' he said, 'they were in reality doing all in their power to "include" me, and were using my previous record to do it.'

He acknowledged later in his letters to the authors from prison, 'I DID have something to hide, I did have knowledge, albeit only limited, of the Shirley Banks affair.' He also maintained that while he did not open up he was careful 'to adhere to the truth and not to lie'. It is probably fair to say that he was economical with the truth in his answers to questions about the Leamington incident.

Bryan Saunders's next step was to question John about his movements on the days prior to Shirley Banks's disappearance – 'to establish your movements to see if they coincide with her movements'. John gave a litany of explanations, the upshot being that he could remember very little. He pointed out that he had no regular routine, hence it was difficult to pinpoint dates and times. 'This sounds rather suave,' he told the detectives, 'but I don't lead a spectacular life. Contrary to what people think.'

John was up against a powerful adversary in DCI Saunders, who pressed on relentlessly with questions about Thursday, 8 October. After dropping off Val Humphreys at Foye House, following her hairdressing appointment between 4.30 and 5pm, John said he drove down to Charlotte's cake shop at Clifton for a cup of tea. He had been there a number of times but he thought it unlikely any of the staff would be able to confirm his visit on this particular day. He did, however, offer to describe the assistants there whom he knew on a 'Hello, how are you?' basis. 'I can describe the girls to you, you know, intimately, I don't mean quite intimately!' Typically, he could not resist making the sexual remark that one of them was a typical Bristol girl with 'long, darkish hair, slim hips', while the other one was a blonde bombshell with a nice figure.

John also said that he had been into the newsagent's just

across Clifton Suspension Bridge from Foye House before going to Charlotte's. Again women came into John's reckoning of events. 'I chatted up the girl,' he said. He seemed to think she was 'sweet' on him and, when he mentioned that he had been on holiday to Crete, she said, 'Oh, I wish you'd taken me with you.' They had a flirty conversation and he described the scenario: 'I've got a black BMW with a flat in Leigh Woods and I think she's, you know...'

After calling in at Charlotte's, John claimed he almost certainly went home to Foye House.

'Would you have gone to a pub at that time of the evening?'

'No.'

'Shopping?'

'No.'

'And you're definite about that?' enquired Saunders, pointing out to John that there were a number of things he was unsure about.

'I'm sure I didn't ... I know what you're trying to get at, you're trying to pin me down, what I was doing after 5.30pm.'

'Yes, that's right.'

'Well, I'll tell you why and this is going to sound awful ...'

'It's not another woman, John, is it?' enquired Bryan Saunders playfully. The officer wasn't far out in his suggestion.

Apparently, it was about buying curtains and John's embarrassment at finding himself in a shop that sold material for dressmaking. He apologised to the shop assistant for his mistake and thought she would probably remember the incident. John described her as young and very blonde and 'very attractive, very attractive'. Saunders asked him if he could remember what he was wearing at the time. John couldn't be sure except, 'I wouldn't be in scruffy gear, I'd be in smart gear, I'd probably be in a blazer and trousers ...'

'Do you ever get mistaken for an Italian?'

John then repeated his previous claim that he was often taken for Sacha Distel or Trevor Francis the football player.

Yet another woman came into the picture that evening. In an attempt to structure his movements, John established that at about 5.30 to 5.45pm he tooted his car horn to a lady he knew at the chemist's shop near Charlotte's. She was leaving work and making her way home. John was known as a customer at the chemist's, and the detective wanted to know if John had it in mind to offer the woman a lift – he thought probably not.

This line of questioning stimulated John to expound on his view of women. He emphasised that he did not regard them only as sexual objects, which he thought might be the detective's opinion because of his conviction for rape. 'I have a very deep dislike of society as a whole,' he confided, 'because I think that society is weak and misguided ... but I have a great deal of love for individual people and I'm not a bastard.'

The detectives brought the questioning back to John's to-ings and fro-ings on Thursday, 8 October. 'We're still sort of bogged down round about sort of half-five to six o'clockish,' Saunders said.

'We will be bogged down on any night that week.'

'Right. OK, did you go home that night?'

'Definitely, definitely ... I phoned my mum.' John denied having a mobile telephone. He said he called his mother from home between 7.30 and 8pm, adding, 'I ring her every night.' He also called her on Friday morning about 8am. Asked if he had made or received any other telephone calls on Thursday evening, John coloured his denial with tetchiness. 'I'm not telling you I have not had a phone call, I'm telling you that I can't remember if I've had a phone call. I can't remember, I don't know.'

John realised that if he could substantiate a telephone call to his mother it would help his alibi for the critical part of that evening. He said he had watched television and mentioned seeing programmes such as *Crossroads*, *Wogan* and, he thought, showjumping as well.

Saunders astutely pointed out that this information could easily be gleaned from a newspaper.

'I can't win, can I?' said John. Indeed, he could not. He was adamant that he did not visit any of his usual haunts like the Avon Gorge Hotel or Colonel Jasper's wine bar that Thursday evening. But he thought there was 'something about Thursday night' but he just could not recall what it was. 'I'll tell you this,' he said. 'If I can, I'm going home.' He was implying that this elusive detail would provide him with a firm alibi for the evening that Shirley Banks disappeared. He was once again buying time as he became more immersed in murky waters.

'Well, that would be in everybody's interests,' said Bryan Saunders, but he added that there was still a problem.

John insisted, 'I phoned my mum on Thursday night; that proves where I was.' He might well have telephoned his mother, but it could have been from a call box at any location. Making that alleged phone call did not put him in his flat and the detectives knew it. Protesting, he carried on. 'The time is the problem.'

'No.'

'It isn't any problem to me.'

'Well, if the time is early evening, we've still got a problem.'

'Why?'

'Because Shirley Banks was seen in town shopping by her friends.' Saunders's point was that, as the missing woman was seen alive and well at 7.45pm, John's insistence that he made a telephone call at 7.30pm did not give him an alibi.

But there were further stumbling blocks to his claims. First, Chrissie Fortune stated that she had rung John at his flat in order to cancel their weekend dinner engagement between 6.30 and 8pm on Thursday evening but obtained no reply. Second, during the crucial hours that John could not account for, his girlfriend Marija Vilcins had tried to contact him at the flat between 6 and 9pm but there was no reply. She had also called during the day but without success.

Always ready with an answer, John explained that his mother had on many occasions tried to ring him but had been unable to get through. Saunders said that Marija could not get through: 'The phone is ringing, but nobody is answering.'

'But that's what my mother gets,' said John, adding, 'Do bear in mind that we're on a party-line system on which we have been having trouble.' Always ready with further suggestions, John said he could have been in the bath when the phone rang, or he might inadvertently have turned down the volume control when he dusted the handset.

Bryan Saunders told John that Shirley Banks made a telephone call to her workplace just before 9am on Friday morning. 'Did she make that from your flat?'

'Let me make this categorically clear,' said John, 'that Shirley Banks did not make a telephone call from my flat on that morning.'

Wogan featured as a time-marker in John's recollection that he had gone out on Thursday evening to an off-licence in Clifton to buy a bottle of wine. He agreed with Bryan Saunders that the programme began at 7.10pm but he was not sure whether he had used his car to drive to the off-licence or if he had walked. The method used would, of course, have affected the timing; by car the journey would have taken three to five minutes and, on foot, 10 to 12 minutes. This was according to John's own estimate.

John mentioned that there had been a dispute over the price of a bottle of Liebfraumilch. Following his description of the shop, detectives had made enquiries in Clifton and determined that the shop was a branch of Peter Dominic in Portland Street. It transpired that the staff of the shop did not remember John. 'Now the possibilities there are that we've got the wrong shop,' said Saunders.

'Super.'

The detective pointed out that, if such was the case, the matter could be resolved by looking at a map.

'Well, how can I remember them if they don't remember me?' asked John.

The two men consulted the map and decided that the shop visited by police officers was the right one. 'I would say you've gone to the right off-licence,' claimed John, 'but you've spoken to the wrong people.'

Saunders said that the man on duty in the shop did not know John Cannan. They discussed the appearance of the staff member and then went on to describe his assistant. 'I think we've got the right shop,' said Saunders.

'I think we have too,' agreed John.

Quizzed about the type of wine and the size of the bottle, John confirmed that it was a standard-size bottle but thought he had also bought some cigarettes or confectionery at the same time. Saunders asked John to try to recall exactly what he had purchased because 'There's timings on the receipts, you see.'

John thought there was something lying deep in the recesses of his memory about that Thursday evening which he had alluded to in an earlier interview but still could not 'bring to the fore'.

'Have you the till receipt there?' asked John.

'Yes.'

'That could be very useful.'

'It could be, that's why I've got it. See the possibilities are this...'

But John interrupted with: 'No, no – I can see the possibilities opening up before my very eyes.'

Saunders continued by saying it was possible that the shopping visit was not on that night or that the purchase was not a combination of wine and cigarettes – 'or that you didn't go in there at all'.

John protested, if that was the case, he would not be able to describe the staff.

'Fair point, John,' replied the detective.

John claimed that he had been wrongly overcharged by 40p for the wine: £3.29 as against £2.89, and it was a bit of a joke between him and the male assistant. He still could not remember if he had bought cigarettes at the same time, but, if he had, reckoned the total bill would have been about £4.39.

'Well, armed with the facts,' said Bryan Saunders, 'we'll go back to the till receipts.' The two detectives explained that the till receipts were quite lengthy and asked, 'What time of day did you go into the shop to buy the Blue Nun?'

'I can tell you precisely,' he answered, and then contradicted himself. 'No, I can't tell you precisely; it was dark, so presumably ... let me think, oh, God, I just can't remember, wait a minute, wait a minute, it was either before *Wogan* or after *Wogan*...'

It was back to the drawing board on the till receipts, and detectives made a further close examination of the off-licence's transactions in an effort to pinpoint John's alleged purchase of a bottle of Blue Nun wine costing £2.89. He still could not remember whether he had bought a packet of mints and, when asked to confirm that he had only bought one bottle of wine, was not sure. In fact, he could not recall if he had bought one, two or maybe three bottles of wine. He simply could not remember. Asked again if he had bought anything else with the wine, excluding cigarettes, which they had already discussed, John thought probably not.

John was trying desperately to outwit Bryan Saunders who had all the cards, or, at least, all the till rolls, in his hand.

'I have to assume,' said John, 'there must be a reference to £2.89.'

Saunders would not be drawn into John's little ploy.

'I'm just reasoning,' John continued, 'that you wouldn't be asking me about a quantity of bottles if it had no direct relationship to £2.89.'

'Just let me ask the questions,' replied the detective.

'Sorry, OK – go on.'

'OK, I'm sure we'll progress if I ask the questions.'

'Yes,' said John, then, ignoring what he had just been told, asked, 'How many did I buy then?'

Saunders referred the question back. 'How many did you buy?'

'I don't know, Bryan.'

'What else did you buy with your wine?'

'I don't know, Bryan.'

Saunders ascertained that John and his girlfriend Marija drank two bottles of wine during their weekend together at his flat. He did not have any wine in the flat beforehand, so it seemed likely that he purchased two bottles sometime between Thursday and Saturday evening. John acknowledged the logic implied here. Asked if he had bought any sherry or beer, he answered, 'No.'

Saunders tried again. 'Are you sure about the sherry?'

'I do drink sherry.'

'Yes, but did you buy a bottle of sherry that day?'

Sensing trouble, John backtracked a little. 'I don't think so. I don't know, I don't know.'

Now Bryan Saunders played his ace. 'There's only one purchase for a bottle of wine at £2.89,' he said indicating the off-licence till receipt.

'Yes.'

'And that was bought with another bottle of wine at £3.15.'

'Yes.'

'The purchase had been completed with some confectionery and beer.'

'I don't drink beer.'

'So the £2.89 that appears that day couldn't have been you, could it?'

'I would say if it's beer, no. What time of day was that, by the way?'

'Twenty-six minutes past seven,' replied the detective.

If this purchase could have been confirmed as John's, it would have helped his alibi for Thursday evening. The timing placed him in Clifton, a mile and a half from Broadmead and ten minutes' or so drive from central Bristol, at the precise moment Shirley Banks paid for her dress at Top Shop in Debenhams department store.

Two different till rolls in two different shops, both time-stamped 19.26 on Thursday, 8 October. One was a prelude to a death for which the other could have been a perfect alibi. The problem for John Cannan was that he was not the customer at the off-licence at that time – the alibi could not work for him.

Realising Saunders had skilfully played a trump card, John tried to make light of it. 'Well, I think we've accounted for my movements about that time anyway.'

'Well, I don't think we have,' replied the officer.

Again, John attempted to backtrack. 'Could I have bought beer?' he mused.

Bryan Saunders was firm. 'If you didn't buy beer, then we're in the situation, the scenario, of not being able to put you in that off-licence on Thursday night.'

'Not true,' insisted John. 'Just because you're not being able to owes more to your incapability to do so, rather than my inability to prove I was.'

John admitted that he was in a vulnerable position. 'I live alone, I don't go out a lot anyway ... I've spent nights alone for the last three weeks.'

Bryan Saunders felt obliged to remind him that he had claimed to have spent the night of Wednesday, 7 October with his neighbour Val Humphreys and also a large part of Friday evening. 'So, of the two nights either side of the really important thing, here you were in company.' The fact that Saturday was also booked up for John with Marija Vilcins had not escaped the officer's mind.

The officers changed tack again and went straight to the nitty-gritty. They kicked off by asking John if he knew Shirley Banks.

'I did not know Shirley Banks,' was the unequivocal reply. Shown a photograph of the missing woman, John reiterated that he was reasonably sure he had not seen her before.

'Has this girl ever been in your flat legitimately?'

'No, she has not.'

Next, Saunders asked John to go over the sequence of events once he realised from the newspapers that he had acquired possession of Shirley's car.

'For days I didn't know what to do,' confessed John, but decided the only sensible course of action would be 'to get rid of the fucking car'.

Having repainted it and wiped it of fingerprints, his intention then was to dump the vehicle, or alternatively to find somewhere to destroy it by fire. John realised the origin of the car the day after he bought it, which prompted Saunders to ask, 'Did you consider that the fellow who'd sold you the car might well be the chap who'd abducted this lady?'

John did not think so.

'But did you ever consider that he might assist us to get this car back? Because he must have bought the car from somebody if your story is right?'

John acknowledged this but believed that suspicion would be directed at him if this man could not be located.

Bryan Saunders again swiftly changed his line of

questioning. On the day he was arrested at Leamington Spa, John took a coat into a dry-cleaning shop at Sutton Coldfield. The belt from this garment was found in his BMW. John described the coat as a trench type 'sold in their millions by a firm called British Home Stores'. He had bought it about 12 months previously, so it was relatively new. Saunders said it was taken to be cleaned because it was covered in mud. John did not deny this, explaining that he had used the coat to protect the boot of his BMW when he took his mother's lawnmower to be serviced. In the process, it was soiled with mud and grass.

'Shall I try and explain what I am getting at?' offered Bryan Saunders. 'Shirley's abducted, OK? Perhaps it was in a field, perhaps it was where it was muddy and perhaps you had the trench coat with you and it got muddy for that reason.' It later transpired after forensic tests had been carried out that the coat was soiled with a red-coloured mud characteristic of the region where Shirley's body was discovered.

John said his mother could vouch for the fact that he put her lawnmower on his coat. The lawnmower was filthy. 'I should have put paper down, but I didn't. In fact, if I remember rightly, I was being a bit pissy because my mum can be a bit of a fusspot.' He added that we all do silly things occasionally, but he felt as if a sneeze on his part was a matter of great significance. Saunders again noted John's comments.

Referring to the weekend when Marija Vilcins stayed at the flat in Bristol, the detective asked John if he wore his mackintosh on a trip to Castle Combe. He couldn't remember if he wore it on that occasion, but confirmed he was a regular customer at Harris's dry cleaners in

Sutton Coldfield. 'I am dreadful, dreadful with my clothes. I fall over, I trip over, I get my clothes absolutely filthy,' he explained.

Asked if the soil at Sutton Coldfield was red, John said, 'I don't know.'

Terry Jones commented that, if the coat had been soiled with mud from the lawnmower, it could be assumed that it would be red.

'You would have to check,' answered John. 'I don't know.'

John mentioned that he had taken his coat on a visit to the Torbay area in Devon. 'I get everything filthy,' he repeated. But he couldn't recall when he last visited a dry-cleaner's. 'I can't remember what happened [last] Tuesday,' he said. When he was confronted with a dry-cleaning receipt dated 23 October 1987 for £4.10, John's memory failed him once again.

'Now wait a minute,' he said. 'I'm just trying to think.' To help his recall he handed out some of Saunders's Polo mints. The officer acknowledged this gesture with dry wit: 'John's kindly handing out the mints which we will replace.'

But John seemed to be less interested in searching for an answer to the question than in working out why it was asked. The detective reminded him: 'Absolutely everything I say is connected with Shirley Banks.'

'Yes. Yes, well.'

Perhaps the mints stimulated John's memory, for, when Saunders asked him a snap question about whether he had used a red Ford Escort car on the occasion he first met Gilly Paige, John agreed readily enough.

'Where was it from?'

'Alpha Car Hire, Birmingham,' came the response.

Still sucking on his peppermint, Saunders replied dryly, 'I am glad that we are in a position to prompt your memory.'

'So am I,' said John.

The two detectives went to great pains to explain to John that he was in serious trouble. He had been arrested following an attempted robbery. He was in possession of various lengths of clothes-line, a replica firearm, a knife and handcuffs. His garage contained a missing woman's car, he had no alibi for the evening she went missing and his account of how he purchased the car did not hold a drop of water. To sum it all up, he had a previous conviction for rape, was a suspect in another rape case, his former girlfriend had filed a complaint for rape and he had been picked out by Julia Holman as the man who had attempted to abduct her the night before Shirley Banks went missing.

Bryan Saunders then appealed to the better side of his suspect's nature. The detective explained that he wanted to find Shirley Banks alive, but, if not, to discover where her body lay. 'I want to be able to say to her parents, we've found her body ... They can then get on with their lives...'

'Yes,' answered John. 'Don't you think this upsets me too? ... Look, I'm not without soul,' John told the officers. 'It doesn't look good with Leamington and all the rest of it, but the point is I have not killed Shirley Banks.'

Saunders said that after eight tape-recorded interviews they had gone down some pretty interesting avenues. 'But let's be quite clear about this, [you've] a pretty good memory when it comes to various points, but the point of time when this girl was abducted, Thursday evening, really, you can't remember.'

'I can't remember last Tuesday,' was John's answer

before telling Saunders, 'You've missed one dreadfully important point.'

'Well, tell me what point I've missed?'

'Well, I think it's for you to consider – you're the detective.'

'You're the man,' said Saunders, 'that for the rest of his life is going to be affected by this ... you go to prison when that body's outstanding and, to be honest, John, natural justice says you don't come out. It's not a threat, it's one human being to another...'

'How am I to respond to that?'

Here, John's solicitor intervened, advising him not to respond.

'I'm just about to hit the ceiling,' shouted John.

This confrontation was a stand-off. Bryan Saunders told John that he hoped he was now aware of the way he was thinking.

'I don't blame you,' John replied, adding before the tape ran out, 'There's something about Thursday night that would help me, but I'll be blowed if I can remember what the damn thing is.'

These evasive thoughts and promises are an integral part of the persona of John David Guise Cannan. Like a carrot dangled in front of the donkey, they allure and tease the mind into believing that there may be, at the end of the day, a logical explanation of events which will secure John's innocence. John's mind was working overtime to gain space and delay the inevitable. But the donkey never gets the carrot and we never get the truth.

12

MONGOOSE AND SNAKE

John Cannan believed that he spent longer in police custody than anyone else in legal history – a total of 17 days at Filton police station. 'There were many times during my confinement at Filton,' said John, 'that I began to doubt my own sanity. I was tired, I was worried and often in pain from the tooth abscess. With every edition of the newspapers, my credibility and legal position was becoming worse.' He realised that his name was being linked to the disappearance of Suzy Lamplugh and he was aware that his former wife and girlfriends were being interviewed by the press and television media.

For a person who liked to be in control, John was completely at a disadvantage. While he expressed the view afterwards about what he saw as the poor quality of the police interviewing, he admitted that, at the time, 'I have never felt so scared and bewildered in my entire life.'

He added that, when he should have been 'making serious admissions and completely letting fly', he reached the stage that he was scared of admitting he betted on horses. Yet he was not averse to making statements that were laced with sexual innuendo or aggression. When asked to describe a young woman of his acquaintance, he told Bryan Saunders she was 'slim, dark hair, southwestern accent, about 5ft 6in at a guess, 18 to 21: wouldn't want to fuck it!' This, and other remarks in a similar vein, were extraordinary statements from a man intent on denying sexually motivated attacks on women.

For their next encounter, Bryan Saunders came prepared with a map of Bristol. He told John he wanted to identify some of the locations that he had referred to earlier. They pinpointed Charlotte's tea room, the chemist's shop, the newsagent's and the establishment John mistook for a curtain shop. It was established that these visits to Clifton were made after he had taken Val Humphreys back to Foye House from the hairdresser's some time between 4.45 and 5.30pm on Thursday, 8 October. John then returned to his flat at Foye House.

'Did you go into Broadmead shopping that evening?' asked Saunders.

John was certain that he had not. When asked if he was a hundred per cent sure, he answered, 'No, no, no, not on the Thursday evening.'

Saunders moved swiftly on to other matters. He wanted to check on a number of items found in John's BMW, namely two umbrellas. A ladies' black umbrella and a gentleman's black umbrella were found in the boot. John explained that he found them in the orange Mini and transferred them to the BMW, 'thinking my luck was in ... I cannot personally keep umbrellas for five minutes ... I think that perhaps we can draw some deduction who they belong to.' This was his acknowledgement that the umbrellas belonged to Shirley Banks.

There was also a riding crop on the back seat of the Mini that he had not removed. John explained that all manner of items were left in cars when they were sold: 'You get a range of weird and wonderful things ... it's no big deal.' When the detective asked him what else he had taken from the Mini, John became a little testy. He acknowledged that finding the umbrellas in his car was 'ominous if you like', but he had been charged with stealing the car and as far as he was concerned that also included the contents.

Saunders patiently pointed out that he was investigating the disappearance of a woman whose car had been found in his possession. 'If you're saying you innocently purchased the Mini,' Saunders said, 'we accept that.' He needed, however, to account for the contents. 'I mean, what was in the vehicle when you acquired it innocently?'

'I'm not going to discuss this any more,' declared John.

'It's the main reason you are here,' emphasised the detective.

'I don't want to answer any more questions appertaining to the Mini. That is my last word on the matter ... we have discussed the Mini time and again.'

The snake and the mongoose were squaring up again. It was time for a tea break and an opportunity for John to talk privately with his solicitor.

When the interview resumed John refused to answer any further questions about the Mini. He said that he might have 'to remain silent under duress because of possible implications and insinuations'.

'I'll put the questions,' said Saunders, 'you draw on your intelligence, your experience, your advice from your solicitor...' He also told John that he was entitled not to answer if he so wished.

Terry Moore tried to break the impasse by suggesting that DCI Saunders put his questions and that John answered as he felt necessary including 'no comment' if he judged that appropriate.

'But I don't want to make "no comment" replies,' John protested, and he went on to tell his solicitor there were implications 'that could be misconstrued in a court of law ... Some of the questions could be improper.'

Bryan Saunders told John he had made his point and asked if they could get back to the matter in hand which was the disappearance of Shirley Banks. 'Be quite clear you are suspected.'

Swiftly he moved to wrongfoot John by referring to the umbrellas and his statement that he had not removed anything else from the Mini. 'I only mention this,' he said, 'because there was of course the excise licence in your...'

John leaped in with an apology. 'Let me say that I was incorrect in my statement. I said to you I only transferred two umbrellas. I apologise.'

'Yes, that's why I jogged your memory because I know you weren't trying to hide the fact.'

'The excise licence truthfully was in my briefcase,' admitted John. His reason for removing the licence disc from the car was interesting. He argued that someone might have broken into his garage and seized the opportunity to steal the car, possibly for joy-riding purposes. If that had happened and the vehicle was eventually dumped and found by the police, the licence disc would have identified it as belonging to Shirley Banks and the fingerprints on it would have been identified as his. 'So I took the excise licence off, purely as a precaution,' was his weak explanation.

When asked why he hadn't destroyed it rather than keeping it, John answered, 'I don't know, I don't know, truthfully I don't know. Truthfully I don't know.' He thought there were times when people did not behave in a sane or rational way.

Continuing his questions about items found in John's BMW, Saunders showed interest in a ladies' white comb.

'Well, actually it isn't a ladies' comb at all,' said John.

'Oh, isn't it? It goes with the BMW does it, John?' said Saunders, adding, 'Injecting a little humour there.'

John said it was his: he'd bought it from Dingles.

'There was a Top Shop carrier bag,' said the detective. 'Do you recall offhand whether it was your bag or not?'

'Do you know, I'm not sure what Top Shop is,' answered John.

'Let me say that we think Shirley was in possession of a Top Shop bag and that's why I'm asking.'

John said he was 'almost 100 per cent certain' he had never been to a Top Shop or ever bought anything from such a store.

John did not recall seeing the bag in the front passenger foot well of his BMW. He asked what it had in it.

'Nothing,' replied Saunders.

'Now wait a minute, boys,' demanded John.

The detective explained that he did not search the car himself but was relying on a list provided by another officer.

'Please will you make extensive efforts to clarify that

point?' asked John. 'I'll tell you why. Because I'm telling you that there was no Top Shop bag in my motor car ... we're in a different ball game altogether.'

Saunders explained that the bag had been found by a Scenes of Crime officer.

John was 'reasonably adamant' there was no such bag in his car. He postulated that it might have been left there 'maybe by some girl', but he had no knowledge of it.

'One of the reasons I keep asking you if you know Shirley Banks,' said Saunders, 'was in case there was any legitimate reason why – and you're an intelligent man – why her fingerprints might be in your car, the BMW.'

'Are you saying that her fingerprints are in my car?'

'No, I'm not...'

'I see, you're purely speculating on this point?'

'No, no, I'm telling you so that you understand.'

Saunders next made reference to a length of white rope found in the BMW.

'I do not deny that.'

'Can I ask you why the rope was in there?'

'No comment.'

'I've just got to go on,' said the officer, referring John to his earlier washing-line explanation.

'I'm sorry to answer that question "no comment".' John said he did not deny there was rope in his car.

'Yes,' said Saunders. 'In the context of me asking you in looking for Shirley Banks, why was there rope in your car?'

'I have to refer to my previous answer,' said John.

Bryan Saunders framed his question differently. 'In the context of that crucial week that we are talking about...'

John finished the question for him: 'Did I buy that rope during the week of the disappearance of Shirley Banks?

That is what you are asking me?'

'Yes, yes.'

'The answer to that question is no, sir, I did not.'

The policeman reeled off the list of articles found in John's BMW – everything from clothes to Paco Rabanne aftershave. 'How long has that stuff been in your boot?'

'Oh, Christ, some of it months.'

'So.'

'Some of it hours.'

Another length of rope had been found in the car's glove compartment.

'I do not deny there may have been some rope...' said John.

'Why was it there, John?'

'I refer to the statement I made at "Nick" [Leamington Spa police station].'

A parking ticket dated 26 October 1987 placed John in Leamington Spa three days before he was arrested there. 'What were you doing there?'

'Basically just looking around. I do get bored, you know.'

'Now then,' said Saunders, still working through his list, 'in the jack well, there are a pair of handcuffs.'

'Yes.'

'Are they yours?'

'So I understand.'

'Are they yours?'

'I was told in Leamington that they were mine, yes.'

'No, forget what you were told in Leamington.'

'I know nothing, I know nothing. I was told in Leamington that they were mine.'

'Where have you seen the handcuffs before?'

'I refer to my statement in Leamington.'

As he had done several times before, DCI Saunders made it plain he would not be deterred by attempts at evasion. 'In the context of the Shirley Banks matter,' he said, 'I'm asking you for an explanation of the handcuffs.'

John said the detective was implying that the handcuffs could have been used for the abduction of Shirley Banks. Saunders probably could not have put it better himself. 'All right, all right, let me make this very clear to you,' said John. 'I have not used any form of restraining on anybody.'

'But I need to ask – are they your handcuffs?'

'I've answered "no comment" in Leamington, haven't I?'

The mongoose was not about to let go. 'Can you give any explanation why there's blood on the handcuffs?' asked the officer.

At this point, John's solicitor suggested he might have a word with his client. The four men reconvened after a few minutes.

'Where were we?' asked Bryan Saunders.

'Well, I think I have something that I ought to tell you,' offered the prisoner. 'The handcuffs that were discovered in the boot well of my BMW are my property. They are owned by me. They were purchased by me some weeks ago and those handcuffs have in part something to do with the matters for which I was questioned in Leamington Spa.'

Saunders pressed home his questions and John admitted that he bought the handcuffs before Shirley Banks went missing. He volunteered the details of where and when he purchased them. He thought the traces of blood on them probably resulted in him trying on the handcuffs. 'You try and get a pair of handcuffs off … it's hard.' He denied that the handcuffs had been put on anyone else's wrists.

'Have they been clamped on anybody by consent?' asked Saunders.

'No.'

'You know what I'm getting at, I think.'

'What you are saying is, is JC kinky? JC is not kinky, no.' After a night's rest and with time to think out his position, John returned to the interview room and asked to make a statement. 'I am beginning to feel disorientated,' he said, remarking that, after spending several days in custody, it was becoming more difficult to give clear answers to questions. 'This puts me in a dilemma,' he claimed, 'since it is becoming difficult to be assured of having a fair trial.' He felt his position was being compromised.

Bryan Saunders acknowledged that he had been in custody 'a good while now', but they were dealing with serious matters which required further discussion.

John said he was not complaining about being put under tremendous pressure but 'the situation is stressful'. After commenting that he was being well treated at Filton, John said, 'Can we press on, gentlemen?'

Keeping John on his toes, Saunders changed tack once again. 'Am I correct in thinking that you applied for a cleaner for the flat?'

'Correct.'

John explained that he'd put postcards advertising for a cleaner in two or three shops in Clifton.

'What were you asking for – a female cleaner, wasn't it?'

'Well, you wouldn't get a man doing the washing and ironing.'

'Did it say female on the advert?'

'Almost certainly. Is that unusual?'

'How many applicants did you get?'

'Millions,' John replied with his characteristic exaggeration. He received many telephone replies and invited applicants to his flat so he could vet them.

'How many came to the flat?'

'About 20.'

'You're a pretty strict employer then, John,' commented Bryan Saunders.

As a result of these interviews, he employed a cleaner for one day. He could not remember her name but, unable to resist a sexual reference, described her as 'early twenties, fairish hair, longish fairish hair, slim, nice little body'. The thought no doubt flashed through the detective's mind that this was another trawling exercise.

John was next quizzed about the knife relating to the incident in Leamington Spa on 29 October. 'Were you in possession of that during the week Shirley Banks went missing?' asked Bryan Saunders.

The pun was probably unintentional, but John said, 'I take your point' and went on to acknowledge that it was a very important question. 'If I hazard a guess,' he said, 'I would say yes.' He repeated his earlier claim that he had bought the knife from a shop in Bristol close to the law courts – a shop that specialised in knives of various kinds. The detective offered to unfold his street map of Bristol in order to help John locate the shop but desisted when told that it wouldn't help. John reiterated that it was a speciality shop: 'everybody would know it.'

John had paid £20 for the knife, which he bought for a purpose which he described with characteristic over-statement. 'Many, many, many, many, many years ago one of my interests was sea fishing and I always had an intention of going sea fishing again, especially like late this year when the cod's running ... so don't put any, you know, just purely ominous motives on that.'

The fact that John did not even own a spool of line, a hook or a rod made this a lame excuse for buying the knife. Saunders was now smiling broadly.

John smiled in return, saying, 'I'm smiling because you're laughing at me. You're laughing your heads off.'

The detective denied any mirth on his part, 'because it's a serious matter'.

When pressed further about the knife, John could not remember when he actually bought it. He could not recall where he parked his car on the day he made the purchase and he did not know if there was a female assistant in the shop. 'You give me far too much credit,' he told Saunders, acknowledging the gentle jibe about his attraction to the opposite sex. Conveniently, John Cannan's memory had failed yet again. But it was soon to return.

Bryan Saunders now suddenly switched the questioning to horse riding. 'Do you mix in sort of horsy circles?' he asked John.

'Yes, the Clifton brigade are nearly all horsy types.'

Saunders asked if he had been horse-riding with a friend or whether one of his stable of girlfriends owned a horse.

'Not to my knowledge,' he answered. John said that he was a fanatical horse-racing fan and had been to Warwick Races in September 1987.

'Did you come into contact with the horses?' enquired Saunders with tongue in cheek.

'It is inevitable.'

All this was leading up to the question of why horsehair should have been found in John's car. Bryan Saunders had earlier made the point about the riding crop having been discovered in Shirley's Mini.

'I've touched a horse,' said John lamely.

'Yes.'

'Ashton Court is full of bloody horses and shit, went to Warwick, been to other racecourses.'

'Yes.'

'Girls who have been in my car, or people who've been in my car, they could be associated with horses, or have touched horses, or I can't see any problem...'

Saunders asked John to name the people in his circle who were horse-lovers.

John mentioned Annabel Rose as a person who had attended race meetings. 'I can think of a hundred and one ways in which horsehair could get in my car,' he said, 'a hundred and one ways.' As an example, John claimed he had picked up a couple of hitchhikers, implying that they might have introduced horsehairs into his BMW.

'I'm tempted to say, was their horse broken down?' quipped Bryan Saunders.

The detectives encouraged John to think if any of his friends owned horses, but there were no names readily forthcoming. John then reverted back to his old tactics and protested that some of his acquaintances were married women and that his sense of principle would not allow him to compromise them. Saunders said that no horse-owning friends seemed to come readily to mind, to which John retorted, 'After nine days here, I don't; nothing's readily to mind.'

'Well, I mean a horse is a pretty big item,' said Saunders.

'I'd know if a horse had sat in my car,' answered John.

'OK, so we've established that a horse hasn't sat in your car.'

As he had done several times before, John tried to short-circuit the detectives' line of questioning. 'If you found horsehair in my car, and I think you have said that Shirley Banks is interested, I don't know, in horses, that would not prove that Shirley Banks had been in my car.'

This cocky remark only served to strengthen the two detectives' resolve, and Saunders, who was beginning to tire of John's barrack-room lawyer attitude, informed John that he was not just talking about horsehair. He said that the BMW was being 'taken apart forensically'.

'I hope you are not putting the clock [milometer] back,' retorted John.

Both officers weighed in with an explanation of the logic of these questions.

'That is one of the silliest questions and lines of thought I think I have ever heard in my life,' John said. 'Open-ended, subject to interpretation ... an extremely spurious point and one which, frankly, I think, no, no – I'm not going to proceed along those lines.'

Biting his tongue, Bryan Saunders suggested there was a danger of getting bogged down on horsehair.

'That's of your choosing,' sniped John.

The two detectives pressed on relentlessly while John, now in cloud cuckoo land, offered that he had been to the zoo and might have picked up some llama dung.

So the hundred and one reasons John said he could list to explain how horsehair could have got into his car were narrowed down to just a few. Hitchhikers who might have touched horses, unnamed married women who might have touched horses, and that he, a supposed horse-racing fan, might have touched a horse at Ashton Court or at Warwick during his one and only visit to the races in 1987.

John's composure had now deserted him and he rambled on pathetically: 'You have my car, you have my house' – neither of which he owned – 'you have every bloody thing I possess. I was stripped off down to next to nothing and, I think, forensically, you know you must get on with it.'

The opponents confronting each other in the interview room at Filton agreed to 'leave it up to the forensics'. The two detectives hardly needed reminding of the powerful cards they held. John was given a cup of tea and returned to the cold confines of his custody cell for the night.

So the pattern continued much as before, with John making regular sorties from his custody cell to the interview room at Filton police station. DCI Bryan Saunders used a mixture of questions covering ground already discussed but swiftly shifting to new territory when it suited him. His plan was to elicit replies from John that could be correlated with what was already known. They would either confirm the established facts or be at variance with them. John was an astute player of this game and commanded a third category of answers that neither confirmed nor denied but merely hedged; he was a master at putting up a smokescreen.

The detectives returned to John's lack of an alibi for the crucial, early part of the evening on Thursday, 8 October. They simply would not let him off the hook. 'Are you a man capable of violence?'

'We are all capable of violence,' came the calculated reply.

'Right.'

'Am I a man inclined to violence? That is a different question.'

'OK, well, answer it in those terms then, John.'

'I am a man capable of violence because we are all capable of violence ... If you wish to discuss violence with me, I will discuss it with you all night because, when you say violence, you must define violence.'

Saunders suggested the way they should play it was that he would put the questions and John should answer them – he could elaborate on the subject of violence later on if he wished. Once again the officers tried to draw Cannan on his ability to use violence against women. Sharon Major came into the questioning, which infuriated the suspected killer. John eventually admitted that he had sexually assaulted his former lover but denied that he had 'horrifically, sexually assaulted her'.

'You asked her for anal intercourse,' said Saunders.

'Not true.'

'She only made good her escape by pretending to get some Vaseline in order that you could penetrate her more easily.'

'Not true.'

'Per anus.'

'Not true, not true.'

The officers then enquired about the occasion John had tried to take his own life with an overdose of paracetamol tablets. 'You told the doctor that you felt that you were schizophrenic, is that correct?'

'Let me think about the word "schizophrenic". Define schizophrenic?'

The detective's disinclination to define the word produced a predictable response from Cannan. 'Unless you are qualified to discuss the subject, I can't discuss the subject with you.'

Saunders said John had told the doctor at the Bristol Royal Infirmary that he had urges he could not control.

'Correct,' snapped John.

'What do you mean by that?'

'What I meant was that I always seemed to be doing the wrong things, getting life out-of-sync when I reflected back on life and things ...I would not make the right decisions.'

'John, did you mean that you were prone to committing horrific sexual attacks or not?'

Turning to his solicitor, John said, 'Mr Moriarty, I think you had better step in, sir.'

Saunders pressed home his attack. Leaning over the table that stood between then, he faced John and looked him firmly in the eye. 'I've got a girl who's missing, you're in possession of her car. I've got a previous girlfriend telling me that you committed a horrific sexual act on her. OK. I ask you...'

John butted in and said he wanted to make it clear that when he spoke to the doctor his remarks were not made 'in a sexual light'.

'So he's mistaken as well, is he, John?'

'I think he's taken it out of context,' was the quick reply.

Saunders's colleague, DI Terry Jones, moved behind John's chair and bent down to the prisoner's right ear. 'He was sufficiently worried, he asked you to go in for psychiatric treatment. Is that correct?'

'Correct.'

Once again Bryan Saunders switched his line of questioning. Referring to John's brief relationship with the ice-skater Gilly Paige, he asked him if he had told her about his preferences for bondage and anal intercourse. This question was bound to produce an angry response from John, who was becoming confused and out of his depth.

'Not true,' came the stock rebuff. He would not say that Gilly was lying but alleged that detectives framed questions to her in such a way as to make her say such things. The master of the smokescreen was up to his tricks again.

At this point, Saunders went into overdrive. 'Is it not the truth,' he asked, 'that you in fact did abduct poor Shirley – you had her at your flat all that night?'

'That is not true.'

'You're into bondage.'

'That is not true.'

'You're into anal intercourse, rape.'

'That is not true.'

'Tying people up.'

John looked desperately at his lawyer. 'Jim?'

'Is it not true that you're into anal intercourse, tying people up, handcuffs, knives and that you abducted Shirley and you kept her at your flat overnight, allowing her to make a phone call the next morning?'

'The answer to your question is no.'

At 5.30pm on 9 November, John was informed that the police had considered the evidence and decided to charge him with kidnapping Shirley Banks.

'You'll look pretty silly if she turned up, wouldn't you?' he replied. The prisoner was taken to the charge room, where he was formally charged by Detective Inspector Terry Jones. John's response was: 'I have been advised to say nothing.'

The following morning he appeared before the Bristol magistrates court where he was remanded in custody at H.M. Prison, Horfield.

John found his appearance before the magistrates an uncomfortable experience because of the hostility that he felt was projected towards him. 'The chill as I stood before the magistrates was such that, as I glanced round at people sitting in the public gallery, I could see and feel the bad feeling that was there.' He said the worst part of it was that he could not blame them as the media painted such a poor image of him. 'Belief was very deep,' he said, 'and belief was rife that I had committed other offences, Lamplugh included. There I was being rubbished, being scandalised, being found guilty before I'd even appeared at trial.'

John said he also had a surprise encounter with Annabel Rose while he was waiting for the proceedings to begin in the magistrates court on another occasion. Opposite the dock was a glass-panelled door leading to the inner regions of the court building. 'Who was standing right in front...?' he asked. 'Annabel Rose, grinning at me as I stood in the dock.' He went mad and complained to his solicitor who instructed the police to ask her to move on. She had official business in the court building and hence every right to be where she was, which, according to John, is what she told the officers.

After being remanded for 14 days, John Cannan was brought before the magistrates on 24 November. Police application for one day's custody was granted and the prisoner was taken to the central police station in Bristol. He was asked in the presence of Jim Moriarty if he would agree to take part in an identification parade.

He said he would. Five witnesses attended and they were separated by a screen from the line-up. Mr Moriarty objected to two of the men in the parade and the officer in charge, Inspector Colin Benson, asked them to leave. Both John and his solicitor were satisfied with the eight remaining men and the identification process began.

The first witness to view the parade was David Jones, a taxi-driver who worked for Blue Spot Taxis in Bristol. Following the publicity after Shirley Banks's disappearance, Jones had told the police that on Friday, 9 October 1987 he had been directed by his radio dispatcher to Flat 2, Foye House, where he was to pick up a female fare and take her to Temple Meads railway station. When he arrived at the address and knocked on the door of Flat 2, a man appeared and told him that no one had ordered a taxi. Now Jones walked along the line-up twice and when Inspector Benson asked, 'Is the person you saw on 9 October here?' he answered, 'Best as I can remember, yes. It's number nine.' This was the position occupied by John Cannan.

The next witness was Carmel Cleary, manageress of Ginger boutique in Leamington Spa. She was asked if the man she saw on 29 October 1987 was present. 'Yes, number nine,' came her reply. Jane Child, the shop assistant at Ginger went through the same procedure. However, she was uncertain whether the person she saw on that day was present on the ID parade. 'I think so,' she said, 'I only saw him with a crash helmet on.' She walked down the line again but said, 'I'm not sure.'

Karen Pearce, one of Shirley Banks's friends at Alexandra Workwear, was positive that she recognised no one in the parade.

There was a long delay before the next witness arrived and John complained to Inspector Benson that he had failed to advise two of the witnesses that the person they saw might not be present. The officer checked his prepared statement and found it to be at fault. The error was rectified before Richard Banks, the missing woman's husband, attended the parade. He twice walked along the line and then stood in front of John Cannan for several seconds. When Benson said to him, 'Is there anyone on this parade that you recognise?' he replied, 'Yes, number nine.' Richard Banks had seen John on more than one occasion at the Avon Gorge Hotel.

The most intriguing witness at the identification parade was David Jones, the taxi-driver who had picked out John as the man he had spoken to at Foye House between 1 and 2pm. When John was questioned about this by DCI Bryan Saunders, he said, 'I did not order a taxi on that day.' The detective suggested that perhaps the taxi-driver was mistaken to the extent that he was referring to another day when perhaps one of John's many girlfriends requested a cab. John thought it unlikely.

Bryan Saunders said either Mr Jones was correct in his statement, or that he had mixed up his dates. 'No taxi-driver ... has come to my door to pick up a friend to go to Temple Meads,' said John, asking if the police had checked the validity of the taxi-driver's statement. Saunders said the statement had been checked. 'And you have absolute one hundred per cent proof that he's right?' snapped John.

Perhaps there was some good reason why John categorically denied that a taxi-driver had ever called at his flat. To start with, there was no record of a late booking for Foye House in the day sheets at Blue Spot Taxis. Further, the duty dispatcher could not recall sending Jones to that call. There was no time showing a booking between 1 and 2pm nor was there a record of Jones radioing in to his controller saying that there was no such booking or requesting other work, which is the usual practice with cab-drivers. Nevertheless, Jones had identified John at the ID parade and, more to the point, identified Flat 2, Foye House as the intended pick-up point.

Following the identification parade, John was told that he was to be formally charged on suspicion of causing grievous bodily harm and indecent assault on Sharon Major. It was now six years after it had happened. Saunders said he proposed to put to John the allegations that Sharon had made against him. John's reaction was that, provided he was given the statements that he had already made on the subject in order to refresh his memory, he was willing to cooperate. This request was refused by Saunders and, after consultation with his solicitor, John remained adamant that he would not change his position. After they spent a fruitless few minutes in which the detective's questions were countered with evasive replies, the session was concluded. At 5pm, John was formally charged with offences committed against Sharon Major. His response was: 'It's total rubbish.'

The prisoner enjoyed little sleep that night. He knew he was in the net with little or no chance of escape. A warder peeking through the cell spy-hole took in the pathetic form of Cannan covered by two grey blankets. Face against the wall, John was fighting himself. One part of his mind knew the truth of it all, but the more dominant half refused to concede to his faults.

The following morning brought John before the detectives once again. There could be no relief in their tenacious search for truth and the whereabouts of Shirley Banks. Saunders and Jones began by throwing the realities of John's position into the session with a warning shot. 'You have now been charged with kidnapping Shirley Banks, and various sexual offences against Sharon Major. Now, John, I still desperately need to find out where Shirley might be.'

'Yes,' acknowledged John.

To this end, the detective asked a series of questions about two sets of keys in John's possession, some of which had not been identified. There was a possibility that Shirley was being held somewhere in locked premises. He sought John's assistance in this but without much success. A Squire padlock key came under particular scrutiny and, when asked if he used lock-ups or premises where such a key might be used, John launched once again into one of his multiple denials.

'Let me make it very clear that at no time have I ever, have I ever, have I ever, ever, had any other property, lock-up garage, or otherwise in Bristol, or elsewhere.'

Bryan Saunders said that he was checking into this and asked John, 'You did in fact arrange for Annabel to rent a lock-up garage?'

'No, no, no, please get it right. I did not arrange for Annabel to hire some lock-up garage from anywhere.' He went on to explain that someone with whom Annabel was associated wanted to hire lock-up premises, but repeated, 'You will not find any lock-up garage in my name either in Bristol or any other part of the country.' By stating 'not in my name', Cannan was teasing the officers, testing them. He simply could not resist the opportunity.

Saunders carried on, 'Well, why were you trying to rent the garage for Annabel Rose then?'

'I wasn't.'

'Forty-seven pounds? She wrote a cheque out, didn't she?'

'That would become evident at a later date.'

'How will it become evident?'

John said she might be a prosecution witness.

'Let's stick to the garage, shall we?' said Saunders. 'Where I might find Shirley Banks, OK?'

John repeated that he had not rented a garage or helped Annabel Rose to rent one. He denied that he had received a cheque for £47. 'By your attitude it seems as if you have a doubt,' said John.

'I have a doubt about what you're saying, OK?'

'So you believe Annabel Rose?'

'Well, I don't believe you,' said Saunders. 'I've got to be quite honest.'

John's reaction was to suggest that the police would not investigate properly any matter concerning a prosecution witness. 'I think that, if you did, you'd be extremely stupid or naive, so, of course, you believe Annabel Rose.'

'I'm just interested in the fact that you contacted a property service with a view to renting a garage – is that true or not?'

'That is untrue.' Asked if he had anything to add, John said, 'No. Have you?'

'Later on, I expect.'

'When you have, let me know,' answered John.

On 26 November, John appeared once more before the Bristol magistrates court and was again remanded in custody. A little over three weeks elapsed before he was questioned further. On 21 December, he was escorted to a police vehicle and driven off on a tour of Clifton by Bryan Saunders and Terry Jones accompanied by Jim Moriarty.

Shown where Shirley had lived in the High Street, Clifton,

he denied all knowledge of having been there or of ever having seen her. With the tour now over, the party drove to Filton police station by way of central Bristol. During the journey, John volunteered the statement that he did not know Shirley Banks and questioned Bryan Saunders regarding his view of police officers who fabricated evidence. The fact is that officers have been known to fabricate evidence against suspected offenders, but Bryan Saunders is not one of them and the senior detective took a very dim view of the question, registering his disapproval with Jim Moriarty.

Soon after their arrival back at Filton, John was taken to the interview room for what would be his penultimate questioning session. This time John was questioned further about his allegations about Annabel Rose.

The final encounter between the mongoose and the snake took place on 22 December 1987. Bristol was buzzing with Christmas spirit. There was a light carpet of snow covering the administrative centre of Avon. Brunel's suspension bridge over the Avon Gorge had turned to a slushy avenue in the rush-hour traffic and Flat 2 was the only occupancy in Foye House without Christmas decorations. It might have seemed incongruous to have a murder inquiry operating less than four days before Christmas Day, a time of peace and goodwill to all men. But the law is never touched by this festive time. The wheels of justice grind on regardless. John Cannan was no special case and he deserved no distinctive consideration. All murders are nasty, brutal and horrible, but there are some crimes, perhaps a handful in a decade, which are so wicked, evil or shocking that they dwarf the others, even in this realm of nightmares. John Cannan was suspected of having committed one of them.

John entered the interview room for the last time. He had heard the carol services outside the cell walls; he had seen tinsel and a few gaily wrapped gifts packed up by officers for their loved ones. He had without doubt missed the fun of Christmastide and his thoughts reflected back to his mother's home and fond memories of the past. Bryan Saunders and Terry Jones had arrived early in the morning wrapped up in heavy coats to protect them from the winter's chill. John sat down to his interview, which would complete more than 20 hours of tape-recorded questions and answers. On this final morning, he said he was getting mentally tired of questioning, although he was prepared to go on.

Saunders began by asking John if he had spoken to a dealer in Soho in August 1987 about purchasing pornographic videos.

'No,' came the curt answer.

The detectives pointed out that John's telephone account showed he rang a particular car phone number on several occasions through the Racal Vodafone network. Asked to explain it, he said that he had been given the number to call for business purposes. 'I got through once and had a garbled conversation for somebody to phone back.' He said he tried several times and finally gave up.

Referring to the itemised telephone bill, Bryan Saunders confirmed that John had called on 9 and 10 September and on several other occasions. 'I asked to speak to somebody on business,' said John with some hesitation.

'What was the business?'

'That I can't say at the moment.'

'Well, I'll try and refresh your memory then, John, OK?' Police enquiries had resulted in a man named 'Karl' being brought in for questioning. It had been his car telephone number that John had called. Karl was a Soho pornographic video dealer and well known to the Metropolitan Police. Under questioning, he said that he had telephoned John on a number of occasions and discussed the purchase of video films.

John answered Saunders's questions with 'No comment.'

Karl also alleged that John had asked him to get him a 'shooter'.

'No comment,' replied the prisoner.

'Well, I'll ask you again,' said Saunders. 'Is it not true or no comment?'

'That's not strictly true.'

'Do you agree that in relation to the videos you asked him to come to Bristol? And in fact he tells me that he came to Bristol on 20 August and he arrived at your place at 2 Foye House, you having given the directions, and you weren't there, and on the door knocker was an envelope with £100 addressed to him. Do you agree that is correct?'

'No comment.'

'Again, John, no comment or not true?'

'No comment. The answer is no comment.'

Saunders agreed he had the right to answer 'no comment' but pointed out the police suspected him of murdering Shirley Banks. The detective said he was not interested in the pornographic videos but he wanted to know about the gun. 'Guns are for killing people,' he added.

DI Terry Jones took over at this point. Leaning towards John, he pointed out that Karl alleged John had asked him to get him 'a fix'. 'Is that correct?'

'You are talking about people who are vipers in a vipers' nest,' replied John.

'Are you a viper in a vipers' nest, John?'

'No, I'm not, but let me tell you that this had nothing to do with the murder of Shirley Banks ... Let me tell you,' offered John, 'there are people who I am more potentially frightened of than you. I would prefer for everybody's safety at this point of time, to say nothing, to remain silent.'

'For the sake of Shirley, I'll put it to you,' said Saunders. 'Was that gun for the purpose of causing harm to a woman?'

'No ... I have not bought a pistol, I have not shot Shirley Banks, I have not shot anybody.'

'Now I've put this to you a number of times,' said Bryan Saunders, 'but I have to put it to you today and this is in the context of I suspect that you have murdered Shirley. I show you again a photograph of Shirley Banks. Have you ever seen this girl before?'

'To my recollection, I have never seen this girl.'

'I take it from that then that you've never had a personal relationship with her?'

'No.'

'Casual relationship?'

'No.'

'Business relationship?' Saunders asked John to reply rather than shake his head, explaining, 'It's for the tape.'

'No, sorry, I haven't.'

The officers next questioned John about items found in his possession when he was arrested. First, there was the imitation firearm discovered in the black BMW. Terry Jones placed it on the table. 'Was that gun in your possession in the motor vehicle at the time of your arrest?'

'Not in that condition.'

'Was that gun in your possession?'

'No. A gun, I would say almost identical to this, was in

my possession at the time.' There followed some discussion as to whether the gun had been damaged during forensic examination.

'My point is,' snapped Saunders, 'were you in possession of an imitation gun?'

'Yes, I was.'

The second item was the pair of handcuffs found in John's car. 'Were these handcuffs in your possession on the day of your arrest?'

'They were.'

'Do you accept that in your possession you had a key capable of operating the handcuffs?'

'I do.'

Next came the orange-handled knife. 'Was this knife in your possession...?'

'It looks very different to how I left it, but certainly a knife similar to that was in my possession.'

Then came the length of washing-line found in John's BMW. 'Was this washing-line, rope, in your possession...?'

'A length of washing-line was in my possession. Whether it's that or not I don't know but a length of washing-line was, yes.'

Finally, there were four lengths of clothes-line discovered in the lavatory cistern. 'I'm showing John four lengths of rope removed from the toilet cistern, Smithfield Motors, Leamington,' stated Saunders for the benefit of the tape-recorder.

'You know I've already answered these questions at Leamington,' replied John.

'I'm talking to you about my allegation that you murdered Shirley Banks, nothing else. You understand, don't you?'

'Yes.'

'Four lengths of rope traced to your possession.'

'If those are the pieces of rope.'

Saunders asked John to accept that those were the pieces found in the cistern.

'I see,' said John. 'I'm accepting whatever you say.'

'The bottom line: were four pieces of rope in your possession?'

'Rope was in my possession.'

'Let's just have a look at them.'

'Well, you know, rope is rope.'

Bryan Saunders acknowledged the point but explained he was talking about four separate lengths, not a continuous length.

'Have you finished with Santa's bag?' enquired John in a festive jibe.

Saunders told John that he did not intend to go over the whole story regarding Shirley Banks's Mini car, for which an explanation had already been given. He asked, though, if he was correct in saying that John claimed to have come by the vehicle innocently.

'Yes.'

'And that you did not take it from the possession of Shirley Banks?'

'No.'

'I'll just recap,' said Saunders, recalling that John had met a man at a motor auction who subsequently came to his flat and sold the car to him.

'Yes.'

'And you took him in good faith as being the genuine owner?'

'At that time, I had no reason not to.'

It was agreed that the sale was made in the week after 8 October, the day on which John took his neighbour to the hairdresser.

'Yes, all right.'

'And you bought the vehicle the week following that?'

'Yes. If I remember rightly, yes, yes.'

John was asked to clarify when he repainted the Mini and agreed that it was probably on the evening of 27 October. 'I would think that's fair,' he conceded.

'So what we have at the moment,' said Saunders, 'we've got you in possession of Shirley Banks's Mini?'

'Yep.'

'We have in your possession at the time of your arrest, an imitation firearm?'

'Yep.'

'Handcuffs?'

'Yeah.'

'Four lengths of rope?'

'Yep.'

'And one longer length of rope?'

'Yep.'

'And a knife?'

'Yes.'

'Did you use those implements to restrain, kidnap, murder Shirley?'

'No, no, why? I didn't, no, no,' protested John.

The mongoose was circling the snake now. 'You know what I'm saying to you, John, don't you?'

'I can see the implications of what you are saying.'

Bryan Saunders reminded John once again – every word had to be clear for the microphone – that he was in possession of Shirley's car, which he claimed to have purchased innocently and, at the same time, happened to be in possession of all the implements...

'Yes,' interrupted John, 'I can see your point.'

'Which could...'

'Yes.'

'By fear...'

'Yes.'

'Or force, restrain a person...'

'Yep.'

'Detain a person...'

'Yes.'

'Terrify a person...'

'Yes.'

'And murder a person.'

'Yes.'

'You are in possession of those implements at the time of your arrest?'

'Correct.'

Bryan Saunders reminded John he was 'talking about this girl going out on 8 October and never returning. Yet very shortly after, you being found in possession of her car.'

'Yes.'

'You see the position you're in, don't you, John?'

'Yes.'

'This is why I keep coming back and saying, has she ever been in your flat?'

'No, not to my knowledge, no.'

'You are the one person in Bristol in possession of Shirley's car.'

'Yes.'

'You are the one person in Bristol who has been picked out ... as the person attempting to abduct a lady the night before?'

'Yes.'

'Your stance is that you're innocent, is it?'

'Is your stance, I'm guilty?'

'Is your stance that you're innocent?' repeated Saunders.

'That is correct,' answered John.

The detective told John that if he was innocent he was also 'a little unlucky' because the facts taken together indicated that he murdered Shirley Banks.

John disagreed, saying that not all the facts were known.

'What are the facts then, John?' asked Saunders.

'This will come out in court.'

Saunders pointed out that the other person who could tell them the truth was Shirley herself, adding, 'She's not here, we've just got a photograph of her ... You insist you've never seen the girl before?' He went on to refer to the surveillance notes, exhibit MR4/A, written for John by Tom Eyles. 'Yesterday, I showed you a photocopy...'

'You did,' acknowledged John.

The mongoose was preparing for the kill now. Bryan Saunders confirmed that he was showing John a photocopy of the surveillance notes – other police officers had the originals. 'There's Shirley's photograph,' he said. 'She can't be here, can she?'

'No.'

'So she's done the next best thing, John – there is her thumbprint on this document removed from your house.' (Soon after Shirley Banks disappeared, fingerprints were lifted from objects in her home and place of work as part of the routine police investigation. Her thumbprint had been matched with one found on Tom Eyles's surveillance notes located in John Cannan's monk's chest.)

The snake coiled back. 'Problem,' said John.

'You have a problem,' Saunders confirmed.

'No, *you* do,' replied John.

'Don't smokescreen ... I don't have a problem at all. You have a problem.'

'I don't.'

'John,' reasoned the detective, 'her thumbprint made from the secretions from her body pressed there – sweat and acid – pressed on to this document...'

'Well, to quote your phrase, we will fight this out in court...'

'I ask you now because later on tonight I'm going to go and see Mum and Dad, Shirley Banks's mum and dad, and I ask you on their behalf...'

'I understand.'

'Where is she?'

'I don't know where she is.'

'Why is her thumbprint in...?'

'Bryan.'

'Your flat?'

'Bryan, that has not been established really as being her thumbprint, has it?'

'I'm telling you that it is the thumbprint of Shirley Banks.'

'I'm sorry, I can't accept that, Bryan.'

'Why can't you accept it?'

'Because...'

'It's like all along, you've told a pack of lies, haven't you?'

'If that's what you wish, that is your prerogative.'

Bryan Saunders asked John to take a close look at the thumbprint: 'That came out of the sweat of her body,' he said. 'You don't care, do you?'

'Yes, of course I care.'

'John, it is verging on the ridiculous, isn't it?'

'Look, you don't know the whole story, Bryan. You don't know.'

Saunders told him to concentrate on the fact that Shirley Banks's thumbprint was found in his flat. 'Direct your mind to the fact that this girl was in your flat.' The logic of the detective's argument failed to penetrate, so he tried appealing to John's humanity. 'I'm not asking you how this girl died,' he said softly. 'I'm saying, please, put two unhappy parents out of their misery.'

'Look, don't you think I care?'

'No.'

'I do care.'

'I think you only care about yourself, John.' Reining in his exasperation, but knowing he had won the battle of wits, Bryan Saunders said, 'John, I don't think I've got anything else to say to you.'

'Well, I don't think really I've got much else to say to you.'

In one final gallant effort the detective referred to the thumbprint again. 'It's one thing you can't give one of your silly stories about ... you can't make an excuse.' Despite his tiredness, he put one last question to John, asking him, 'As one man to another, please tell me where Shirley Banks's body is?'

'I haven't got a clue,' was John's obstinate reply.

At 3.16pm on Tuesday, 22 December 1987, John Cannan was charged with the murder of Shirley Anne Banks. When cautioned, he made no reply.

13
THE BODY

On Easter Sunday, 3 April 1988, Basil Hooper and his wife Jill decided to take their niece and two teenage children for a walk along a forest trail in the Quantock Hills in Somerset. They drove to Adscombe near Over Stowey and parked their car at the top of the track leading to Crowcombe Hill. Their walk would take them through part of the 2,000-acre conifer plantation known as Great Wood, which lay just over a mile from the A39 Bridgwater to Minehead road.

Jill was intent on finding some moss to line her hanging baskets at home, and, when she made her way down through the bushes to a stream, she called out to her niece to follow her. It was then, as she turned to her right, that she saw some 30 to 35 yards upstream what she thought 'appeared to be the body of a human being'. As any reasoning person would, she thought it was more likely to be a tailor's dummy or something similar, rather than a body. Nevertheless, she decided not to investigate but scrambled up the bank to tell her husband.

'I believe there's a body down there,' she told Basil, who was sitting with his son on a log by the track. He accompanied her down to the stream and walked to within 15 or 20 feet of the object in the water. Moving closer, he observed what looked like a body lying face down in the water with both arms outstretched in front of it. Like his wife, Basil Hooper thought it was not really a body but a 'blown-up dummy' because it seemed bloated. But, on closer scrutiny, he saw a ring on the left hand that convinced him that he was indeed looking at a human corpse. Because of its size, he took it to be a man.

Rapidly, the Hoopers retraced their steps to the track and there encountered a friend, Dave Smith, who was also out with his family. Hooper asked Smith to go down with him to the stream to confirm that the object was a body. Smith picked up a stick and handed it to his companion so that he could reach out and poke the object. 'Having done this,' said Hooper in his statement to the police, 'I was then convinced it was ... a human being.'

After marking the spot on the track with a black plastic bag tied to a stick pushed into the ground, Hooper began to walk back to his car with the intention of fetching the police.

After a short distance, he was overtaken by a Land Rover which he waved down. Breathlessly, he told the driver, Kevin Morley, what had happened. Morley suggested they inform the Forestry Commission warden who was working near by. Before long, Bob Garrard of the Forestry Commission was looking at the corpse. He saw the ring and also noticed an earring. He also formed the opinion that the body had been attacked by animals.

Garrard telephoned the police and sensibly began to

seal off the area with tape to prevent people descending into the gully known locally as Barr's Bottom. At about 4.45pm, PC Mervyn Bradner of Bridgwater police station arrived at the scene. He looked at the body which everyone now agreed was human and, in police parlance, 'preserved the scene until officers arrived'. Within an hour, officers were present in numbers, backed up by a mobile support unit and carrying out preliminary searches. Acting Detective Superintendent Barry Stone arrived from the Avon and Somerset Constabulary's headquarters at Bristol at around 6pm

Stone was preceded by Dr Helen Jago, a police surgeon who had been called out by Taunton police. She made a close examination of the body, describing its position as: 'lying with the undersurface immersed in water. The face was on the left side and pointing downwards. The right arm was stretched out to the right and the left arm was underneath the body [contradicting Jill Hooper's statement that both arms had been outstretched], with the fingers projecting from the undersurface of the right side of the trunk under the water.' Dr Jago noted 'that the flesh over the buttocks had an orange hue and the back of the left thigh appeared to have been partly eaten by birds or animals. There was mud and debris over the body and the hair was matted and muddy.' She also noticed an earring on the exposed ear and rings on the third and fourth fingers of the right hand.

Death was certified at 6.34pm and Dr Jago reported, 'The body would appear to have been dead for many weeks but it was not possible to be more specific ... I was not able to give cause of death at this stage.'

Professor Bernard Knight of the University of Wales

College of Medicine, Cardiff was summoned to contribute his forensic expertise to the investigation. Professor Knight, a distinguished forensic pathologist, was recognised internationally for his work on dating human skeletal remains. He arrived at the floodlit scene just after 10.28pm and immediately began his own examination under a tent erected over the corpse. A mortuary technician had already been called out to prepare the autopsy room at Taunton's Musgrove Park hospital to receive the remains.

Professor Knight took in the details of the scene for himself, noting the same features as Dr Jago. He decided that the difficulties of the location combined with poor illumination, made further examination impossible. The body was therefore removed to the mortuary at Musgrove Park hospital by Geoffrey Grandfield, a Bridgwater undertaker who had been asked to stand by. The remains arrived at the hospital between midnight and 1am and Knight began his full post-mortem examination immediately.

At this stage, the body was unidentifiable and scientists from the Forensic Science Laboratory at Chepstow were in attendance at the examination to receive specimens that would assist identification. The initial reaction by the police examining the scene at Barr's Bottom was that they were investigating a suspicious death so a police photographer recorded every stage as Professor Knight made a thorough extended examination of the remains. Knight determined that this had been an adult white female, about 5ft 3in tall with a stocky build, although this may have been partly due to bloating resulting from decomposition. He estimated the weight at between eight and nine stone.

The back of the body was a yellowish-orange colour over

large areas due to the underlying fat being exposed as the result of loss of skin tissue. Other areas, particularly over the thighs and buttocks, were white as the result of the fatty tissue emulsifying to form a waxy material known as adipocere. This is a natural process in which normal body fat, when subjected to moist conditions, becomes hydrolysed and breaks down into fatty acids. Much of the adipocerous material and skin and material around the buttocks and back of the left thigh had been removed, probably by foxes whose teeth marks were evident. The front of the body, which had been in contact with the stream water, was less affected by adipocere, being pale and discoloured with patches of decomposition.

The liquid stage of putrefaction was not evident, probably due to the cold water and the wet conditions in which the body had lain. The face was unrecognisable due to distortion caused by the features being compressed against the stones lining the stream. The eyes were collapsed into their sockets and the pathologist noted no petechiae, or pinpoint haemorrhages, that might have denoted strangulation. While the lips were distorted, there were no signs of laceration or bruising. The teeth were all natural and the front upper and lower dentition was in excellent condition, being very white and rather prominent. Most of the back teeth, upper and lower on both sides, showed signs of extensive fillings. The teeth would shortly provide vital evidence in establishing the identity of this dead woman.

When discovered, the body was naked apart from several items of jewellery. Around the neck was a plain gold chain. In the right earlobe was a pendant earring. On the ring finger of the left hand was a plain gold wedding ring. On the middle finger of the right hand was a similar gold ring and on the ring finger of the right hand was a gold ring with a single stone setting. The earring was a distinctive piece of jewellery in the form of an elongated ellipse with a multi-coloured enamel design on one side. These adornments, like the teeth, would be powerful aids to identification. Each was allocated an exhibit number, identified by Bernard Knight's initials 'B.K.' and taken into the charge of a police exhibits officer at the mortuary.

The pathologist then turned his expertise to the head of the body. As yet it had not been washed clean of debris. There was loosely attached hair at the back and on the right side of the head but very little on the crown or left side. The hair was matted and had dead leaves, twigs and insect larvae entangled in the strands. When later washed, the hair's natural colour was a combination of pale brown and blonde. It was quite long in places but its condition made it difficult to measure.

The top and left side of the head felt fractured when palpated by the pathologist. His report showed mottled discoloration on the scalp and nothing to indicate any definite ante-mortem bruising. Professor Knight recorded four lacerations through the full thickness of the scalp between the left ear and the crown of the head. There was a triangular laceration measuring 40mm by 30mm above the ear, a straight oblique laceration 30mm long above it, and a ragged vertical laceration behind the ear. There was also a small punctured wound immediately behind the ear, a small punctured wound immediately in front, and a 60mm-long vertical laceration behind the other three towards the back of the head. Finally, there was a vertical laceration about 25mm long near the back of the head to the left of the mid-line.

All of these wounds appeared to have crushed edges that were dark in colour, suggesting old haemorrhages. The skull was shattered into many fragments: the whole of the rear left side, crown, back and rearmost part of the right side were comminuted into numerous fragments of various sizes. Further fracture lines traversed the skull and some ran into the natural sutures where the plates of the skull joined together. Professor Knight observed that the sutures were unfused which was characteristic of a young adult. Although it was not possible to give an accurate assessment of age from the condition of the skull sutures, the absence of fusion was indicative of an individual aged under 30 years.

One fragment of the skull had deeply penetrated the underlying brain tissue, but the pathologist thought this might have been a post-mortem occurrence. The dural membrane of the brain, lining the skull, was largely intact except where it had been penetrated by the one skull fragment. On opening the dura, the brain was found to be totally decomposed which reduced the value of the examination.

The neck and spine were intact and there were no fractured ribs. The mouth was normal, apart from decomposition, as were the tongue and larynx. The hyoid bone (at the base of the tongue) and thyroid bones of the larynx were intact and the air passages showed no signs of obstruction.

The lungs were flabby as a result of decomposition but were otherwise normal; the heart was normal and the coronary arteries were free of disease. The stomach was empty and the organs of the abdomen all appeared normal. A careful examination of the exterior of the body had established an absence of any marks around the throat and there were no defence wounds on the hands. The fingers were too decomposed with loss of the nails to ascertain whether any fingernail scrapings might have been of value. There appeared to be no abnormality of the vagina or anus, although the tissues were swollen due to decomposition.

Professor Knight concluded that the body was that of a young adult female with fair to blonde hair whose teeth had been subject to considerable treatment. She had not borne children and he put her age at between 20 and 40. The pathologist acknowledged the difficulty of establishing the time that had elapsed since death. Taking into account the conditions in which the body had been found – partly immersed in cold running water during the colder months of the year – he put the minimum time at one month. 'No maximum can be given,' he stated in his report, 'though it would be unlikely that the body was there in the warmer months of 1987, otherwise it would have decomposed and had extensive maggot damage'.

'As to the cause of death,' wrote Knight, 'it seems very likely that severe head injuries killed the deceased.' He continued, 'The fractures of the skull are very severe indeed and suggest crushing with a heavy object. Together with the multiple jagged lacerations, the possibility of repeated blows with a heavy stone is a reasonable possibility.' He then considered the likelihood of the injuries having been caused by the body being washed around in the small stream or by a fall from a considerable height. Bearing in mind the naked state of the body and the absence of any sufficiently precipitous high ground, however, he concluded that 'the most likely explanation is repeated blows on the head from a heavy object such as a rock'.

The body was taken from the mortuary at Musgrove Park hospital early on Monday afternoon and conveyed to Yeovil general hospital to await burial.

While the post-mortem team had been working into the small hours of the night, Bristol detectives working on the disappearance of Shirley Banks had joined forces with murder squad officers in Somerset. The supposition that the woman's body found by the Easter Sunday walkers was Shirley's was widespread. All that was needed was confirmation of identity and this lay in the realm of forensic odontology.

Professor Knight had removed the upper and lower jaws from the corpse. Armed with these grim artefacts in a sealed container, Detective Constable Brian Evans called on Anthony Pitter, a forensic odontologist who practised in Bath. Evans also had with him the National Health dental record of Shirley Banks (the document had been completed under her maiden name of Reynolds) and a number of X-rays. At 2.15pm on Easter Monday, Pitter carried out a detailed comparison of the teeth in the jaws with the records of dental treatment carried out on Shirley Banks. He discovered 32 permanent teeth in the jaws, 16 in each of the upper and lower parts. A number of the teeth had silver amalgam fillings in them, two of which were markedly less tarnished than the rest. X-rays of the left side of the upper jaw showed a root filling in the upper left second premolar. There were signs of long-standing infection between the two upper premolar teeth on the left side in the form of a buccal sinus.

The odontologist compared his findings with the X-rays and dental records of Shirley Banks. There was a match between the characteristics of the teeth in each instance. The treatment records mentioned a sinus in the same position as that noted by Pitter and showed that the untarnished fillings had been made on 15 September 1986. 'Because of the overwhelming similarity between the appearance of the fillings seen post-mortem and the appearance of the fillings seen on the X-rays, plus the presence of the sinus mentioned in the dental records, I am sure that the records in the name of Miss S. Reynolds and the jaws seen at post-mortem conform one to the other,' Pitter reported.

The body found at Over Stowey was thus identified as Shirley Banks, and Chief Inspector Pieter Biesheuval of the Avon and Somerset police was able to confirm this at a packed press conference. Even before Anthony Pitter had produced the clinching dental evidence, police were virtually sure of the identity of the woman's body.

At 12.15pm on Easter Monday, Detective Constable Ian Gibson of Avon and Somerset Constabulary's crime squad had made a call on Richard Banks. Gibson had with him five pieces of jewellery that had been found on and near the body. Banks identified the gold necklace as one worn by his wife over a number of years. He also identified one of the gold wedding rings as similar in every respect to one given to Shirley by her mother and confirmed that the gold ring set with an amethyst was willed to Shirley by an aunt. 'I have no doubts about Shirley wearing it,' he said, 'as she was particularly fond of it'. He was positive that the second gold wedding ring was Shirley's.

If further corroboration were needed, it was provided by Gillian Reynolds, Shirley's sister, who was a student at a College of Further Education in Scotland. She positively identified all the items of jewellery including the oval-shaped earring, which she had seen Shirley wearing.

The dental evidence was the proof positive required by the police to confirm that the missing woman had been found dead. But for her husband, sister and parents it was the jewellery, each item with its personal association with family history and with Shirley's tastes for personal adornment, that really showed what they had long suspected – that she was dead. They could now let go of hope and begin to grieve. The *Western Daily Press* of 5 April 1988 carried the headline: MISSING BRIDE'S BODY FOUND, and the report spoke of the news which Mr Banks 'had dreaded for so long'.

Meanwhile, police Scenes of Crime officers were scouring the area in which the body was found for any clues that might be obscured by the undergrowth or lie in the water of the little stream at Barr's Bottom. The search area was divided into sections (lanes) by means of ribbons of white tape. The ground in the vicinity of the spot where the body was found was subjected to a fingertip search and the outer area to a walk-through search. The first discovery was made by PC Gregory Gough at 10.06am on Monday morning when he spotted a rock about the size of a 2lb sugar bag some nine feet downstream of the corpse. The rock had a strand of blonde hair attached to it.

As the day progressed, the discoveries came thick and fast: clumps of hair attached to branches and rocks, a pair of women's black knickers and a few green buttons. PC Raymond Humphries combined his fingertip search with the use of a metal detector. At a spot some 18 feet from the stream, the detector emitted a signal and, on probing the dead leaves and twigs, he found an oval-shaped metal earring decorated in yellow, red and blue enamel. A total of 21 exhibits was logged at the scene of discovery by PC

Michael Hague and, late on Monday evening, he handed these over to colleagues at Bridgwater police station.

Three green buttons found in soil sifted from the bank about 10 feet from the stream caused particular interest. There was a possibility that they had been attached to the clothing worn by Shirley Banks when she met her death. It was known that she had bought a new dress at Debenhams in Bristol on the evening she disappeared. This was a navy and white print, spun viscose dress, fastened at the front with 13 buttons, made exclusively for Top Shop. Six of them had been delivered to their shop within the Debenhams store from the company's central warehouse in September 1987. The dresses were made for Ann Reeves & Co Ltd who supplied the pattern, materials and buttons to Picrrs Fashions the manufacturers. The buttons were supplied by M. & M. Frazer Ltd who had them dyed navy to meet Reeves's specification by S. W. Turpin's Chequer Works. Taking with them a navy and white dress identical to that purchased by Shirley Banks, police officers visited each of the companies concerned in its manufacture.

A director of Ann Reeves & Co Ltd confirmed the instructions given to their button suppliers, stating that the same buttons were used for all 600 dresses in the design batch. Shown the three green buttons found at Barr's Bottom, Ann Reeves acknowledged that they were identical to the buttons used on the particular navy and white dress sold by her company. Jeffrey Curnew, sales director of S.W. Pleaters Ltd, confirmed that the buttons he was shown by the police had been manufactured by his company. Edwin Cheeseman had worked for M. & M. Frazer for 35 years dealing with buttons. Of the buttons shown him by the police, he said, 'These three buttons are identical to the ones supplied to Ann Reeves & Co Ltd.'

The life history of the buttons was completed by Christopher Jones, owner of Turpins, who had been in the business of dyeing buttons and buckles for 25 years. Looking at the three buttons produced by the officers, Mr Jones said, 'These are identical in every way to buttons supplied by M. & M. Frazer Ltd and are identical to the ones supplied to me on the 7 August 1987 to dye.' He also examined the specimen navy and white dress and confirmed that its buttons matched in every respect those supplied by his company.

The last word on the buttons was provided by Michael Sayce, a forensic scientist working at the Home Office Forensic Laboratory at Chepstow. In light of the information provided by the garment manufacturers, he concluded that the three buttons were similar in size, dimensions and construction to those on the dress and shared two of the same mould impression numbers, namely 21 and 10. He found that each button had threaded through it remnants of the thread with which it had been stitched to the garment to which it originally belonged. The vestiges of thread were of black polyester, which tests demonstrated was similar in colour, chemical composition and dye to the thread used to stitch the buttons to the Top Shop navy and white dress. 'This indicated,' Sayce noted in his report, 'that the buttons had been ripped from the garment.'

On 6 April 1988, the coroner for West Somerset, Mr Michael Rose, conducted the inquest on Shirley Banks. Professor Knight's report of his post-mortem examination was read out and the pathologist gave the most likely cause of death as the victim having been battered to death with a heavy rock. It was impossible to say how long the body had lain where it was found, but it was likely to have been several months. Identification had been made using dental records and the jewellery found on and near the victim. Inspector Roger Grimshaw told the inquest that John Cannan, a Bristol businessman, had been charged with Mrs Banks's murder. The coroner adjourned the inquest indefinitely and granted a certificate allowing the funeral to proceed after a second post-mortem had been carried out.

The clinical, matter-of-fact forensic procedure proved beyond doubt that Shirley Banks was dead. It was probably no more than her family and friends expected after she had been missing for six months. The anguish of those who cared for Suzy Lamplugh, missing now for 20 months, could only be imagined. As their hopes dwindled, so the uncertainties increased.

What the forensic reports also showed was the manner and circumstances of Shirley's death. The young woman, probably wearing the dress she had bought with such delight at Top Shop, had been taken to a remote killing field in the Quantock Hills. There the dress had been torn from her body, spilling its buttons on the ground, and she had been battered to death with a heavy rock. Her killer made no attempt at concealment; his victim was left naked and dead in a woodland stream.

14
THE TRIAL

John first learned that Shirley Banks's body had been found when he was given the news by a prison officer on 4 April 1988. He was told that the newspaper reports mentioned the dead woman had not been sexually assaulted. According to John, the officer said, 'You must ... get straight on to your solicitor; surely they've got to let you go now.'

'That, I very much doubt,' concluded Cannan.

It would be a year almost to the day before he appeared on trial at Exeter Crown Court. In the meantime, he faced committal proceedings at Bristol magistrates court on 14 July 1988. He was charged with 16 offences as follows:

1. 'For that you on 30th December 1980 at Sutton Coldfield in the City of Birmingham had sexual intercourse with Sharon Major without her consent.' *CONTRARY to Section 1 (1) of the Sexual Offences Act*, 1956.

2. 'On 30th December 1980 at Sutton Coldfield in the City

of Birmingham did attempt to commit buggery with Sharon Major, a woman.' *CONTRARY to Section 1 (1) of the Criminal Attempts Act*, 1981.

3. 'For that you on 30th December 1980 at Sutton Coldfield in the City of Birmingham did make an indecent assault on a woman called Sharon Major.' *CONTRARY to Section 14 (1) of the Sexual Offences Act*, 1956.

4. 'For that you on 30th December 1980 at Sutton Coldfield in the City of Birmingham did unlawfully and maliciously cause grievous bodily harm upon Sharon Major.' *CONTRARY to Section 20 of the Offences Against the Persons Act*, 1861.

5. 'On 6th October 1986 at Reading in the County of Berkshire did rape Donna Tucker.' *CONTRARY to Section 1 (1) of the Sexual Offences Act*, 1956.

6. 'On 6th October 1986 at Reading in the County of Berkshire did commit buggery with Donna Tucker, a woman.' *CONTRARY to Section 12 (1) of the Sexual Offences Act*, 1956.

7. 'On 6th October 1986 at Reading in the County of Berkshire did indecently assault Donna Tucker, a woman.' *CONTRARY to Section 14 (1) of the Sexual Offences Act*, 1956.

8. 'On 6th October 1986 at Reading in the County of Berkshire did take away Donna Tucker against her will and by force with the intention she should have unlawful sexual intercourse with you.' *CONTRARY to Section 17 (1) of the Sexual Offences Act*, 1956.

9. 'For that you on 7th October at Canon's Road car park in the City of Bristol did attempt to forcibly abduct and to carry away Julia Pauline Holman against the will of the said Julia Pauline Holman.' *CONTRARY to Section 1 of the Criminal Attempts Act*, 1981 and *Common Law*.

10. 'On the 7th October 1987 in the City of Bristol did attempt to take away Julia Pauline Holman against her will and by force with the intention that she should have unlawful sexual intercourse with you.' *CONTRARY to Section 1 (1) of the Criminal Attempts Act*, 1981.

11. 'For that you between 7th October and 31st October 1987 in the City of Bristol did steal a motor vehicle, namely a Mini Clubman saloon, registration number HWL 507N, to the value of £175, the property of Shirley Anne Banks.' *CONTRARY to Sections 1 and 7 of the Theft Act*, 1968.

12. 'For that you on 8th October 1987 in the City of Bristol or elsewhere did forcibly abduct and carry away Shirley Anne Banks against the will of the said Shirley Anne Banks.' *CONTRARY to Common Law*.

13. 'On 8th October 1987 in the City of Bristol did take away Shirley Anne Banks against her will and by force with the intention that she should have unlawful sexual intercourse with you.' *CONTRARY to Section 17 (1) of the Sexual Offences Act*, 1956.

14. 'For that you between 7th and 30th October 1987 in the City of Bristol or elsewhere did murder Shirley Anne Banks.' *CONTRARY to Common Law*.

15. 'On 29th October 1987 at Leamington Spa in the County of Warwickshire did assault Carmel Cleary with intent to rob.' *CONTRARY to Section 8 of the Theft Act*, 1968.

16. 'On 29th October 1987 at Leamington Spa in the County of Warwickshire did detain Carmel Cleary against her will and by force with the intention that she should have unlawful sexual intercourse with you.' *CONTRARY to Section 17 (1) of the Sexual Offences Act*, 1956.

On 23 September, John Cannan was committed for trial, charged with the murder of Shirley Banks. The indictment totalled eight charges, including those of rape, buggery, kidnap, attempted abduction, indecent assault and abduction for sex.

The trial proceedings, which were to last 23 days, began on Wednesday, 5 April 1989. John described in his letters the moment when he arrived at court in Exeter in a white prison van with its blue light flashing, 'heralding my arrival to an entire corps of TV and press photographers'. With the jury already sworn and in their seats – eight women and four men – the clerk of the court asked John Cannan to rise and the customary expectant hush settled on the courtroom. 'It was all pure theatre,' said John, adding that the atmosphere could have been cut with a knife.

The Honourable Mr Justice Drake DFC presided. He had served in the Royal Air Force during the Second World War and was called to the Bar in 1950. He was made a judge of the High Court of Justice, Queen's Bench Division in 1978. Defending John was Anthony Palmer QC, widely regarded as one of the most effective exponents of cross-examination and equally at home as a defender or prosecutor. Indeed, a few weeks after the conclusion of the trial at Exeter, he led for the prosecution at the trial for murder of Baroness Susan de Stempel at Worcester. John's prosecutor was Paul Chadd QC.

What some might regard as the awesome majesty of the court, John regarded glibly as 'cant'. He disliked the theatricality of the robed and wigged judge and counsel. 'I couldn't come to terms with how artificial and stage-managed it all seemed,' he said to the authors. He was not keen either on Paul Chadd, who as prosecuting counsel held centre-stage as the trial proceedings began. 'Deliberately accentuating every word,' complained John, 'he allowed the charges to hang in the air – abduction – rape – buggery – murder': charges which John denied and to which he pleaded not guilty.

Counsel told an attentive jury that John Cannan had 'preyed on three women in a year'. He had been identified by means of DNA profiling as the man who had raped a woman in Reading in October 1986. A year later, almost to the day, 'We say, this man went to Canon's Marsh car park in Bristol ... and, armed with a handgun, he tried to take away Miss Julia Holman,' declared Paul Chadd. The third incident alleged against John was that, on the following night, he was successful – 'He got possession of Mrs Banks.' He had the tax disc from her car and other items belonging to her, including her car, and 'one of Mrs Banks's fingerprints was found on a document in his flat'. The prosecution contended that John kidnapped and murdered Shirley Banks between the time of her disappearance on 8 October and his arrest on 29 October 1987. 'This man,' said Chadd, 'has committed the gravest of sexual offences and the murder of Mrs Banks.'

Warming to his theme, Paul Chadd described John as a vicious sex beast, who had lied when he said he only knew Shirley Banks by reading reports about her disappearance in the newspapers. 'A fingerprint of the newlywed found in Cannan's Leigh Woods flat proved she had been there,' he said.

He then told the jury of another vital link, which was the discovery of the tax disc from Mrs Banks's car in John Cannan's possession when he was arrested. This brought the Avon and Somerset police further into the enquiry and the car belonging to the missing Shirley Banks was discovered, in a repainted state, sporting false number plates at John Cannan's flat in Bristol. Cannan's explanation was that he had bought the vehicle honestly and not knowing that it belonged to the missing woman. This transpired to be an extreme example of 'I bought it from a bloke in a pub' excuse. When he realised the connection, he wiped the car clean of fingerprints, repainted it and changed the registration number with the intention of driving it later to a lonely spot and setting it on fire.

The prosecution witnesses were headed by Donna Tucker, whose courtroom testimony was headlined in the *Evening Post* covering the trial as 'CANNAN IN KNIFE RAPE'. In her account of the terrifying experience to which she was subjected by the rapist, she said, 'I felt he would have killed me with the knife if I had not done what he wanted.'

Paul Chadd referred to her ordeal and spoke of a victim 'subjected in terror to the foulest of indecencies'. He said that genetic profiling tests carried out on semen stains found on the victim's clothing had positively identified John Cannan as her attacker. The chances of John Cannan not being her assailant were said to be *one in 260 million*. A Home Office forensic scientist, called to give expert evidence, outlined the procedure used to test a sample from the victim's knickers. The defence disputed that the clothing sample was the correct one. It was pointed out that samples of body fluids from paper tissues found at the scene of the rape were semen traces which tests had shown were 'not Cannan's'.

Courts are traditionally said to be 'spellbound' or

'enthralled' by the performance of important witnesses. The Exeter trial was no exception and the press reported the 'spellbinding' evidence of Julia Holman. 'BRAVE JULIA TELLS HOW SHE CHEATED GUNMAN' ran one of the newspaper headlines. The young woman related what happened when she returned to her car at Canon's Marsh car park on 7 October 1987. In hushed tones she explained, 'I did not have a chance to put my seat belt on...' Julia paused for a moment, clearly upset, before resuming, 'before a man appeared at the door, leaned down into the car and produced a handgun.'

She said her immediate reaction was one of anger: 'I swore at him and pushed him away.' As she drove off, the horror of what had happened sank in and she swerved out of the car park 'in total panic'. She later picked John Cannan out at an identification parade 'without hesitation'. Under Anthony Palmer's cross-examination, she denied that she might have seen Cannan before or recognised him from newspaper photographs.

Another 'spellbinding' moment occurred on the fifth day of the trial when Richard Banks, the dead woman's husband, faced John Cannan across the courtroom. A handsome man with a firm jaw and distinctive red hair, 32-year-old Banks answered Paul Chadd's opening questions in a hesitant voice. He recalled the events leading up to his wife's disappearance, vividly describing his anxiety when she did not return home. He spent the night in a state of mounting panic wondering where she was: 'I was beside myself with worry for her,' he said.

Under cross-examination his character changed and he denied not knowing his wife's whereabouts because he was away in London at the time. Such claims were 'absolute nonsense', he said. He also strongly denied the suggestion that he and Shirley had engaged in a furious row. 'I fully expected Shirley to return home,' he told Anthony Palmer. He denied too the imputation that he did not make any telephone calls about her absence because he was not expecting her back. 'Absolutely not,' he snapped.

It was revealed that the six weeks of married life shared by Richard and Shirley Banks had not been without problems. Friends said there had been arguments about Richard's late nights out on occasions and suggestions of a trial separation. Banks acknowledged that since Shirley's death he had built a new life, paying off their mortgage and establishing his own property business. Banks told the court that he had seen John Cannan several times in the bar of the Avon Gorge Hotel. He could not be certain though that Shirley was with him on those occasions. He picked Cannan out at a police identity parade in November 1987 as a man he had seen in the bar 'more than once'. According to press reports, Richard Banks glowered at Cannan across the court when he confirmed that he had seen him before.

A moment of real drama in the trial arrived with the appearance of Annabel Rose. The 32-year-old solicitor looked pale and drawn. Holding in her emotions, she stood shaking as she began her evidence before a packed, hushed court. With her hands clasped tightly in front of her, she answered questions put to her by Paul Chadd. Tearfully she admitted to close 'association' with John Cannan. Asked if it was a sexual affair, she answered shakily, 'I'm afraid so,' but she could not remember how long it lasted.

Annabel Rose's cross-examination spared her nothing and Anthony Palmer QC reminded her that the affair to which she had admitted lasted 11 months. 'During the period of the affair with Mr Cannan you would regularly have sexual intercourse with him, would you not?' he asked. She agreed, acknowledging that she had a key to his flat and often visited him there. Anthony Palmer named four places where they made love: in two hotels, Cannan's flat and outdoors. The witness shook her head vigorously at this last suggestion. 'I suggest to you,' counsel persisted, 'that you made love on that mackintosh in Ashton Park.' 'No,' she replied. When it was further suggested that she had refused to cooperate with the police, she became angry. Gripping the sides of the witness box, she sobbed, 'I have always cooperated with the police throughout the inquiry. I have done everything possible to help them. It is not fair to say that.' Annabel Rose appeared to be near the point of collapse but continued after taking a sip of water and drying her eyes with a handkerchief.

Annabel Rose said the affair ended in August 1987 and John Cannan began to threaten her 'in a most unpleasant way'. He did not want their relationship to end. He told her that he knew where her parents lived and if she did not conform to his wishes they, and her husband, would be harmed.

'I know he contacted the police on a regular basis and persistently made complaints about me which were without foundation,' she said. He told her that he had 'manufactured evidence' implicating her in offences and would act on it if she did not do as he demanded. She was aware that he had hired a private detective to follow her parents.

At the close of her cross-examination, Annabel Rose sank wearily into her seat in the witness box. Mr Justice Drake said he would adjourn the proceedings briefly in order to confer with counsel. At this point John leaned forward in the dock and shouted out, 'It is time the whole truth came out. She is play-acting, she is play-acting – this is madness.'

The judge rebuked him and said that if he had any instructions to give his solicitor he should do so in the proper manner. John apologised for his outburst. Annabel Rose left the witness box in tears.

The newspapers had a field day with its coverage of Annabel Rose's evidence: 'SOBBING LAWYER TELLS OF HER AFFAIR', 'CANNAN: MY LOVER' and 'SOLICITOR'S NIGHTS OF LOVE' were typical. The Bristol *Evening Post* defended its reporting of the trial, offering some solace to Annabel Rose who, the paper recognised, was not accused of having committed any criminal offence and had been submitted to considerable publicity. 'Perhaps, as she recovers from the trauma of the occasion, she may reflect that, although she may have lost some reputation and her job, she still has her life.' Shirley Banks had been less fortunate.

John had no sympathy for Annabel Rose's evident distress. 'When she entered the court,' he wrote later, she was 'stooped and physically shaking, wringing her hands and had to be supported by her own solicitor ... she took the oath and the rattle of the water glass between her teeth was plainly audible. It was utterly transparent...' he concluded coldly.

Meanwhile he had to face the testimony of 69-year-old Amelia Hart. She told the court about the strange incident she had witnessed. The bespectacled old lady spoke about an occurrence in Leigh Woods on 9 October 1987, a date she remembered because it was her cousin's birthday. What followed was possibly a prelude to murder and the jury sat transfixed as her words drifted across the quiet courtroom.

'I could hear something being dragged through the trees,' she said, 'like breaking trees. Something was being dragged.' Then she heard sounds. 'Like someone had a punch-bag in the woods and was practising on it.' She saw a man standing in the woods with his back to her. 'He was punching something I could not see. His arms were moving in a semi-circle beating something with his hands. He was beating something and then jumping on it. I thought it was a one-sided wrestling match – that is how it looked. But, whatever it was, he was hitting it in the undergrowth. He ran back and fell on it, and I heard a youth's or a girl's voice shout out, "No, oh no!" A man's voice said, "I warned you what I would do, I warned you, I warned you." Then there was the most dreadful, blood-curdling scream...'

Tim Raggett, junior defence counsel, tried to shake Mrs Hart's testimony. She said she had been too frightened to report the incident to the police straight away. In her first statement to the law officers, she did not mention that any violence had taken place; her description of the violent beating she had witnessed came in her second statement almost two months later. She said she was too frightened at first to tell detectives the whole story. When police Scenes of Crime officers searched Leigh Woods in the vicinity of the incident described by Mrs Hart, they could find no signs of any struggle or disturbance.

'The jury can see that you are a well-intentioned woman,' said Tim Raggett, 'but I put it to you that you have a lot of time on your hands and you have a vivid imagination.'

'No, definitely not,' replied Amelia Hart.

Counsel put the question several times, but Mrs Hart insisted she was telling the truth. She denied that she had let her imagination run away with her. Tim Raggett showed her a copy of the Bristol *Evening Post* dated 7 December 1987 and, pointing to a photograph of John Cannan, asked, 'Know him?'

She admitted having read newspaper accounts of Shirley Banks's disappearance and of seeing photographs of John Cannan. But, she said, 'I'm sure that someone was killed in those few moments when we were going past. I did not sleep afterwards and a few days later I began saying to my husband that this girl, Shirley Banks, was missing and perhaps there was a connection with what I had seen.'

Mr George Hart, who was partly deaf, said he only saw a figure in the woods.

The prosecution alleged that Shirley Banks had been held in Cannan's flat at Leigh Woods because her thumbprint was found there. The discovery of this vital clue had been made by senior fingerprint officer Paul Jobbins. 'On the document found in the chest at the flat there was a left thumbprint,' he explained to the jury. 'It would appear at some stage the document had been folded and held in the left hand. It is an excellent-quality mark – a very good mark for paper.'

When Shirley Banks's body was discovered in April 1988, the only surviving skin on her hands was part of the palm on her left hand. This, combined with the impressions taken from objects she had handled on a day-to-day basis, was sufficient to prove that the thumbprint in John Cannan's flat was hers. 'There is no doubt at all,' stated Jobbins, 'that she handled that document.'

It is worth pausing here for a moment to consider the

fact that no other fingerprints belonging to Shirley Banks were found in John's flat. It has been argued in several quarters that Shirley was never at John's flat and there was a slim probability that the document was planted by another person. This scenario can easily be dismissed. During the time she spent in the flat, Shirley's movements would certainly have been controlled. She was probably held under restraint, either tied up or handcuffed. Consequently, there were few opportunities to leave fingerprints behind. Moreover, John was adept at removing such traces, as we know from the meticulous way in which he wiped Shirley's Mini clean of any fingerprints.

Marija Vilcins, the girlfriend who spent the weekend of 10/11 October at John's flat, allegedly 24 hours after Shirley Banks had been held captive there, was questioned about a telephone call she had made. In her statement to the police, she said she had called John at the flat at about 7.30pm on Thursday, 8 October and spoken to him. Replying in court to Anthony Palmer's questions, she said she was in fact mistaken and that she had called John not on the Thursday but on the following day. 'At that time,' she said, 'I did believe the statement was correct. But I was under a lot of pressure.' She described her weekend with John as 'very pleasant'.

It was for the Saturday of Marija's visit that John had invited dinner guests: Chrissie Fortune and her husband who ran Rainbow, the plant shop in Clifton. Chrissie Fortune told the jury that she tried to call John at his flat during the day of Thursday 8 October and also between 7.30 and 9pm that evening. There was no reply. She eventually got through on Friday morning to give her apologies and say that they were unable to come to dinner.

On the 13th day of the trial, Detective Chief Inspector Bryan Saunders gave evidence regarding his interviews with John Cannan. The detective read out the questions from the 500-page transcript of the tape-recorded interviews. Prosecution lawyers responded with the replies given by John in a double act that lasted four days. John complained later that the replies were read out in a 'bland and insipid way' which was very different to the tone of voice he had used when answering Saunders at the time of the interviews. He was particularly critical that his words 'I stumbled on something I shouldn't have' were not read out at all.

The video-dating episode, about which John had answered questions in the taped interviews, was singled out for special treatment by the press. 'Smooth-talking John Cannan made a lonely hearts dating video to find a wife,' reported the *Western Daily Press*, adding, 'and had women queuing up to go out with him.' The *Daily Mirror*, after the trial, referred to him as a 'psychopath who only wanted clean-living girls'. In an exclusive article, the paper reproduced frames from the video showing the smooth-talking lady-killer, dark-suited, animated and smiling into the camera. 'But behind all the charm was a murderous sex plot.' DCI Bryan Saunders was widely quoted as saying of the video, 'It is a pretty professional tape and it took me by surprise.'

John was fairly scathing about his interviews with the police and remains so to this day. 'There was ...from day one,' he complained, 'an invisible strategic thread that wove their questions together in order to arrive at their own crime design, a picture of their own making.' He claimed that, after Shirley's body was discovered, he volunteered to answer further questions but his offer was declined. 'If that wasn't important,' he railed, 'then what in God's name was?'

The Bristol *Evening News'* coverage of the trial drew criticism from some of its readers. A letter from the Bristol Women's Committee expressed concern that much of the reporting seemed to imply that the women in the case were guilty rather than being innocent victims for whom the publicity caused distress. The newspaper defended its reporting on the grounds that it sought to keep its readers legitimately informed about the cunning of men such as John Cannan.

While controversy continued to rage outside the courtroom, the trial proceeded at a steady pace. On 21 April, the jury, together with Mr Justice Drake and various counsel, visited Foye House at Leigh Woods. They had already been told by Professor Bernard Knight that Shirley Banks's skull had been shattered by blows struck with a rock. 'Her skull was shattered into many fragments. It was like an egg struck by a spoon.' Michael Sayce, a Home Office forensic scientist, had told the court that John Cannan's overcoat had blood spots on it but they could not be identified. He had also said there was no evidence of any struggle having taken place in the flat. No doubt, the jury were also mindful of Mrs Amelia Hart's graphic evidence in which she claimed to have witnessed a violent beating in Leigh Woods.

The eight women and four men comprising the jury viewed Flat 2 from the entrance foyer but did not go inside. They walked round to the side of the building to see the garage where Shirley's Mini had been found. Then they moved to the area of Leigh Woods adjacent to Foye House where Mrs Hart said she saw a man beating someone. During the 45 minutes of the visit, John sat quietly with his lawyers watching events from inside a prison van.

On 26 April, it was announced that Annabel Rose had resigned from the Bristol law practice of Gerald Davey and Co. A friend told newspaper reporters that Miss Rose was staying out of the city for a while. On the same day it became known at Exeter that John had opted for the right to remain silent at his trial. After hearing the prosecution case against him for nearly four weeks, he had decided not to give evidence.

This was a decision over which John had been agonising. 'I offered no defence,' he wrote later to the authors, 'because of the prejudicial legal circumstances surrounding my trial, therefore the jury did not hear my account.' His contention is that the inclusion of the Reading rape charge made his defence 'a nightmare'. He believes that it was used as a way of preventing him telling the court what he knew about organised crime. Those were the things he had 'stumbled on' and were part of the conspiracy theory to which he would return time and time again. '...all we could do,' he wrote, 'was to use my trial as an old style committal, probing, illiciting [sic] answers, finding things out.'

Anthony Palmer QC opened and closed his case for the defence in one sentence: 'On behalf of the defence, we call no evidence,' he told the court. He explained to the jury that John Cannan's right to remain silent should not be thrown in his face. He stressed that his client had been questioned by the police for more than 22 hours, answering every question put to him. He also gave hair and blood samples and had his fingerprints taken.

Defence counsel's remarks were described as having a

272

stunning effect on the case. In reality, Anthony Palmer was trying to make bricks out of straw. His short address was limp in the extreme. Of course John Cannan had given body samples and had his fingerprints taken. There was nothing remarkable about that. Certainly he was questioned for some considerable time. Nothing unusual about that either. That he had answered every question put to him took no account of his evasive tactics to avoid the truth. The upshot was that there was nothing the defence could say.

Summing-up for the prosecution was a different matter altogether. Paul Chadd claimed that John Cannan had kidnapped Shirley Banks, held her captive in his flat and then battered her to death.

Even the quick-witted John Cannan could not explain how Mrs Banks's thumbprint came to be on a document in his flat, said counsel. He alluded to the fact that Cannan had handcuffs and a knife. Holding up the five-and-a-half-inch knife, he asked, 'What woman could face up to this?' He said the spot where the body was found was just an hour's drive from Bristol and in an area well known to the prisoner.

Prosecuting counsel went on to say there was over-whelming evidence proving that Cannan had subjected another woman to 'indescribable indecencies' at knife-point. He reminded the jury that genetic tests showed the chances against John Cannan being the rapist were one in 200 million. 'Scientists have used these odds to show the impossibility – there might be another man with the same DNA in Tibet, but I ask you to use your common sense.' He continued, 'Do you believe this woman was lying or do you believe she came here in her agony to relive her hell?'

Chadd also claimed John Cannan also tried to kidnap Julia Holman in Bristol but was 'thwarted by that young woman's spirit'. She picked him out of an identity parade as soon as she entered the room. 'Have you any doubts that she was right?' He then asked the jury if they would have any difficulty recognising John Cannan's distinctive features.

Referring to Amelia Hart's testimony, Chadd said she admitted reading newspaper accounts of Shirley's disappearance, 'But,' he added, 'all the newspapers in the world could not have told her of the things she told you.' He concluded, 'Rapists are not ordinary men. In a rapist lies an element of cruelty which sometimes goes further and circumstances engineer disaster ... Some women would submit and were then stigmatised as having consented ... Some women object and in that protest lies danger. One can never know what has produced the appalling result that obviously occurred here.'

Anthony Palmer dismissed the prosecution's claims as 'absolute nonsense'. He said there was no proof that John Cannan had abducted and murdered Shirley Banks. She could have been kidnapped by someone else. He asked the jury to ignore the intense publicity that surrounded the case.

He said, 'The sheer weight of prejudice around his [John's] neck is enormous unless you act like a British jury and are determined to be fair.' He suggested it was quite possible that Mrs Banks had met someone other than John Cannan whose connection with her arose because he later came into possession of her car. Counsel stated no witnesses had come forward to say they saw Banks's car being driven to his flat and when she telephoned her place of work she had not sounded like a frightened person held under duress. 'If Cannan had abducted her,' he said, 'the last thing he would have allowed would be for her to telephone someone who might suspect something was wrong.'

'We have to face the real facts raised in the evidence,' Palmer said. He thought the jury might make a diary of the times for Friday, 9 October, calling it 'an ordinary day' to show the sheer impossibility of John Cannan killing someone or dumping their body. 'Cannan was woken that morning by a telephone call from an acquaintance, he then rang his mother and later went out to buy food at Marks & Spencer. He made a further telephone call and at lunchtime cashed a cheque for £25 ... an ordinary day, no panic or odd behaviour.'

Palmer also suggested that Shirley Banks was not a prisoner when she was driven to the Quantocks. There was no intent to rape or kill her. She went there voluntarily 'and something happened there to cause her to be killed ... killing on the spur of the moment'. 'Had there been any intention to kill the woman,' he argued, 'the man would have armed himself with a weapon – a gun, knife or rope. Cannan had some of these things.

'If it be said, he took this lady to the Quantocks to kill her, why didn't he either use his knife to stab her or the rope to strangle her? I submit,' he said, 'that the killer was not this man Cannan.'

It had probably crossed the jury's mind that Mrs Banks was already dead, murdered in front of Amelia Hart's very eyes in Leigh Woods. Anthony Palmer's address to the jury was weak, full of supposition and contained little that could help his client.

In his summing-up, which was a model of fairness, Mr Justice Drake drew attention to the prosecution's vital piece of evidence – the thumbprint on the document in Cannan's flat. He complimented the defence counsel on his presentation of doubts concerning the evidence and said he had waited with great interest to hear his explanation of the thumbprint. 'I was reminded,' he said, 'of Sherlock Holmes [and] the dog that did not bark in the night.' This was a reference to the story of *Silver Blaze*, in which a racehorse was stolen from training stables at dead of night. In his investigation of the crime, Holmes discovered that a dog was kept at the stables. The animal had not barked at the intruder, so the detective concluded the thief knew the dog well.

'I was struck, as I must say,' continued Mr Justice Drake, 'in that very full and persuasive speech of Mr Palmer's, by the dog that did not bark, the point that never came. What of the thumbprint found on the document in the flat?'

With telling logic, the judge reviewed the manner in which Anthony Palmer had dismissed the thumbprint. The defence counsel, he said, had concluded that the print on the document only proved that Shirley Banks held it at some time. 'Was it not a vital point that a document in which the defendant professed no interest should be found with Shirley Banks's fingerprint on it? This was a vital piece of evidence, which surely connects Shirley Banks with this man.' The evidence, the judge said, 'only proves that she held it at some time. How? Unless she was in his flat.'

The jury deliberated for ten hours before bringing in their verdicts. John stood impassively in the dock, dressed as he had been throughout his trial in a blue blazer and grey flannels. His face betrayed no sign of emotion as the jury foreman told the court that unanimous verdicts had been reached on all charges. Guilty to the charges of abducting and murdering Shirley Banks and guilty to the other six charges of rape, buggery, abduction and attempted kidnapping.

Sentencing John Cannan, the judge told him, 'I have to bear in mind mercy, but I also have to deter others who might be minded to have the inclination to attack and violate women. Above all, my duty is to protect others from you and the possibility that you may ever have the opportunity to commit such offences.

'The sentence for the murder of Shirley Banks is that fixed by law – imprisonment for life. But I add the recommendation that the period you serve in prison shall be the period of your life. You should never again be allowed liberty outside prison walls. Take him down.'

John Cannan the killer paled and staggered to the top of the steps leading down to the holding cells beneath the court. It was one of the few signs of emotion he had portrayed throughout the proceedings.

As he was taken away to begin his life sentence, it became known that Scotland Yard detectives planned to question him about the disappearance of Suzy Lamplugh. 'NOW CANNAN TO FACE "MR KIPPER" QUIZ' ran the Bristol *Evening Post*'s headline under the single word 'GUILTY' printed in heavy type. Then the analysis and scrutiny of events began. John's refusal to confess to the killing of Shirley Banks gave free rein to those who wanted to reconstruct events as they imagined them. One theory was that he kept his victim at Foye House overnight and, the following morning, set out to drive down to Somerset.

While waiting to pull out on to the main road, Shirley made a run for it into Leigh Woods. It was there that he caught up with her and subjected her to the beating witnessed by Amelia Hart, before bundling her back into the car. Once in the privacy of the woods at Over Stowey, he battered her to death with a rock and abandoned her body in the stream.

In a lengthy interview with DCI Bryan Saunders at the Avon and Somerset police headquarters, author Christopher Berry-Dee put this theory to the detective. Although John has persistently pooh-poohed Amelia Hart's testimony as 'utter rubbish', DCI Saunders believes this was the likely tragic scenario. Shirley Banks may have died in Leigh Woods, sometime during the journey to Over Stowey, or after being dragged down the muddy bank to the stream.

John was described in the press as a 'woman hater with a lust for power', a 'killer in love with knife and gun', and an 'evil character' and much else. There were plaudits for the police and interviews with Shirley's family. Her father paid tribute to the Avon and Somerset police who, he said, had always given every consideration to his feelings and those of his wife despite the demands of their job.

The police had interviewed over 2,500 people, taken 1,672 statements and processed countless enquiries during the course of the murder hunt. But there were complaints when it became known that the 70 detectives who had worked on the investigation – the longest and costliest in the history of the Avon and Somerset police – intended having a tie made to signify its completion.

A reader in a letter to the Bristol *Evening Post* said she was upset by the lack of sensitivity shown by the police in striking a tie. The motif was a cannon with a wheel that had come off. 'It's not a joking matter,' she wrote. 'It smacks more of a rugby club dinner than a murder enquiry.'

DCI Bryan Saunders was reported as saying that it was a well-established practice to strike a tie at the end of a major enquiry. The idea was to mark the teamwork and friendship of the men who took part in the 18-month inquiry. The design of the tie was a matter for approval by the chief constable.

John commented on 'the orgy of self-congratulation' following the trial. He wrote that the police were dishonest in exploiting his weak position to make up for their own ineptitude. He also referred to prosecution counsel's praise for a 'clever piece of old-fashioned detective work' and added bitterly, 'Well, you know it all ... you're the fucking experts.' This remark was directed towards the authors.

Under the headline 'KILLER OF MY SUZY IS CAGED' in the *Today* newspaper, Claire Rayner wrote about Mrs Diana Lamplugh's reactions to the news that John Cannan had been convicted of murder. The feeling was 'that her daughter's killer had also been caught and convicted'. The *Daily Mirror* pursued the Suzy Lamplugh angle with a headline 'IS HE MR KIPPER?' and gave ten vital clues supposedly linking John Cannan to the missing estate agent.

The *Sun* published an interview with Gilly Paige, the ice-show dancer, who said she had been affected by nightmares since she'd heard of John Cannan's crimes. Under the headline 'HAUNTED BY HIS EYES' the paper printed a close-up of the piercing 'blue eyes of John Cannan that made girls swoon with love or shiver with fear'.

John's brother and sister were also interviewed by the press. Anthony Cannan was reported as saying that their father never recovered from the shock of John's conviction for rape in 1981. 'He just used to break down over it all.' Anthony said there could be no sympathy for his brother who 'had no thoughts for anyone except himself'.

John's sister, Heather, believed he and 'Mr Kipper' were the same person. Her outspoken views included an appeal to him to admit that he killed Suzy Lamplugh and to tell the police where he had hidden her body. 'You are locked up now until you are an old man,' she was reported as saying, 'so what have you got to lose?' She said that the family had tried to blot out the horror of John's first rape offence, but 'it was impossible to ever look him straight in the eye again knowing what he'd done ... He was born with the Devil in him and he's turned into a black-hearted monster. We are all so ashamed.'

According to another press report, while John was on remand at Horfield prison, Bristol, he had told a visitor that he had already thought out an escape plan and would flee to Colombia in South America because he could not face imprisonment. He was alleged to have said that as an individual he had no boundaries and that the gap between the two sides of his nature was getting greater. 'I am beyond help. I am beyond redemption,' he was quoted as saying.

Seemingly without a friend in the world, except his loving mother who kept faith in her son, John was locked away in a cell at Wakefield prison. Jim Moriarty, his solicitor, announced that they would appeal against the conviction and sentence for murder. The grounds for appeal were that the judge erred in law at the start of the trial by rejecting defence submissions not to try the offences together. The offences were regarded as of such a 'scandalous' and 'prejudicial' nature as to make it impossible for a jury to consider them separately. It was thought inevitable that they would have a cumulative effect on the jury with the result that a fair trial was not possible.

The appeal was heard at the Royal Courts of Justice on 23 July 1991 before the Lord Chief Justice of England, Lord Lane, sitting with Mr Justice Kennedy and Mr Justice Rougier. John appeared looking nervous and pasty-faced, handcuffed to a prison warder. He was wearing the now familiar blazer and flannels with an open-neck shirt. He looked drawn and appeared to have lost weight. His owl-like eyes scanned the court seeking out one of the authors, to whom he smiled in recognition.

Anthony Palmer QC, defence counsel at the trial, argued the grounds for appeal. The thrust was essentially that evidence from one case, for example the Reading rape, coloured the jury's consideration of the other charges. In the best traditions of the English adversarial system of justice, Paul Chadd, prosecution counsel, argued the opposite position. He maintained there was no possible room for a mistake regarding the DNA evidence in the Reading rape and said the presence of Shirley Banks's thumbprint in John Cannan's flat and of her car in his garage were irrefutable. He quoted from the transcript of the tape-recorded interview in which DCI Bryan Saunders confronted John Cannan with the thumbprint. He contended that the trial judge had discretion to try offences together or separately. When that discretion was exercised lawfully, as he believed was so in this case, it was not a matter for another court to overturn.

The judges retired to consider their judgment, which was duly given by Lord Lane. He said there were no grounds for miscarriage of justice and the trial judge had made a lawful decision to try the offences together. The appeal was therefore dismissed. John hung his head briefly and was led below to the cells. In contrast to the huge headlines that greeted his conviction at Exeter, the failure of his appeal captured only a few lines on the inside pages of the newspapers.

Moves had also been started by John's legal advisers to halt plans by the BBC to show a programme about him in their *Crimewatch* series. A special documentary was scheduled for screening which was thought to be in contempt of the appeal hearing. An injunction was sought in the High Court to prevent the film being transmitted. The 50-minute programme, described as 'a chillingly realistic reconstruction' of the police investigation, was made in Bristol with the assistance of officers involved in the case. The part of John Cannan was played by Joe Hall, a local actor whose circle of friends included Andrew Riley, one of the men who had chased John through the streets of Leamington Spa prior to his arrest.

The *Crimewatch* programme was screened in the autumn of 1989 despite the protests. John was not pleased with it. Among his various criticisms, he highlighted the incident in which a taxi-driver was allegedly called to Foye House. He wondered 'how a girl, snatched from her car, the driver's door of which didn't open, abducted, imprisoned, tied up, beaten up, raped and buggered, orally sexed, ravished and generally abused, could then ... be allowed to pick up a telephone to book, I repeat, book a taxi to take her to a railway station. After, that is, telephoning work sounding perfectly normal and at ease to a colleague who knew her well...' He added that there was no record to support the taxi-driver's contention that a telephone request for a cab had been made.

It was during his early months of solitary confinement at Wakefield prison that John began writing to the authors setting out his reactions and giving his interpretations of events. He denied at his trial, and still denies, that he even met Shirley Banks, let alone abducted and murdered her. He also denies committing rape at Reading or attempting to abduct a woman from Canon's Marsh car park in Bristol.

The Reading rape charge he calls a 'limpet' designed to ensure his silence when he came to trial. In other words, he was the victim of a conspiracy. It is a theory that he argues with all the intensity and close attention to detail of which we know him to be capable. Above all, it is a scenario in which everyone has lied except John and one in which he knows more than anyone, including the police.

His strongly held conviction is that he was framed for the murder of Shirley Banks. Far from trying to kill her, he argues that he was endeavouring to protect her. He did not know Mrs Banks personally or by sight, but he had heard of her name and the dreadful position she was in. For John claims to have discovered that Shirley Reynolds [her maiden name] had been, probably unwittingly, drawn into the drug scene and 'had been used for a delivery ... and largely confirmed a suspicion I'd held for some time. She later became a victim of a contract killing.'

There is something strangely disconcerting about the way John uses Shirley's maiden name. Naturally, she was known as Shirley Reynolds up to the time she married Richard Banks, which included the period when John was enjoying a relationship with Annabel Rose. From the time she disappeared to the moment her body was found, she was always referred to in the media as Shirley Banks. Yet John used her maiden name almost as if he was accustomed to calling her by it. He asserts 'There is a man who enforces for them [the Bristol criminal underworld], he's not strikingly similar to me, he isn't, but there are physical similarities between us and I doubt very much if his name was Hodgeson.'

The St Paul's area of Bristol is notorious for its drug-trafficking activities and an 'enforcer' is known to have worked in the district.

Referring to Shirley's Mini, one of the most incriminating pieces of evidence against him, he says vehemently, 'I was steered into that bloody car; Hodgeson DOES exist!' They met at the car auction and John had no reason to suspect the man's genuineness and, at that time, no connection with Shirley was evident.

John has described Hodgeson as around mid- to late thirties, of medium build and height. He had dark, swept-back hair, 'a little longer and thinner than mine'. He was friendly, spoke with a slight southwest accent and did not seem in the least nervous. 'In the cold light of day,' said John, 'if you stood him next to me, side-by-side, you would notice differences in appearance: he was I remember, a little stockier than me but, facially, we were not dissimilar.' Hodgeson had wanted £150 for the Mini but accepted John's offer of £125. 'There was no paperwork, nor was there any need for any,' said John. 'I asked him if the Mini was "hot". He replied that it wasn't.'

John's reason for buying the car was so that he could use it in connection with a building society raid. It was 'just a cheap old banger and purely a means to an end'. The transaction took place at about 7.30pm, probably on 14 October, in the road outside John's flat at Foye House. His mother was inside watching television. He accompanied

Hodgeson to the car, which was parked in Bridge Road by the kerb facing towards Clifton Suspension Bridge and, hence, towards Bristol.

'The transaction was without fuss and took only 10–15 minutes.' The two men completed their deal in the entrance to the flat after John test-drove the vehicle for five minutes. 'I didn't invite him in my flat because I had my mum with me and because the car may have been used for illegal purposes.' He handed over £125 in cash. He also noticed a car parked about 50 yards further down Bridge Road with its side lights on.

This account of John's has several fundamental flaws. The major one is that if the date for the transaction – 'probably 14 October' – is correct, then this was some four days after Shirley disappeared. Most of the county's police force were looking for the distinctive orange Mini, with most police vehicles having a note of the registration number pinned to their dashboards. It seems highly unlikely that a group of conspirators would drive the car in its original state, sporting its original number plates around the very city from which Shirley Banks went missing.

Nevertheless, it was only later that John realised the car he had bought was being searched for by the police in their investigation of Shirley Banks's disappearance. He claims to have received an anonymous telephone call alerting him to the car's true owner. He realised – and this is John's account and his alone – that he had to get the car out of sight immediately, which he did by locking it in his garage while he thought of the best way to dispose of it altogether. This statement implies that, up until either the press reports of Shirley Banks's disappearance or the anonymous telephone call, the Mini had been parked outside his home at Foye House. This smacks of an untruth as no witness came forward to claim they had seen the distinctive car parked near Foye House.

John recollected sitting in his flat trying calmly to think things through: 'I was sitting on a car that had deliberately been sold to me to get me into trouble,' he said. He resolved that 'Hodgeson had to be found' and his plan was to use Tom Eyles to trace him, follow his movements and then, 'I would have been in a strong position to go to the police.' The trouble was that he had no money with which to pay the private detective – hence the attempted robbery at Leamington Spa that led to his arrest.

When being questioned at Filton after his arrested, he said, 'I feel as though everybody is looking at me and expecting me to be able to solve Shirley's murder, to dot every "i" and cross every "t".' His dilemma was that, 'Whilst I knew much more than the police ... and some I can prove, my problem was that I didn't know things, and that is what made it necessary to find out.'

The police, he was firmly convinced, would not believe his story. 'So I decided to contain my explanation of the car purchase.' That is why, he claimed, 'the police failed to discover Shirley's body.' The logic of this is not at all clear, but he said, 'I, with Shirley gone, was on my own,' implying that he was up against overwhelming odds which included both the forces of law and order and also the power of the criminal world.

John claimed to have told the police about a drug ring operating in Bristol that involved a 'heavy criminal family'. He was concerned about his own safety if he were unveiled as an informer and also that of his mother and daughter. 'I honestly didn't kill Shirley Banks,' John insists. 'The opposite in fact is true. It was me who under the most impossible of circumstances was trying to intervene ... I'd never met her and hadn't a clue who she was, all I was able to determine ... was the nature of the girl's predicament.'

John's reconstruction in one of his letters of what, according to the prosecution, he was supposed to have done to Shirley Banks, makes absorbing reading. Having abducted her he was charged with taking her back to his flat where he sexually abused her but allowed her to telephone her place of work the next morning to explain her absence in an apparently normal voice. 'Then, dressed in my blue suit,' says John, 'I went to the bank at 1pm. Upon my return I borrowed Val Humphreys's vacuum cleaner, the contents of which were forensically examined and nothing untoward was found.

'Then I allowed her to PRE-BOOK a taxi to take her to the railway station, NOT I add to the police or her husband which, given that I am accused of abducting, imprisoning, raping etc, seems a little odd.

'Then, a taxi-driver allegedly comes despite there being no paperwork to cover it and a firm denial by the taxi controller that a taxi for Leigh Woods was ever ordered.

'Then I bundle her into my car, which was cleared forensically, whereupon she escaped, some 20 yards down the road. Instead of screaming "RAPE" and trying to attract attention, she dives into the woods next to my flat. I follow her in and, according to Mrs Hart, pound her with my fists and thoroughly beat Shirley severely, despite pathology reports which showed no bruise or laceration on Shirley's body.

'Then, leaving her senseless and unconscious, I try to

strangle Mrs Hart through the open window of her car despite her driver husband hearing and seeing nothing.

'They, the Harts, then continue their journey to Clevedon where they partake in afternoon tea.

'Meanwhile, with traffic passing, I bundle Shirley into the black BMW again despite a finger search revealing no such violent event ever having occured [sic], and drove to the Quantock Hills.

'I then apparently dressed her up in my mac despite her being unconscious, because, if you recall, I left Shirley in the wood next to Foye House and tried to murder Mrs Hart!

'(NO, I couldn't have left Shirley tied up in the wood because she escaped from my car, if you remember.)

'After laying her down on my mac, I decided to rape her again but, instead of removing her underwear, I pulled her pants to one side and raped her despite there being no evidence of sexual assault, no signs of injury or rope marks to either wrists or ankles.

'Having raped her again, I waited until my sperm had impregnated her knickers which must have taken some time, then I stood her up unconscious and gave her a blow to the head which killed her.

'Then I took her knickers off along with the rest of her clothes, leaving however her knickers behind at the scene of the crime to be found by the police.

'You might, of course, be tempted to think that I'm joking or EXAGERATING [sic] what PRECISELY the prosecution alleged.'

This extraordinary and mocking account of the murder that he denied contains some interesting points. First, although Shirley's car was in John's possession, no forensic traces of his presence were found in the vehicle. This is not surprising as John admitted wiping it clean of fingerprints. Similarly, there were no forensic traces indicating that Shirley had ever been in his BMW. For a possible explanation, it is necessary to look no further than the Reading rape and Donna Tucker's gloved attacker who was so meticulous about removing any fingerprint impressions and ordered her to brush the seats clean before he left her.

The same incident also provides a partial answer to another of John's points, which was the absence of any signs of sexual assault on Shirley Banks's body. It is true that Professor Knight's post-mortem examination revealed no abnormality of the genitalia or anus, nor were there any marks on the throat or bruises indicating that the victim had been tied up or constrained. It should be remembered, however, that the body had been dead for several months and had deteriorated accordingly. Large areas of the body's surface had become macerated and swollen due to prolonged immersion in water and some skin tissue had been destroyed by animals.

Nevertheless, no indications of sexual assault were found. Once again, the Reading rape incident is instructive. The victim had been subjected to rape and buggery, yet on medical examination within hours of the attack was found not to have a mark on her. The attacker in this case was John Cannan, so perhaps the absence of injuries associated with sexual attack on Shirley Banks's body was not so remarkable.

John had concluded that the authorities feared he would give evidence in court 'and reveal to the jury the events leading up to Shirley's disappearance, embracing within its compass my calls to the police and the leaks which had occurred. They couldn't afford to let the Banks' murder go to separate trial, so they bolstered the prosecution with the Reading rape – a 'limpet charge' as he liked to call it – knowing that he could not defend himself. 'The Avon and Somerset police,' he argued, 'with the help of legal counsel, deliberately manoeuvred me into a corner making it virtually impossible for me to give evidence and to reveal the facts of the Shirley Banks case. I was in effect gagged.'

John was really whistling in the dark with these arguments, probably because he knew his defence was unbelievable. Perhaps, by withholding information, or the truth as he saw it, he believed he could cling on to some kind of power. It was then no surprise that he declined to use his conspiracy argument to defend himself when he was on trial, if not for his life, at least for his liberty. 'I offered no defence,' he said, 'because of the prejudicial legal circumstances surrounding my trial, therefore the jury did not hear my account or the testimony of my witnesses ... All my side is therefore "new evidence". When to disclose,' he proclaimed, 'is up to Mr Palmer,' adding, 'and of course, me!'

One of his purported reasons for not giving evidence was that he would have 'to testify against many people, many of whom, and one in particular, is a solicitor(s)'. John claimed that 'Everything I did was for a reason. There was no way after Shirley Banks disappeared, that I wanted the Avon and Somerset police any further involved.'

'The biggest mistake I made was telephoning them in the first place.' John contended the police used the press to discredit him by timing their various charges against him in order to keep his name in the public eye. He also alleged that certain witnesses were assisted with their statements, 'dovetailing one to follow the sentiments of preceding ones.' With a hint of bitterness, he said, 'They wanted me convicted ... I've lost my life for things I haven't done.'

But what of the clinching evidence against him – the discovery of Shirley Banks's thumbprint on the surveillance document found in his flat? John acknowledged that the thumbprint and his possession of the Mini were the two primary pieces of evidence against him. He had explained the Mini, at least to his own satisfaction, and naturally had a theory about the thumbprint.

John acknowledged that it 'is probably genuine' but drew attention to what he viewed as an anomaly. Bryan Saunders confronted him with the print during the final interview at Filton in December 1988. But he claimed the police fingerprint expert did not confirm that the control sample (one of Shirley's perfume bottles) matched the impression on the document, exhibit (MR4/A) until the following January. 'The point being,' he wrote, 'how would Saunders know that that was Shirley's thumbprint when it had not been examined?' He said that, if it was genuine, he could not account for it. 'I genuinely don't know; others I think, however, might know ... if it's a legitimate print.'

This rather vague theory was John Cannan at his best. The police transcript of John's final interview shows without doubt that they had already identified Shirley Banks's thumbprint well before that interview and had presented it to John as such.

John persisted in his view that he did not have a fair trial and likes to hint in his letters at what he would have said 'had I given evidence'. His correspondence paints a picture of himself as the lone crusader standing up for what is right while all around him conspire and lie. It was the fault of the police that Shirley was killed and then that her body was not found quickly. If they had listened to him and pursued the allegations he made instead of leaking information, Shirley might not have died.

He did his level best to obtain additional information at his own expense. 'After I had promised the police to try and obtain further information,' he said, 'I did two things: (a) I employed Tom Eyles Legal Services, and (b) I enrolled at Suitor Dating Agency...' The latter move, he explained, was to pursue enquiries into drug dealing. 'There were certain people I had to chip away at and it was becoming increasingly difficult on my own.' He concluded that, if he had been successful, 'I would have been in a position to cause absolute mayhem.'

Despite everything – the trial with its overwhelming weight of evidence against him, the loss of his appeal and the bleak future ahead of him – John persists in his denials. He did not murder Shirley Banks, and did not rape Sharon Major. He did not rape Donna Tucker, he did not perform buggery, he did not attempt abduction and he was not implicated in the disappearance of Suzy Lamplugh or the death of Sandra Court. On the contrary, he maintains that he was trying to prevent Shirley Banks falling into the clutches of evildoers.

By not telling all he knew in order to give himself some kind of defence at his trial – for that is what he claims – he added to the crushing burden of his self-proclaimed innocence. Perhaps he consoles himself with the thought that, by retaining some secret knowledge, he also retains power. He has told the authors as much: 'I AM IN CONTROL because information is power.' But such information as he may have is valueless while he keeps it in his head. He has neither power nor control. His life is regulated for him. The system controls every movement he will ever make again. John acknowledges, 'I am doing NATURAL LIFE precisely [the] same sentence as the NAZI war criminal Rudolf Hess.'

Since he wrote those words, Hess has been released from prison by death – John faces the same expectation.

15

THE MIND OF A
SERIAL KILLER

'I put my faith in you to preserve me some measure of dignity,' John Cannan told the authors when this book was started. He also said that it was important he should not lay down any preconditions for his cooperation. 'You should write it as you see it.'

We have tried to be objective in our approach and fair to John. Whatever he may have been convicted of and whatever secrets he has retained, John has been courteous and helpful throughout. We recognise that he is a person capable of warmth and friendship and also of strong, loving relationships as he has demonstrated throughout his life. But there is also violence in his soul and it is the dichotomy between these two intense emotions – love and hatred – which lies at the heart of understanding John Cannan. In seeking to reach that understanding, we hope we have not impaired his dignity as a human being. That was never our intention but, if John's life is to be worth anything, holding back from the truth will not help. We have tried to adhere to the facts, the known evidence and statements, venturing into speculation only for the sake of completeness and when others have opened up questions.

We have to ask: has John Cannan committed more than one murder? In this chapter we shall examine the patterns of behaviour of serial killers, and we shall also assess John's connections with the unresolved cases of Sandra Court and Suzy Lamplugh, although no involvement by John can be proved. We have put these issues to him many times and he has consistently denied being involved. With the known facts that are available, we have to suggest that, on balance, John Cannan knows more about Suzy Lamplugh than he cares to admit. As we know, he has also always denied the offences for which he is serving a life sentence.

But one must also be careful not to jump to conclusions. After John had been arrested, other unsolved murders were linked to John Cannan, particularly those with a sexual motive. The body of 13-year-old Candice Williams, for example, was found on the 12th-storey landing of a block of flats at Erdington, Birmingham on 25 July 1978. She had been raped and strangled. Her murder initiated the greatest manhunt ever staged in Birmingham. Despite an extensive investigation, including 7,000 door-to-door enquiries, the killer eluded the police.

In November 1987, a West Midlands press report stated that the investigation into Candice Williams's death was being reopened following the arrest of a man for another offence. Although his name was not mentioned, this could only have been a reference to John Cannan. Indeed, at the time, John and his wife, June, often walked their dog in the park adjacent to the block of flats at Erdington where the young girl was murdered. Like many other men in the area, John was interviewed during the course of the murder inquiry. He gave two accounts for his movements that day which contradicted each other, but he was not asked to give a blood sample. He was reinterviewed in 1987 by West Midlands police, whose aim was to see if there was any connection between him and the crime. It seemed too much of a coincidence that there might have been two prospective killers in the same park on the same day...

'I did not kill Candice Williams,' John said categorically, and complained that the 'police are trying to use me as a dumping ground to offload offences they haven't solved and are trying to shroud me in a veil of suspicion'. His denial was borne out in March 1991 when it was reported in the Birmingham *Evening Mail* that, after 13 years, a man was being charged with the murder of Candice Williams. In March 1992, Patrick Hassett was jailed for life at Birmingham Crown Court on the strength of DNA profiling. Hassett had confessed to a fellow prisoner at Winson Green where he was serving a ten-year sentence for a previous sex crime. The DNA profile of semen samples taken from the 1978 murder victim and stored for over a decade was matched to the DNA in a sample of Hassett's hair. It was another dramatic demonstration of the power of genetic-fingerprinting techniques.

Having given an account of John's life and of the crimes for which he was convicted, we have to reach some conclusion. What kind of person is he and what were the forces that drove him to violence? And can anything constructive be derived from the life of a man who has already served years in custody and who is unlikely ever again to be a free person?

John had a child's quick temper, which, as he matured, became an adult's 'short fuse'. Totally self-centred, he liked to get his own way in everything, whether it was winning an argument or in the conduct of his relationships.

He claimed he was beaten at school and sexually abused by a teacher. He spoke later about the shame and guilt that this experience engendered and of his helplessness that he could not talk to his parents. John believed this had stigmatised him. No one should make light of what even a mild experience of this kind can have on a young mind, although for many boys subjected to this kind of incident there are no harmful personality effects in later life.

Sexual abuse, however, is one of the childhood experiences that has become recognised as a common factor in the background of men who have become sexual deviants. John showed behavioural instability as he approached his teenage years to the extent that he was referred for psychiatric examination. He felt a sense of humiliation and resentment rising in him. Possibly, that led to his first known offence as a young teenager when he put his hand up a woman's skirt.

John's behaviour, playing truant from school, showed the instincts of a loner. The responsibilities of a wife and child did not appeal to John and the marriage broke down after a year. He was leading a promiscuous life at this time and drinking and smoking heavily. When his father learned about his son's irresponsible ways, there was a showdown and John deserted his wife and daughter.

By his mid-twenties, John was practically an alcoholic, reduced to committing robbery to pay for his drink. He was at a low ebb and his failure to cope with life weighed heavily on him.

Then he met Sharon Major, a mature vivacious woman with a stable personality. They were attracted to each other and were drawn into a relationship. For John, this was something of a fresh start, a way out of the doldrums and a return to a normal way of life. The affair might have lasted longer than it did if John had not wanted to dominate his partner. However, he brought into this new relationship all the messy baggage of his past. When his immature, vain and violent tendencies surfaced, Sharon glimpsed something unwelcome, even evil, in his behaviour. Her instincts told her it would be wise to terminate their time together.

That was the flashpoint. John cared for her but his needs were really those of dependency. Consequently, when the end came he lost control of his emotions. His attack on Sharon was elemental, brutal revenge: 'You've hurt me so badly. I'm going to hurt you too' were his uncompromising words to her. He came close to killing her: indeed, he said that was his intention.

When it was all over and his fury had abated, John reverted to his normal self. Contemplating the injuries that he had inflicted on the woman he professed to love, he was full of apologies. Recalling the incident much later during a police interview, he distanced himself from the violent attack by saying, 'It was as if it was not me.'

He tried to make amends but to no avail. When she resisted his continuing attempts to talk her round, he realised he had failed and took his revenge on her reputation. His anger at rejection spilled out in words damning her character and accusing her of seedy practices. John lapsed once more into a despairing state; feeling sorry for himself was part of his inability to cope with his own emotional reverses. He resorted to alcohol but his anger over the break with Sharon was not yet spent.

Two months after raping Sharon Major, John committed a second brutal sexual assault. His victim was a pregnant woman whom he raped in the presence of her mother and child. He had threatened her with a knife and tied her up. Before leaving, he told her, 'I'll be dead within a fortnight.' John served five years in prison for this crime and it is the only offence in the list of charges against him that he acknowledges. While he protests his sorrow for this brutal act, he also explains, even tries to justify, it on the grounds that, because he had been humiliated by Sharon, he wanted to inflict pain on someone else. As in his recollection of the attack on Sharon, he again distanced himself from the act by saying the man in the shop 'wasn't the real John Cannan'.

His failure to cope with the disappointment and emotional aftermath of losing Sharon's affection created such a rage in him that he committed two rapes in the space of just over two months. The spiral of violence, temporarily halted by his period of imprisonment, was quickly resumed after his release. If John was responsible for Sandra Court's death or Suzy Lamplugh's disappearance, he waited only a few days before seeking out a new victim. The alternative scenario is that he waited three months. For, beyond doubt, he committed rape at Reading in October 1986. The attack bore all his hallmarks: the knife threat, verbal intimidation laced with 'fucking', a word he characteristically used under pressure, and anal as well as normal intercourse.

The Reading rape seemed to quieten John's rage, at least for a few months as he began to develop a relationship with Annabel Rose. He was not having much luck with his jobs but, as he turned progressively to crime as a source of income, having a job mattered less and less. The important development was that he could afford to run a car and stay at hotels. He was mobile and looking for opportunities. With money to spend and helped by a family legacy, he could shed the vestiges of his previous abject existence and create a little style for himself. He liked to dress well and with his natural charm and plausible manner easily portrayed himself as a successful businessman. He had a string of girlfriends and was able to indulge his powerful sexual inclinations.

John used his gifts to the full and the complete repertoire was employed when he sighted Gilly Paige. Their relationship to all intents and purposes was a conventional affair of the kind that unattached individuals subscribe to on impulse. Two attractive people sat at separate tables in a hotel restaurant, both at a loose end. His adventurous approach won her over and they became lovers that very night. Gilly Paige was literally dicing with death. It was during the follow-up that Gilly, like Sharon, sensed something ugly in her companion's character – the way he talked and the subjects he chose to talk about. Suzy Lamplugh was one of the topics, and John mentioned that the missing estate agent was probably buried under concrete. While out on a drive with Gilly, John had placed his hands around her neck with the comment, 'Maybe this is the way Suzy died.'

There were strong echoes in this chance meeting of the experience that Sandy Fawkes, a London journalist, had in the USA when she met a handsome stranger calling himself Daryl Golden. They also met in a hotel bar – in Atlanta, Georgia in 1974 – and became lovers, spending six days and nights together. She found him charming and captivating at first but then detected an evil side to his character. This was confirmed when he pulled a gun on her. She escaped to tell her story in a book called *Killing Time*, the story of her encounter with John Paul Knowles who had killed twice the day before meeting her. A few days after they parted company, Knowles committed two further murders.

Dubbed by the press 'The Casanova Killer', Knowles was a serial killer with an unhappy childhood and dreams of fame and success which subsided into petty crime and eventually murder. During the time he spent with Sandy Fawkes he talked of having made some tapes about his life which would be the basis for a book. He also told her, correctly as it turned out, 'within a year I will be dead'. John Cannan expressed similar sentiments to his rape victim.

John's liaison with Gilly Paige was one of a number of affairs which he engaged in at this time. They were mostly chance encounters when he saw an opportunity and exercised his charm to win over the girl. It was a kind of gentle trawling for which nature had provided him with the necessary gifts – good looks and a pleasing manner. But the relationship on which he wanted to build was that with Annabel Rose. She was an intelligent, professional woman with all the attributes of success that John would have liked for himself. In her case, he wanted more than a quick conquest – he was looking for a more stable, long-lasting relationship. Perhaps the kind of relationship he had started to establish with Sharon but which had gone so disastrously wrong.

When the affair with Annabel Rose started to deteriorate, John became aggressive and threatening. His reactions to the first signs of rejection were explosive, verbal and menacing. Annabel was too much of an individual and had too high a social profile for him to be able to rule her life. When she made it clear she wanted to terminate the relationship, he became angry and vindictive. His initial ploy was to harass her by employing a private detective, Tom Eyles, to carry out surveillance on her parents. Eventually he made outrageous and unfounded allegations against her to the police to try to ruin her. But much of Annabel Rose's problem with John was brought on by her own foolishness. As a solicitor advising him while he was serving a prison sentence, she knew all about his criminal past and of the circumstances surrounding the rape attack for which he was convicted. Yet she disregarded all caution and common sense and entered into a relationship with a rapist.

The scene in Colonel Jasper's wine bar when John, falsely portraying himself as John Peterson, met Tom Eyles and his wife Janet showed the opportunist's instincts. Suntanned after his holiday in Crete, well dressed and smiling, the schemer, even while seeking to make life difficult for his former lover, was also sizing up a very attractive Janet Eyles in a way which she found immediately disturbing.

John's rejection by Annabel Rose – the second time he had been subjected to what he regarded as a humiliating experience – triggered off a brooding violence. It was to be a re-run of the Sharon Major rejection incident. The visit to the Bristol video-dating agency – an amusing diversion on the face of it – had a more sinister interpretation in the light of subsequent events. It was by design a very convenient way to seek a companion, but for John there was the prospect of finding a subject for his frustration. A way of targeting another Jean Bradford or Donna Tucker perhaps. As events turned out, he found there were ample opportunities in the environs of Bristol, in the city's car parks and shopping areas.

First there was the failed abduction attempt at Canon's Marsh car park. This was followed the next day by the disappearance of Shirley Banks and a few weeks later by the attempted robbery at Leamington Spa. The result was one dead victim out of three attempted assaults by a man whose travelling equipment included a knife, handcuffs, replica revolver and various lengths of rope. It may be said that John had bad luck; certainly two of his intended victims had good fortune.

Whatever the urge driving him on, it seems clear that his aggression was so consuming as not to be deflected by failure nor, it seems, easily satisfied by success. Only 24 hours elapsed between the attempted abduction in Canon's Marsh car park and the successful abduction of Shirley Banks. Following Shirley's disappearance, 21 days passed before he appeared in Ginger boutique at Leamington Spa. Although ostensibly bent on robbery, he was equipped at Leamington with the paraphernalia of restraint and abduction, and with his car parked close by for a quick escape. This incident, particularly its location, had much in common with the 1981 rape attack on Jean Bradford in Sutton Coldfield.

Three attacks on women in the space of as many weeks clearly indicated that the forces propelling John towards serial violence were quickening their pace. The story of his life between 1980 and 1987 was a tale of rejection by two women he claimed to love. He had demonstrated a range of relationships with the opposite sex: one-night stands, as he liked to call these short-term promiscuous relationships, and intensely emotional affairs. It was the experience of rejection that triggered off his violent moods and drove him to seek victims on whom he could exact a humiliating revenge. By the time he was arrested, his lapses into violence were coming closer together and he had become a terrifying menace to society.

To understand what was happening to John Cannan, it is instructive to turn to America and to a man who has come to represent the stereotypical serial killer, Theodore Robert Bundy, executed in Florida in 1989.

Bundy was attributed with killing 31 women in several states over a four-year period. An illegitimate child whose mother refused to identify the father, Ted was four when his mother married John Bundy, thus providing him with a stepfather whom he came to resent and regard as an interloper. Ted grew up to be a good-looking, blue-eyed boy with a strong temper. He was shy and something of a daydreamer, fantasising about becoming rich and famous. He grew up into what some might call a handsome, athletic young man, good at skiing, although he was too self-conscious to engage in team sports.

Bundy's relationships with the opposite sex were not very successful; apparently he had only one high-school date in three years. His friends saw him as scholarly and articulate but lacking in self-confidence. In his late teens, he formed a strong attachment to a young student, a sophisticated girl called Stephanie Brooks who came from a well-off family. She had beauty and poise; Ted was so smitten that he enrolled at Stanford University to study Chinese to please her. The course exposed his shortcomings, however, and Stephanie grew tired of his immature ways. When she dropped him, Ted was said to have been devastated. He left university, becoming increasingly withdrawn and worked, among numerous occupations, as a supermarket shelf-stacker. He lived in a small rented apartment and slid into stealing and shoplifting.

Bundy also developed a liking for violent pornography and became a Peeping Tom. He suffered periodic depression, but in 1970 was persuaded to resume his studies. He enrolled in a psychology course at Washington State University and for a short time worked at the Seattle Crisis Clinic as a counsellor. His ambition was to go to law school but his applications were repeatedly turned down. Despite these reverses, he had a number of girlfriends who regarded him as handsome and charming. They also liked his good manners and dress sense.

His regular relationship was with a girl named Liz. Eventually she, too, grew tired of him and the affair began to show signs of strain. She also saw another side to his character when he threatened to 'break her fucking neck' if she revealed that he was a thief. He also asked her for anal sex, which she refused, but she did allow him on one or two occasions to tie her up. Ted secretly enrolled at the University of Utah College of Law and renewed his acquaintance with Stephanie. Seven years after their first relationship, they spent Christmas together. She thought he had become more positive in his outlook but it was not sufficient for her to want to build a lasting relationship with him. For a second time, she told him she did not want to see him again. Within weeks of being rejected by the girl of his desires, Bundy committed his first murder in February 1974. Soon afterwards he met Carole Boone, who would eventually marry him and become the mother of his child.

In the meantime, he continued to see Liz but his behaviour towards her was erratic and his treatment of her was rough. He and Liz parted company.

Young women began disappearing in his home area of Washington State in 1974 at the alarming rate of one a month until mid-1975. In July 1974, a girl out picnicking was approached by a good-looking man who asked her to help him with his boat. She declined but heard the man make the same request to another girl, introducing himself as Ted. Stories began to circulate from a number of female students of a man called Ted who had tried to pick them up. The disappearances continued but the action switched to Utah and Colorado.

On 16 August 1975, Ted Bundy was arrested in Salt Lake City and charged with murder. Handcuffs, a crowbar, lengths of rope and a face-mask fashioned out of pantyhose were found in his car. In 1977, he was extradited to Colorado where he studied law in prison while he waited to appear on trial. On 7 June 1977, he escaped from prison only to be recaptured a few days later. But in December he escaped again and made his way to Florida.

In January 1978, posing as a student at Florida State University at Tallahassee, Bundy attacked and killed two women and assaulted three others. He was arrested at the beginning of 1979 and was tried at Miami for three counts of murder. He pleaded not guilty and claimed that the forensic evidence which linked him to one of the victims had been planted by the police. He said he was subjected to incompetent defence lawyers and prejudiced media attention. Bundy also aired his opinions on justice, which he said was just a game in which the outcome was predetermined.

Ted Bundy's trial for murder was the first to be seen on national television; 250 reporters had applied for press status. Despite his views that witnesses' descriptions of him were tainted by prior publicity and that the whole judicial process was ludicrous, Bundy was convicted and sentenced to death. He was on Death Row for nearly ten years before finally going to the electric chair. Throughout a decade in custody, he maintained his innocence and never confessed.

A number of books have been written about Ted Bundy and probably the most important are the two by journalists Stephen G. Michaud and Hugh Aynesworth. They gained access to Bundy before he was executed. He told them that a malignant force ('the entity') resided within him, gradually taking over his conscious self and inducing him to commit rape and murder. Ted was not admitting guilt for himself but for his inner self. When he was sentenced to death by Judge Edward D. Cowart, he replied, 'The sentence is not a sentence of me. It's a sentence of someone who is not standing here today.'

In *Ted Bundy: Conversations with a Killer*, Michaud and Aynesworth persuaded Bundy to talk in the third person, thereby revealing a great deal about himself without needing to confess to the crimes. These exchanges produced some remarkable insights into the mind of a serial killer. Ted admitted feeling indifferent to other people and he was aware of his mood changes. He dismissed his burglary activities almost in one breath – there was no question of guilt; he simply took what he needed.

His attitude to women was much the same – he took them as victims in order to kill them and thereby achieve their ultimate possession. He said he had no hatred of women, but spoke of a weakness that gave rise to sexual activity involving violence. This in turn absorbed some of his fantasy.

He talked about a divided personality and of the 'entity' or 'disordered self' – that part which was fascinated by sexual violence and worked in harmony with the other, normal self. It was the 'entity' that organised the abduction of the victim and the normal self that planned the killing. The abnormal entity took over with increasing frequency, forming a partnership with the normal self. Ted emphasised that he was not talking about two different minds but two different behaviour patterns of the same mind.

Bundy described the feelings of excitement mixed with anticipation as he began looking for his next victim. When making his approach, he felt like an actor playing a role. He would engage her in conversation, be charming and entertaining – he wooed her while keeping himself mentally at a distance in order to resist feelings of compassion. He saw her in depersonalised terms as if he were watching a film. Methods used to intimidate the victim included a knife or a gun and she might be tied up. Once control over the victim had been established, the rape would follow and then the slaughter. By the time the compulsive frenzy abated, he realised the danger he was in and his normal self would resume control and start the process of concealing the crime. When this was achieved, exhaustion and sleep ensued.

In the immediate aftermath of the killing, he resolved never to do it again. During this contrition phase, ordinary relationships were possible in which the normal self remained in control and opportunities to claim another victim could be avoided. A feeling of having accomplished something resulted, a feeling of satisfaction that his urges were under control. Then the resolution 'never to do it again' would begin to evaporate, to be overtaken by the resolve not to get caught. This desire would come into stronger focus as the preceding event faded and anticipation of the next became all-consuming. He reasoned that, since they were opportunistic, the very nature of the killings made them easy to commit and get away with.

He felt as if he was always one jump ahead of the police and virtually immune from detection. Success fed upon success and he would become completely emboldened and that part of his personality which needed the stimulation of violence would increase in appetite.

Bundy described this behaviour as an illness and tried to rationalise its causes for the benefit of Michaud and Aynesworth. He talked about stress as a trigger – the kind of stress which arose randomly either from personal circumstances or from environmental causes. This might be due to lack of fulfilment, low personal esteem, a sense of failure or an adverse emotional experience; external causes might lie in fluctuating job prospects or business and financial considerations. While these events might be random, their effect on the individual was specific. People vary in their ability to deal with stress: some might cope well whereas others react poorly, exhibiting confusion, frustration and anger. Individuals in this second group, if they had a predisposition or weakness that lessened their self-control, might react by seeking a target for their frustration and turn anger and hostility into something malevolent. In some people this manifested itself in a need to seize something that was highly prized by society – human life itself. The motive then became the hunting of humans and their ultimate possession by killing them.

According to Ted Bundy, the philosophising killer, society is driving some of its members past the point where they are capable of conforming to its rules – their genetic make-up is being tested to its limits. Individuals with a predisposition to react violently when subjected to stress are increasingly emerging in society as deviants. Bundy predicted there would be an increase in serial killings as more individuals became alienated and vented their frustration on their fellows. At the same time, more people were dropping out of a declining culture and emerging as potential victims. In other words, there were both more hunters and more prey.

Bundy also made the observation that such predators were not susceptible to a rational analysis of their problems. He was particularly outspoken on the subject of guilt, which he described as an encumbrance that most people carried with them. His view was that guilt was a mechanism used to control people and he claimed not to feel guilty about anything he had done in the past, believing he had the gift of living entirely in the present. He did not worry, think or concern himself about the past and bore no burden apart from his confinement in prison. Not surprisingly, therefore, Ted did not acknowledge he had anything to confess.

While Ted Bundy is only one of a number of serial killers, there is a great deal in common between the lives of Ted Bundy and John Cannan, and much that they shared in their outlook and views.

PHYSICAL COMPARISONS

Both were very good-looking men who excited comment. They were natural athletes. Their general appearance was of decent-looking, clean-cut and well-dressed individuals. Their physiques were almost identical.

FAMILY BACKGROUND

We know nothing of Bundy's father, so we do not know if he inherited his characteristics, but both men had overbearing father figures in childhood and doting mothers. At school they proved to be intelligent, although both were shy, lonely boys with no close friends. This detachment extended into later life. As youths, both took to robbery and sexual offending: Bundy was a 'Peeping Tom' and Cannan was convicted of sexual assault.

PERSONALITY

They shared an air of charm and sophistication that proved attractive to women. They were vain, bordering on narcissistic, and articulate, and both dreamed of acquiring wealth and fame – they wanted to be 'somebody'. Bundy was aware of his mood changes, while Cannan probably was not; they switched from a placid outlook to aggressive behaviour very quickly.

Both men were emotionally immature with a capacity for self-deception. They resorted to lying, hedging and self-justification with ease: they were always right, others always wrong, even in the face of overwhelming evidence contradicting their views. When facing the charges against them, they insisted on their innocence, pleaded faulty memory and complained of planted evidence. They were fascinated by legal procedure:

Bundy studied law and represented himself in court, while Cannan was a natural barrack-room lawyer who took pleasure in laying down the rules at his police interviews. He also contacted the police on numerous occasions to discuss allegations of blackmail.

TRIGGERS OF VIOLENCE

Both men experienced rejection by women they loved: Bundy was rejected twice by the same woman and Cannan by two different women. Bundy was eventually accepted by the woman he had pursued but, in John Cannan's case, rejection was final. These incidents resulted in feelings of humiliation and deep resentment, precipitating violent behaviour that included rape.

VICTIMS

Bundy and Cannan selected their victims from a particular physical type in which hair colour was an important factor. Bundy targeted brunettes for murder, while he enjoyed normal relationships with blondes. John was the reverse: he singled out blondes as victims and experienced conventional relationships with brunettes.

MODUS OPERANDI

Both men carried firearms (an imitation gun in Cannan's case), handcuffs and ropes. These items were found in their cars when they were arrested. Bundy and Cannan regularly travelled by car from town to town – they were highly mobile. They favoured abduction by car, followed up by rape, battering to death and disposal of the victim in an isolated spot.

STATEMENTS

In statements made following their convictions, a number of common threads emerged. They refused to confess or admit any guilt whatsoever. Both believed their defence was strong enough to have succeeded and they criticised the system of justice as a sham.

Each man professed to be unafraid of death, claiming a kind of moral high ground over their fellows. They also shared a common bond in their pursuit of mysticism and eastern philosophy and they laid claim to a knowledge of economics.

Of course, a few points of comparison with just one serial killer, however compelling they may be, do not necessarily turn John Cannan into a serial killer. But there is sufficient substance in the common ground with a known serial killer such as Ted Bundy to merit further consideration. The term 'serial killing' came into use in the mid-1970s to denote a change in the observed patterns of murder. The mass murders of earlier decades, committed for gain or elimination in an essentially domestic environment, gave way to multiple murders for which the motives were so obscure as to be accorded the label 'motiveless'. These were the beginnings of what is now termed serial killing, in which murder is committed for its own sake. An example was the 'Son of Sam' murders in New York in 1977, which embodied an important element of serial murders in that the killer and his victims were strangers.

Such murders are serial acts and distinguishable from mass murder in that they are committed singly in different places and at different times. Another distinctive feature is the lack of any relationship between killer and victim. This is by no means a new phenomenon: serial killers have been in our midst for at least a century. What is new is the increase in their frequency. It is only relatively recently, as a number of serial killers have been caught and convicted, principally in the USA, that it has been possible to study their occurrence and gain sufficient information to improve our understanding.

Crime statistics for the USA in 1990 quote a total of 23,000 murders, some 5,000 of which are unsolved. The proportion of stranger murders has risen from 8.5 per cent of the total in 1976 to more than 22 per cent by 1984 and is still rising. Authorities differ over the proportion of serial killings contained in these figures; a conservative estimate is one per cent of the total. In 1986, the FBI reported that there might be as many as 40 serial killers responsible for several hundred deaths roaming the country and as yet uncaught. Again, this estimate has been challenged but the upward trend is undeniable.

FBI researchers and staff at Northeastern University have analysed the details of all known US serial killers since the early 1950s, providing a great deal of data for further sociological and criminological study. What has emerged is that 94 per cent of serial killers are men and 80 per cent are white. A sexual component is nearly always present in these crimes and the killers usually restrict their victims to their own race.

By looking at the methods used in new cases of serial murder, it is possible to build up a psychological profile of a killer. Indications of his likely occupation, background, status and lifestyle will be evident in his methods and enable detectives to define the type of person for whom they are searching. Psychological profiling was pioneered by the FBI's Behavioral Science

Investigative Support Unit at Quantico, Virginia. Such profiles have been available to assist police agencies throughout the USA since 1977 as part of VICAP, the Violent Criminal Apprehension Program.

Refinement of detailed interviews with 36 known serial killers has created a set of characteristics that they have in common. They are men mostly in their thirties or early forties with a strong compulsion to control others. A common feature in their backgrounds is an unhappy childhood with episodes of abandonment, abuse or rejection. Their crimes are sexual in nature and involve escalating torture and mutilation – they kill not for gain or passion but for pleasure. Their victims are usually young women who are strangers to them and they tend to dispose of their bodies in a superficial way by burying them in shallow graves, or by throwing them into garbage dumps or in water.

The Canadian anthropologist Elliott Leyton has made a study of modern multiple killers. He traces the origins of the present surge of killing to the late 1960s and the social changes taking place at that time in the USA. The tremendous economic expansion following the end of the Second World War created jobs in industry for many individuals with only meagre ability. Nevertheless, they prospered and gained a quality of life that fulfilled their ambitions. But, as job quotas were filled and employment opportunities then began to decline, a growing number of individuals found it impossible to achieve their ambitions. Disappointment gave way to disenchantment and rising resentment against society. Young men whose dreams of success had been thwarted turned to fantasies of revenge, and frustration spilled over into violence. These changes occurred in a society that for decades had accepted, even extolled, violence as a response to frustration. Leyton put it succinctly when he wrote, 'No single quality of American culture is so distinctive as its continued assertion of the nobility and beauty of violence.'

Another trend, which was a reversal of the previously observed patterns of murder, was that the social status of the killers declined while that of their victims increased. The murderers of the 1970s and 1980s were largely low achievers, holding jobs accorded low social recognition, whereas their victims were university students or young professionals. A look at the backgrounds of a number of recent multiple killers in the USA, including Ted Bundy, shows that they all came from disturbed backgrounds or thought they did. Adoption, illegitimacy and institutionalisation are easily identifiable characteristics, but a host of other features are apparent. These point to individuals who feel themselves to be different from their fellows: individuals outside the normal bounds of society who feel they have no recognisable place in its structure; individuals who for either real or imagined reasons feel themselves to be alienated from the world around them.

With feelings of low personal esteem and unattainable ambitions, they resort to the substitutes of dreaming and fantasising. When life lets them down or they suffer rejection in a desired relationship they experience a crisis which they are neither emotionally nor socially equipped to handle. These are the weaknesses that Ted Bundy spoke about so clearly which combine to push the individual over the edge towards violence. The desire is to strike out at society, to hurt and humiliate others as they believe themselves to have been hurt and humiliated. They punish the innocent, destroying human life as their ultimate act of revenge and gaining temporary relief from their anger in the process.

Dr Joel Norris, an American psychologist, has made a study of episodic violence and his researches have included interviews with a number of convicted serial killers. He published his initial findings in 1988 in a book called *Serial Killers: The Growing Menace*, in which he discussed the symptoms of what he believes is a form of illness. Episodic killing may be viewed as a disease in the sense that its sufferers demonstrate common symptoms. These embrace social, psychological and biochemical factors of which child abuse, chronic malnutrition, drug and alcohol abuse and inherited neurological disorders may be precursors.

Episodic violence depends on an individual's arousal to a stimulus and his need to satisfy it. This reaction, like the instincts of fear and anxiety, is controlled by the body's hormones. If the hormonal functions are impaired due to biochemical or neurological changes, loss of control will result.

In their attempts to explain the phenomenon of serial killing, some commentators have used the electronic vernacular, suggesting that such killers are wrongly 'wired-up'. Explanations that reflect the desire to find physically related causes for the upsurge in violent behaviour may not be too wide of the mark. Breakdown or malfunction of the body's biochemical pathways that trip the brain beyond its normal restraints is an explanation deserving greater study. Experts acknowledge that serial murder considered as a form of illness is not a concept that falls into any accepted medical or legal classification. Because it cannot be assessed by traditional techniques does not mean it is lacking in validity. New ground is being broken and every success in applying profiling to apprehend serial killers provides fresh data for the researchers.

While we are groping our way towards root causes of episodic violence and possibly to a level of understanding sufficient to exercise prevention, there are few doubts about the effects once an individual is in its grip. Serial killers may seem to spring up from nowhere, but killing is only an advanced stage in a gradual build-up of offending and violent behaviour. The beginnings may lie in voyeurism, minor sexual offences and thieving, escalating through aggressive sexual relations to violent rape and finally to murder. The fully emerged serial killer is apparent when the killing becomes repetitive and routine.

The build-up to each incident in the individual also follows a pattern, once he is in the clutches of episodic violence. There is a behaviour pattern that is repeated on each occasion, virtually taking the form of a ritual. Reliance on ritual has been identified as a common aspect of known serial killers' behaviour. Psychologists have pinpointed a number of distinct phases. First is a state that involves withdrawal from everyday existence into a condition bordering on hallucination in which the normal moral restraints cease to be of significance. This phase may be accompanied by drug or alcohol intake and is one in which personal control is subsumed by the idea of violence. Dr Norris likens this to 'a portal between two realities' in which the individual is simply driven to satisfy a lust.

The next development is one in which the intending killer begins to trawl for a victim. He frequents areas where he is likely to find a suitable victim for abduction – car parks, shopping centres or dark, deserted streets in which a woman alone and vulnerable may be found. The killer is directed by a keen sense of purpose yet his outward behaviour is, to all intents and purposes, normal. Once the prey is identified, the killer stalks from a distance, sizing up the situation in terms of the opportunities open to him. He looks for escape routes and a mode of operation that will bring him quick success.

Once he has his victim within reach, the killer begins a kind of seduction. He talks disarmingly, using a mixture of charm and plausibility, to secure confidence. As his blandishments begin to succeed, so the victim is drawn irrevocably into the predator's grasp. Because many serial killers are handsome men, they find and seduce their victims with relative ease. Dr Norris says that only those who resist at the outset have any chance of escape. Once they allow themselves to become ensnared they are doomed.

The next phase is capture – it is the moment when the trap closes. In the cases of most serial killers, it is the instant that their victim willingly enters the space that the predator controls, such as his car or apartment. Alone with his victim he tortures, rapes and kills her.

His elation is followed by a gradual realisation of what he has done as normality begins to return. Some serial killers, driven to relive their moment of triumph, attempt to preserve their victim by means of grotesque rituals involving dismemberment. There is also a need for concealment as the rational elements of their personality assume more control.

The body is disposed of, often in a remote area, with sufficient cunning to keep the police guessing.

Finally comes the depression phase when the killer realises that his triumph is short-lived and that he has achieved nothing. Indeed, he has failed because his sense of frustration, which the murder was supposed to have erased, is still there.

While he feels no guilt, he experiences sorrow, although only for himself, and resolves not to kill again. But soon the fantasies begin to reassert themselves and the moment arrives once again when he gives up normal control and is taken over by his violent urges. The whole pattern is then repeated and another victim in another place is at risk. This time the suffering and pain he inflicts will be greater than the last in an effort to satisfy the cravings that left him short of total satisfaction after the previous killing.

This bizarre sequence of events is not an imagined or academic scenario – it is what happens when a full-blown serial killer emerges in society. It is clear that, once he is in the grip of a bout of episodic violence, he is beyond the reach of external forces. While able to distinguish between right and wrong, he experiences a reduced ability to judge the quality of his actions. Dr Norris says that, once in this state, he has lost his free will. He may be thought of as mad but, because his condition defies medical and legal definition, the normal criteria for defining sanity cannot be properly applied. Serial killers distort reality by merging their killing instincts into normal behaviour patterns. This enables them to lead outwardly conventional lives with normal activity interspersed with killing episodes. This is why they are so dangerous and so successful.

A characteristic of serial killers, as demonstrated by Ted Bundy and others of his ilk, is the ease with which they attain a state of guiltlessness. They slither away from acknowledging their crimes despite overwhelming evidence of their involvement, as if responsibility rests with someone else. This attitude is assisted by a convenient loss of memory about events, which enables them to lie with impunity or to change their accounts at random. Psychologists say that the loss of memory is real because when they are at their most violent they block out the memory of their crimes. For these reasons, they are difficult to interrogate and frustrate their questioners by their facility to lie and manipulate.

John Cannan was on the verge of becoming a serial killer. Had he not been apprehended at Leamington Spa, his increasingly frequent bouts of violence would most probably have led him further down the destructive path to more killings. His personality and behaviour bear the hallmarks of an emerging serial killer. His arrest in October 1987 was timely in that it prevented other victims falling into his path.

The pattern of John's activities and what is known about his background, behaviour and outlook fit him with eerie precision into the world of the modern serial killer. In John's case, with the killing of Shirley Banks, he had possibly only just emerged in that role. If he was responsible for the murders of Suzy Lamplugh and Sandra Court, he was already matured as a serial murderer.

Perhaps now is the appropriate time to look into John's mind, taking into account what we know about the make-up of a serial killer, and try to draw other parallels. We have already discussed the dismissal of guilt and the 'other self' which is common to serial killers. There is also the convenient real or false memory loss. To understand this in John Cannan, we have to seek out not what he says but what he doesn't say – what he conveniently forgets or refuses to explain.

An important illustration of this emerged in the correspondence between John and the authors. He was reminded that Shirley Banks's body was discovered near Over Stowey in the Quantock Hills, a mere mile and a half from the route which he had frequently travelled to Ilfracombe when visiting Sharon Major's parents in north Devon. John dismissed this as 'simply academic' and said that he did not know where Over Stowey was. 'It is NOT a place that I have any knowledge of at all,' he said.

This contrasts sharply with Sharon's clear recollection of the route that they took on these visits. They drove south from Bristol on the M5 motorway, coming off at junction 23, the Bridgwater exit. The obvious way to proceed at this point would have been to follow the main road, the A39, heading for the coast and skirting to the north of the Quantocks. But, in her statement to the police on 12 April 1988, Sharon described a route that took them along minor roads across the Quantocks through the villages of Durleigh, Enmore and Bishops Lydeard, where they joined the A358 north to Minehead. Her memory of this itinerary, which took them so close to the spot where Shirley Banks's corpse was later found, was uncompromisingly precise, whereas John professed to have no knowledge of it at all. In her statement, Sharon also mentioned that she and John often went for car rides in the countryside, sometimes stopping for a picnic. 'He would always prefer to go off the beaten track,' she said, 'along small country lanes to find isolated beauty spots.'

Another example was drawn to John's attention after he had repeatedly claimed that he had only visited Poole in Dorset twice in his life, once to attend a motor auction, once to stay in a hotel for the night with Gilly Paige. But, as we have said, the police have very specific evidence that Cannan was in Poole the weekend that Sandra Court was murdered, a coincidence that cannot be discounted.

Despite a huge police effort, the killer of Sandra Court has never been tracked down. After his appeal failed, John was interviewed by Dorset CID because of similarities between the deaths of Shirley Banks and Sandra Court, and similarities in the circumstances in which their bodies were found. The case remains open.

A further example concerns the missing, presumed dead, Suzy Lamplugh. The authors drew together the known facts about her disappearance and put them to John on several occasions. John replied, claiming that our synopsis of the facts, given in Chapter 5, was 'seriously flawed' and repeating his denial of any involvement with Suzy. Bearing in mind his stated willingness to assist in every possible way, John was pressed further to account for his movements over the weekend prior to the estate agent's disappearance. He could not, or would not, answer these questions and used the same evasive techniques he had employed over the geographical location of Shirley Banks's body and the trip to Poole on the Bank Holiday weekend that Sandra Court was murdered.

Serial killers like to keep on the move and John Cannan was no exception to the rule. Many of their victims are either lured or forced into their cars. This is another characteristic that John shares. It applied in the case of Shirley Banks. (Shirley was most probably approached in a threatening manner similar to the way John had approached Julia Holman, and forced to drive her car to Foye House.) Donna Tucker was raped in her own car and Julia Holman escaped an abduction attempt when returning to her parked car. It was also the case that Sandra Court had been in a vehicle prior to her death.

We know that Shirley Banks's body was found in water, and it is at least an interesting coincidence that Sandra Court's body was also found in water. If John abducted and killed Suzy Lamplugh, where might her remains be expected to lie? Only her abductor knows the answer to that question but navigational ideas used in crime investigation might offer some hints. For example, a direct line can be drawn in the case of Shirley Banks from Bristol through to Ilfracombe with her body being discovered along that route in an area familiar to John Cannan.

A direct line can also be followed in connection with the murder of Sandra Court. Her body was found on a main road leading out of Poole through Bournemouth towards Ringwood and Southampton, and, probably, thence to London. The young woman's personal effects were found strewn about the verges of the road that led through the New Forest and up to Ringwood. It might be postulated that driving home along the main road, the killer spotted Sandra Court, a little the worse for drink, and enticed her into his car with the offer of a lift. Murder followed and the killer left his pre-planned direct route to Ringwood and diverted through the country lanes, disposing of his victim's personal effects along the way before rejoining his intended route east of Ringwood.

The letter sent to the Dorset police claiming that Sandra's death was an accident was posted in Southampton. John Cannan knew Southampton well as he had worked in the city for a time. He was also familiar with the New Forest area, having walked in the woods there, and at the time of Sandra's murder he was living at a prison hostel in London. Once again, John conveniently forgot to mention that he had visited Poole during the weekend that Sandra was murdered.

In the case of Suzy Lamplugh, we know that John frequented a wine bar in the same street that Suzy worked. We know that he had access to the hostel cook's car and had made use of the vehicle on his visit to Poole. After Suzy went missing, John stayed at his mother's home in Sutton Coldfield. He can account for his movements for the days either side of Monday 28 July 1986 when Suzy was abducted, but cannot recall his activities on the day in question. Many of the known facts about her disappearance point to John Cannan as her possible abductor and, if a navigational theory of crime investigation is applied, her body may lie at some point accessible from the route between London and Birmingham.

John will deny these conclusions as he has denied everything else, but that is in keeping with his state of mind. It is doubtful that he understands his own nature. His protestations of innocence in the face of what an objective observer, and indeed a trial jury, regarded as overwhelming evidence may seem wilful and arrogant. But, if his mind has isolated his memory from some of his violent acts by putting them into compartments of forgetfulness, he might indeed have convinced himself, as he has suspected all along, that the world was against him. In that sense, perhaps he too is a victim.

His trial jury did not doubt his sanity – that was not an issue. He portrayed himself as an intelligent, articulate man who, if judged by his statements, was well able to argue his case. In the light of the crimes with which he was charged, the lust that motivated them and the brutality demonstrated in their commission, the layman's conclusion is that he was bad rather than mad. It cannot be said that he did not know what he was doing, but without doubt he did not care. 'I don't give a fuck' was his answer to Sharon Major when she pleaded with him to stop hurting her. In the grip of episodic violence, his victims were expendable objects of lust. At the moment of climactic frenzy, he was beyond notions of right and wrong.

John Cannan's mental powers are demonstrated in his letters to the authors which show a clear, logical mind at work, albeit one capable of deception in depth. The budding serial killer has graphically illustrated his abilities over the 18-month period in which he has given his own account of the events that brought him a life sentence. Taken at face value, his letters show a grasp of detail and articulate expression that beguiles and tempts belief.

Without benefit of reference to documents or records, he can recall times, dates, places and names with masterful accuracy. He knows every exhibit in the case by description and number and can recall the first names of witnesses and police officers. He weaves these verifiable facts into an interpretation of events based partly on fact and partly on fiction, creating a plausible, almost hypnotic account that is intended to seduce the reader.

This plausibility is seemingly strengthened by John's

declared intention to publish the truth and to hold nothing back. But, when details of his letters are compared with the police interview files, it may be seen that he has used the same wooing tactics with detectives: expressing an earnest desire to help but all the time striving to manipulate and create confusion. It was a version of this technique coldly practised by the handsome, well-groomed and charming John Cannan that disarmed his female acquaintances and drew some of them into a trap that closed violently.

Serial murder is fortunately a relatively rare phenomenon in Britain, and BBC *Crimewatch* presenters always end their programme by saying that one should not worry unduly about the ever-increasing crime rate: 'Sleep well!' Denis Nilsen, the mild-mannered civil servant who murdered 15 down-and-outs in the late 1970s, was a homosexual exponent of serial killings, with the exception that he always used the same location for his murders: his home. Peter Sutcliffe, the so-called 'Yorkshire Ripper', murdered 13 women, mostly prostitutes, also during the late 1970s. He had the roaming nature of the serial killer and sufficient plausibility to avoid capture, despite being interviewed nine times by the police. Sutcliffe was a full-blown serial killer. A more recent example is Kenneth Erskine, dubbed the 'Stockwell Strangler' by the press. He murdered seven elderly people of both sexes. The FBI assisted the Metropolitan Police in their murder inquiry by providing a profile of the killer from details of his crime. The FBI were spot on.

Although late starters, senior police officers and forensic specialists in Britain are now well versed in the trends taking place in the USA and are familiar with the latest profiling techniques used to apprehend serial killers.

Following criticism of their shortcomings in handling the great mass of information which accumulated during the Yorkshire Ripper investigation, the police have installed a computerised data management system called HOLMES (Home Office Large Major Enquiry System) to enable nationwide crime inquiries to be coordinated. The speed with which information was exchanged between police forces was an important factor in John Cannan's arrest for the murder of Shirley Banks.

Crime specialists are also well aware that the social and environmental factors that create the breeding grounds for serial killers in the USA already exist in Britain. All the stress factors and other pressures that push individuals towards failure and probe their weaknesses are evident in today's society. There is also a strong public awareness of the phenomenon gained through the medium of entertainment. The horrifying sub-culture of the serial killer has been introduced into ordinary people's lives by way of books, films and television. David Lynch's weird television series *Twin Peaks* proved highly successful and was followed by the thriller movie *Silence of the Lambs*.

The film, based on Thomas Harris's novel of the same title, portrayed a transvestite serial killer who kills and skins his victims. The storyline also featured an imprisoned psychopathic doctor, Hannibal Lecter, who rapidly became a cult figure, and in true Hollywood fashion the plot included a beautiful rookie FBI agent for good measure. In ten weeks, the film grossed $100 million in the USA and £8 million in three weeks in Britain. During those weeks, millions of people were exposed to the celluloid terror of serial killing. Stephen King, the horror writer, was reported to have likened the phenomenon to 'feeding the alligators'. But what did we learn from this feast of terror, gore and depravity? Very little. Apart from combining several serial killers into the same plot, and the ineptitude of the police in allowing Lecter to escape, there was little to ring true with reality. There was an outstanding performance by Anthony Hopkins who played Hannibal Lecter, masterfully portraying a cunning and plausible serial killer, but the whole film disintegrated into a farce when it ended by contriving a sequel to entertain future cinema audiences.

What was phenomenal was that the public wanted to flirt with horror and brutality of the worst kind and to be entertained by it. Hard on the heels of these visual dramas came a verbal battering from Bret Easton Ellis in the form of his novel *American Psycho*. The central character is a handsome, charming and intelligent yuppie working on Wall Street who also happens to be a violent psychopath. The descriptions of his depraved crimes are horrific and close to pornography. The publishers described the book as a bitter novel about a world we recognised but refused to accept.

The 1990s opened as a decade in which serial killing – murder for the fun of it – would be raised to cult status. As often happens, art became reality in August 1991 in the form of Jeffrey L Dahmer, a mild-mannered man who worked in a Milwaukee chocolate factory. His foul-smelling apartment contained the rotting remains of some of his mutilated murder victims – he had killed at least 17 times. *Newsweek* made the inevitable connection with *Silence of the Lambs* and quoted a forensic psychiatrist who said, 'Every time you think it's the most bizarre thing you've ever heard, something worse happens.'

Is serial violence worth worrying about in this country, when it is so rare – just a few convicted killers during the last two decades? Some specialists in the study of violence believe that, like other diseases, serial killing can be prevented if it is identified in time. Greater awareness would make it feasible to recognise its early signs and to help individuals before their periodic outbursts of violence progress to murder. The climate for dealing with the victims of rape and sexual assault needs to improve in order to encourage them to discuss their experiences with trained professionals. To some limited extent, physicians and healthcare workers with greater knowledge of the subject and able to interpret offenders' descriptions and details of attacks would be in a position to raise the alert about potentially dangerous individuals. This approach carries with it all the inherent problems that are evident now in persuading victims of sexual offences to come forward and discuss the intimate details of their experience. This is especially the case when disclosure may involve past sexual experiences in the context of a long-standing relationship.

Many violent offenders know that something is wrong with them. Some make faltering attempts to seek advice and some attempt suicide. John Cannan, for example, was twice referred for psychiatric consultation and made one unsuccessful attempt on his own life. Unless these cries for help are recognised for what they are, the chance to take a family history, the first step in recognising the telltale signs of developing aggression, will be lost. The causes of episodic violence may be traced through definable malfunctions revealed in personal histories, such as incidents of sexual abuse, alcoholism, personality disorders and previous offences.

If individuals in the early stages of episodic violence can be identified through medical and professional advice, they can be helped. Environmental medicine is a young discipline but it too has a part to play by creating more public awareness.

Individuals in the workplace observing personality changes in colleagues, perhaps becoming uncharacteristically aggressive or unhealthily withdrawn, should have a channel open to them to express their concern. Some serial killers have worked in offices or premises where there is a structured environment and continuity of contact. Others operate as loners, thus presenting few opportunities for informal observation. Even so, they have acquaintances who drift in and out of their lives, like travellers in the night. In the case of John Cannan, at least three women friends observed enough of his behaviour at first hand to realise that he could be dangerously obsessive and aggressive. They backed away, and their experiences only became known when it was too late to help.

There are limited opportunities for picking up incipient serial killers at a stage early enough to head them away from destruction. There are obvious dangers in resorting to Orwellian solutions where everyone reports on everyone else. A colleague's well-intentioned concern may simply be regarded as unwarranted intrusion. The most acceptable remedy will probably lie in medical care and the early identification of genetic and physiological abnormalities in childhood and developing anti-social personality traits. This is idealistic insofar as it depends on the wide provision of community medicine; the reality is that available resources are unlikely to penetrate deeply enough into those recesses of society where they are most needed. The thought of preventing the emergence and flowering of serial killing at source is a fine concept but one that is likely to remain an ideal.

The knowledge that would make early identification and treatment of serial killers possible is in its infancy. While the problem is more urgent in the USA, it has lower recognition in Britain. It is only when men like Peter Sutcliffe and John Cannan erupt on society to take their violent toll that the public takes stock. The news and entertainment media feed off the horror but the shock waves quickly subside, leaving the menace of serial killing still lurking in the shadows.

One practical answer is to make potential victims more 'streetwise' in their approach to personal relationships. Of course, it would be sad for the human race if individuals of either sex denied themselves the chance of instantaneous attraction and romance – human nature would not permit it anyway. But, if people were more aware of the dangers of making unthinking commitments to strangers, there would be less scope for cynical opportunists and, possibly, fewer victims of serial violence. It has to be said that many victims show an amazing degree of gullibility in the ease with which any caution they may have is disarmed. At the same time, it should also be stressed that individuals like John Cannan are a relatively rare phenomenon.

It is nevertheless desirable that potential victims, young women in particular, deny the opportunist any encouragement in his chosen killing fields. It is not just the lone woman at night taking a shortcut through a deserted, badly lit street, but the more familiar territories of shopping malls and car parks where individuals can be abducted from apparently safe surroundings. Shirley Banks was just such a victim, as was Suzy Lamplugh and, save for her quick thinking, Julia Holman. Awareness is perhaps a matter of common sense and it is that faculty which will protect women from the evil of deviant individuals. The reality is that serial killers will continue to emerge from time to time and, while society struggles to come to terms with the phenomenon, individuals need to be vigilant about personal security.

Ultimately, the solution to the problem of serial killing lies in diminishing the root causes. It means creating social conditions in which there are employment and career opportunities for those of modest talents so that they are not shut out. It means eliminating child sexual abuse through the better education of parents and raising living standards to give families space in which to grow. These things are, of course, wildly idealistic. As Colin Wilson put it in his book *The Serial Killers*: 'Theoretically, a Utopian society with a low birth rate, ample living space and a high general level of prosperity should cease to produce serial killers.'

In addition to raising the level of individual awareness, improvements are continually being made in criminal investigation methods. The hope is that refinements in profiling will enable more serial killers to be caught earlier in their careers. Their mobility that has so frustrated the police will become less effective as information is computerised and made accessible on a nationwide basis. Forensic techniques such as DNA 'fingerprinting' are being constantly upgraded to make the identification of offenders a swifter and more accurate process. And our knowledge of this subject will be increased when convicted offenders such as Ted Bundy, Denis Nilsen and John Cannan can be persuaded to share their thoughts and feelings.

The police have come under a great deal of criticism of late, with their professionalism and integrity being called into question. Their stock has gone down in public esteem as a result of a number of highly publicised miscarriages of justice in which evidence used to win convictions was found to be unsafe. Officers of the Avon and Somerset Constabulary were rightly commended at the end of John Cannan's trial, along with Andrew Riley and Robert Filer, two spirited members of the public who chased a would-be robber without concern for their own safety. In this case, the police officers involved achieved high standards of professionalism and, through their determined efforts, an emerging serial killer was apprehended.

The transcription of the long hours of interviews between Bryan Saunders and John Cannan reads like a novel. Here was a battle of wits between an experienced detective and an intelligent suspect who liked to think of himself as 'Top Gun' and was accustomed to having his own way. It proved an unequal struggle in the end because Saunders held all the cards and, like an experienced player, did not reveal his hand. John nevertheless gave him a run for his money, having every admission wrung from him as his mind raced ahead to the next question. Whether it was car auctions or schizophrenia, he argued the toss about everything.

It was perhaps a fitting reward for Bryan Saunders that he was later promoted to detective superintendent and held the appointment of deputy coordinator, South West Regional Crime Squad. This self-effacing police officer makes the point that he was only part of a large dedicated team of policemen who brought John Cannan to justice. He stresses that his superior, Detective Superintendent Tim

Bryan, was the senior investigating officer during the Banks investigation. Tim Bryan went on to be transferred to Wiltshire Constabulary and became the detective chief superintendent in charge of Wiltshire CID.

It would be difficult to name all the officers and police personnel who deserve merit in the investigation, but one name does require a mention, and the officer concerned was praised by senior detectives at an interview with the authors at Reading. Detective Constable Terry Caine interviewed the taxi-driver following the Reading rape of Donna Tucker. It was this officer who tracked down Cannan to London and, with the help of a Metropolitan Police collator, identified him as a possible suspect.

The encounter between the snake and the mongoose proved John's guilt but also showed he had intelligence and wit that might have helped him create a different life had they been channelled more constructively.

And what of John? Despite everything, he is a human individual, unique in his qualities and personality. He may experience extremes of emotion that exceed his powers of control and have placed him beyond the pale as far as society is concerned. Nevertheless, we deny the very humanity we seek to protect if we take away his dignity. He is a vehicle for forces that have condemned him to destruction as much as they have destroyed his victims.

John feels let down by society, by the system and by the people in it. But it is all one way – what others owe to him, no mention of what he might give in return. It is the self-centred outlook of an immature personality. As a boy wanting to be the centre of attraction and falling into a tantrum when he did not succeed in getting his own way, so it was when he grew up. When he failed to get what he desired, his anger was so corrosive as to demand satisfaction through violence. One man may vent his frustration by discharging a shotgun at a masterpiece by Leonardo da Vinci exhibited in a public gallery; another may express his frustration by destroying a human being. John elected the latter course and, sadly, where the artistic masterpiece may be repaired, the human life is lost forever.

John continues to deny the crimes for which he is serving life imprisonment. There are no admissions of guilt or remorse and he has resisted suggestions that his sense of alienation would be eased if he accepted what he had done. He at least conceded in a letter written in autumn 1991 that he is 'someone who has a record of sexual offending' but his bitter resentment at what he regards as unfair treatment by the police remains. He also persists with his conspiracy theories and his judgement on the legal system is as critical as that of Ted Bundy. While John's indignation may keep his mind occupied, it will do nothing to alter his circumstances. What he can learn about himself may yet give him composure.

John has taken his revenge and there is no adequate measure for the agony he has wrought. Death is tangible, grief less so. The death of Shirley Banks, the abuse and violence which he cruelly inflicted on Sharon Major, Jean Bradford and Donna Tucker and the anguish caused to Julia Holman and Carmel Cleary are his responsibility. Nor should his family be forgotten: his brother and late sister were victims too and his mother has suffered indelible pain. In the service of his savage condition, John has marked many people with permanent grief.

This book is largely about distress – that of the offender and of his several victims. With that in mind it is worth looking to those who are condemned by John for their views about him. Lord Lane, the former Lord Chief Justice of England, presided over John's appeal. In a letter to the authors, Lord Lane wrote, 'The prospect of a young man spending the rest of his life in prison is appalling. It is a pity that there seems to be no humane alternative. There is good in the worst of us. Oddly enough, prison sometimes serves to allow that fact to be proved.'

This sentiment by the nation's most senior criminal judge is echoed by one of John's victims. Sharon Major suffered terribly at his hands and the memory will probably haunt her for the rest of her life. Yet, of the man who claimed he was let down by the people he knew and loved, she has this to say: 'I know what John did to me was wicked but there is a good side to John which is desperately trying to get out. He almost killed me and I still live in terror of him today but one has to learn to forgive and that I have done.'

Did John Cannan kill more than once? Did he abduct and murder Suzy Lamplugh and perhaps Sandra Court? Suzy's mother was reported as believing he was involved in her daughter's disappearance and others were similarly persuaded.

We are aware that circumstantial evidence has the power both to confirm suspicion and also to mislead. In John Cannan's case, it can be said with confidence that he was in the grip of serial violence. His urges tipped him over the edge with Shirley Banks and circumstances strongly suggest he had been to the precipice before.

It is uncanny how his known movements place him so close to these unsolved crimes and how the incidents so accurately reflect his behaviour traits and *modus operandi*. His denials of the obvious in the attacks on Sharon Major, Donna Tucker and Julia Holman and the murder of Shirley Banks tend to strengthen the notion that he knows more about Suzy Lamplugh and perhaps Sandra Court than he is prepared to admit.

Ever mobile, always available, opportunistic and charming to a fault, John Cannan belongs to that part of the human race that, for reasons of heredity or upbringing, harbours a predatory instinct.

EPILOGUE

Christopher Berry-Dee spent two years writing to John Cannan. Partly as a result of John's copious, well-presented correspondence, the Suzy Lamplugh case may yet be solved. Much of what follows has never before been placed in the public domain.

Sometime in 2009 or 2010, we may see newspaper headlines screaming: JOHN CANNAN, ONE OF THE COUNTRY'S VILEST RAPISTS AND A CONVICTED SEX KILLER, WILL BE FREED WITHIN DAYS. AN INDEPENDENT JUDGE, WHO HAS CONSIDERED HUMAN RIGHTS LEGISLATION, SAYS THAT CANNAN HAS SERVED HIS TARIFF AND HAS ORDERED THAT HE BE RELEASED. POLICE OFFICERS, WHO STILL CONSIDER CANNAN TO BE THE PRIME SUSPECT IN THE MURDER OF ESTATE AGENT SUZY LAMPLUGH IN 1986, ARE HORRIFIED.

If Suzy Lamplugh were alive today, she would be 45 years old. She might be married to a doting husband and have children, but fate brought her across the path of the man who has come to be known as Mr Kipper. The year was 1986, and it seems all but certain that it was on the afternoon of Monday, 28 July that Suzy met him. Whether the estate agent met her death that afternoon or evening, we may never know. She may have survived the night and have been subjected to restraint, terror and rape, as Shirley Banks was in 1987. Like Shirley, Suzy may have lived until the following day, but her killer would certainly not have allowed her to breathe a day longer.

At the time of writing, April 2007, John Cannan is 54. For his sins he has spent half his life behind bars of one sort or another; currently he is into his 20th year for the murder of Shirley Banks. At present John is serving his time at Full Sutton, a modern, purpose-built, maximum-security prison about 11 miles east of York in open countryside near the village of Full Sutton. The prison's primary function is to hold men in category A and category B: some of the most difficult and dangerous criminals in the country.

Prison life has not been kind to John. Long gone is his fine, lean physique. He is fat and his skin is yellowish. No longer the proud, well-dressed and immaculately coiffed car dealer who boasted of his worldly travels and hundreds of sexual conquests, he now stoops when he shuffles around and his eyes have a hunted look – nervous and shifty at the same time. Those who know him say he has a few friends but prefers his own company, reading anything about motor cars and philosophy that he can get his hands on. He is still prone to being a big mouth when he feels it safe to boast; other cons call him 'Billy Liar'. In this respect, nothing much has changed.

Concerning the grim details of the abduction and murder of Suzy Lamplugh, he staunchly maintains his innocence.

Jim Dickie, one of the country's top police detectives, is convinced that, if John Cannan is let out, he will rape and kill again. The prospect of his being freed from prison is a disturbing one, yet it remains a distinct possibility, as Mark Townsend, crime correspondent of the *Observer*, reported on 30 July 2006: 'It is understood that Cannan has already lodged appeals over the tariff, using human rights legislation. Amid increasing concern among officers investigating the disappearance of Suzy Lamplugh, New Scotland Yard has taken the rare step of pre-empting these moves by announcing publicly that he must never be freed.'

During this press conference, Jim Dickie leaned forward, thumped his desk and said, 'Cannan will reoffend. He should never be released. If you look at his profile, I have no doubt he will strike again. He has been released from prison before and committed crimes. He is a danger to the female population, particularly the blonde, 20-something professionals like Suzy. Even if he wasn't released until he was 60, he would go on to abduct, rape and murder women.'

It has been almost 20 years since Suzy's abduction and murder. Much muddy water has passed under the bridge in those two decades but most people, including the Lamplughs and the police, are convinced that John Cannan remains the prime suspect in the Lamplugh case.

John has been reinterviewed twice (most recently in 2000), but, although his denial has not changed, the state of forensic science has. On Tuesday, 5 November 2002, a press conference was held at New Scotland Yard. It is worth reproducing Deputy Assistant Commissioner Bill Griffiths's review of the situation in full.

'As a result of the re-investigation into the murder of Suzy Lamplugh, we have submitted a file of evidence to the CPS in June of this year recommending a prosecution. They recently advised us that they felt we had insufficient evidence at this time.

'The current investigation began on 12 May 2000. The team of detectives has left no stone unturned to seek justice for the Lamplugh family. It has been a lengthy and complex process that has been driven with vigour and determination by DCS Shaun Sawyer and DCI Jim Dickie.

'We have had the benefit of cutting-edge technology. Every piece of forensic evidence available has been revisited and re-examined. I and the officers involved honestly believe that we are now closer to a prosecution than we have ever been before.

'DCS Sawyer and DCI Dickie, I know, have become closely involved with the Lamplugh family over the past two and a half years. Although they are proud to have been able to progress the investigation this far, they are both personally and professionally disappointed that they could not yet bring this investigation finally to a close.

'When Suzy first went missing on 28 July 1986, the Metropolitan Police dealt with missing people and murders very differently. Officers did not have access to information technology. Everything was logged using a card index. There was huge media and public interest in Suzy's disappearance that inundated the investigation team with a massive amount of information. No management systems were put in place to cope with this influx of calls.

'It is a matter of great regret for all of us at the Metropolitan Police that significant opportunities were missed during the initial inquiry. If these opportunities had been grasped at the time, it may have led us to a prosecution many years ago, but that did not happen.

'The detailed investigation of the last few years has demonstrated to us what a lovely person Suzy was and that it was a matter of great misfortune that, apparently through her work as an estate agent, she was stalked and murdered. Although we have not lost hope that Suzy's body will eventually be discovered, we greatly regret that we have not been able to find her so far.

'The Suzy Lamplugh Trust is very much alive. It is vigorous and moves from strength to strength. As a result of hard work and determination of the Trust so much has been achieved.

'John Cannan has been interviewed twice by police in connection with Suzy's murder since his arrest. He has not been eliminated from our enquiries as a suspect. As this investigation has progressed – more and more questions about his involvement remain unanswered.

'We know that there are still people who have not come forward to us for no matter what reason – maybe they think what they saw was unconnected or maybe they were trying to protect someone they cared about. It is never too late to speak to us. We would like to see that final piece of the jigsaw falling into place to allow the Lamplugh family to move on and for us to see justice has been done.

'While the CPS advice is that there is not enough evidence to prosecute at this time, this investigation is not over.'

There is always light and dark, sunshine and shade. There are always matters brought into the light, while others are left, for whatever reason, hidden from public scrutiny in darkness or at best left to cool in the shade. What follows is fact, not hearsay.

In 2000, the Metropolitan Police called me, explaining that they had read the first edition of this book and had confronted John with some of the content. John had retorted that the claims in this book, specifically about him ever using a red Ford Fiesta car while he was on a pre-release scheme at Wormwood Scrubs, were 'bullshit'.

'Every word is a lie,' John claimed. 'Berry-Dee has invented it all.'

So it was quite proper for the police to ask if I still had John's letters – could I substantiate everything I had written in the book?

Within days, DCI Jim Dickie and his partner, DI Stuart Ault, were reading through the hundred or so letters penned to me by John Cannan. Everything attributed to John and reported in this book was word perfect.

A week later, the police called me again. They knew that I understood the workings of John's mind, perhaps better than he did himself. Stuart Ault asked me if I could revisit the letters, to look for anything that I felt might assist them in their future investigation. This was a request I could not refuse. So what emerged from this reappraisal of the correspondence?

THE RED FORD FIESTA

Of specific interest to police was the red Ford Fiesta that Cannan had borrowed from the prison hostel cook in 1986. Until they had read this book, the police had been unaware that their prime suspect had use of this vehicle around the time Suzy vanished, although John denied saying any such thing. Why, they asked, would he now deny having used this car, having earlier written that he drove it often?

Clearly, Suzy's killer had been mobile and had the use of a vehicle. Later, on the day of her abduction, the woman's car had been found abandoned not far from where she had last been seen, so it seemed clear that she had been moved elsewhere, probably in a car other than her own. It was therefore paramount that Jim Dickie and his squad locate the hostel cook and the red Ford Fiesta.

DI Stuart Ault discovered that the hostel cook had since died, so any confirmation from him whether or not John used the car during the fateful time was now out of the question. The car itself was discovered in a scrap yard. The vehicle might yet reveal forensic evidence.

In fact, the police did find DNA evidence that suggested Suzy had been in the red Ford Fiesta, as had John Cannan. The problem they faced was that the CPS felt that the evidence could not place both people in the car at the same time.

In 2006, Mark Townsend of the *Observer* wrote, 'Now the investigation into the chief suspect has entered a new stage. Scotland Yard has confirmed for the first time that a fresh review of the entire case has been launched by forensic scientists alongside intensive new co-operation with the Crown Prosecution Service. A previous file against Cannan – which culminated in the November 2002 press conference – led to the CPS deciding four years ago that it did not justify a charge. Forensics technology has developed remarkably in the meantime. The jigsaw puzzle of a case – characterised by its contradictions, conundrums and controversy – could yet lead to a conviction.'

'SARAH' AND THE MYSTERIOUS 'POLICEMAN'

John was known to have frequented several of the wine bars and pubs used by Suzy Lamplugh, and he may very well have been trawling for his next victim. John's *modus operandi* fits hand-in-glove with that used by Suzy's abductor: a smooth, plausible and charming operator with a convincing line of chat, perhaps topped off by a bottle of champagne and a bunch of roses. How many young women could resist such a charm onslaught? Dozens of John Cannan's conquests could not.

John can fully explain away his movements for the days either side of 28 July 1986. In relation to the fateful day, he claims he visited his mother on 29 July. When I interviewed her some years ago, she said that 'Johnny' did not see her that day – although, and she paused to think again, 'he might have called in later that evening but I don't think so.'

In his book *The Suzy Lamplugh Story: The Search for the Truth*, Andrew Stephen says that on the Friday before Suzy vanished – the same day John Cannan was released from his night-curfew restrictions at the prison hostel – Suzy dined at Mossops restaurant on Upper Richmond Road. When she left, she inadvertently dropped her chequebook, pocket diary and a postcard on the steps. These items were found by Keith Heminsley, acting landlord of nearby The Prince of Wales pub, who duly reported his find to Suzy's bank on the Monday morning. The bank then telephoned Suzy at work that morning, telling her that her personal property had been found and was in the safe possession of Heminsley. She then telephoned the landlord and they made an arrangement for her to collect the property at the pub around 6pm that evening. She never arrived.

That afternoon, Suzy went missing. The same afternoon a woman, who gave her name as Sarah, called Heminsley at the pub and left a message for Suzy – apparently for her when she arrived at the pub – to phone her number, which Heminsley wrote down on a scrap of paper. Sometime later a man, who said he was a policeman, called Heminsley and asked if he had Suzy's diary and chequebook, which the landlord confirmed.

When Heminsley told all this to the detectives handling the case, they were taken aback. They knew of no policeman who could have spoken to him on the afternoon Suzy went missing – well before her disappearance had even been reported. Heminsley was adamant, too, that he had given the scrap of paper on which he had written Sarah's name and telephone number to the police when he was interviewed a day or so later. But the police had no such piece of paper, which would have been of immense importance. They spoke to Suzy's bank but no one there had phoned the pub. It was certainly not Sarah 'Puff' Hough, one of Suzy's friends. In fact, the police could find no trace of any Sarah.

Only a few people could have known that Suzy had made an appointment that morning to collect her property from the pub at 6pm, as her call to Heminsley was the last phone call she made before rushing off to meet 'Mr Kipper'. So the callers could only have been office colleagues – and none of Sturgis's staff had phoned the pub – or someone Suzy had encountered later that Monday afternoon.

Was the call to Heminsley from 'Sarah' made by Suzy herself, possibly under duress? Was it a plea for help? Who was the policeman? It was all very baffling, especially as the two detective constables – who had first interviewed

Heminsley soon after Suzy was reported missing – strongly insisted that they were not given any scrap of paper.

The officers charged with bringing Suzy's killer to justice firmly believe Heminsley to be an honest and straightforward man who told the truth. We may never know what happened to the scrap of paper bearing Sarah's contact details. One theory from the original investigation – and still privately maintained by senior detectives today – was that Suzy's abductor did not work alone. It is certainly possible that the woman who called the landlord was a female accomplice, but the police believe it was Suzy.

MOTIVE

One does not need to prove motive to prove the crime, and Jim Dickie is right on the nail when he says that Cannan is an out-of-control, highly dangerous sexual predator; and that if he were released he would rape and kill again.

John is still a suspect in the murder of Sandra Court, although he says he is not. He denies the killing of Shirley Banks. He initially denied the rape of Jean Bradford before confessing to it. He denies the attempted abduction of Julia Holman. He flatly denies the murder of Suzy Lamplugh and the abduction and rape of Donna Tucker, or that he ever raped his first true love Sharon Major.

Despite all this, John says that his human rights have been breached – mainly, it seems, because he is being denied fair use of a telephone in prison. He also knows full well that no evidence has come to light with which the police can make a charge of the murder of Suzy Lamplugh. He knows too that, should he ever be brought before a jury, he can claim – despite the finest refereeing by a judge that such a high-profile case would inevitably demand – he could never receive a fair trial because he has already been tried by the media.

In so many respects, John is not dissimilar to the pathological American serial killer Kenneth Bianchi. Both men are sexual psychopaths, and both men killed women because they enjoyed the trawling and trapping of their prey before abusing, raping and killing them. Yet both killers hold on to a warped dream that one day they will be set free from their life sentence, simply because they believe they are more intelligent than those who have 'conspired' to have them locked away and that there is no 'real' evidence they committed any murders.

There can be little doubt that, while John was serving the five years of his eight-year sentence for the rape of Mrs Bradford, his mind became truly split. As Sharon Major said years later, 'There is a good side of John which is desperately trying to get out.' He is a real-life Dr Jekyll and Mr Hyde.

I believe that, while he was serving his five years for Mrs Bradford's rape, he really wanted to turn over a new leaf and make something of himself – to somehow make amends for all the grief he had laid upon his mother's doorstep. I think that he had sincere ambitions about returning to the car trade, and that is why he visited the car auction at Poole in May 1986.

JOHN CANNAN TODAY

All authorities will agree that John Cannan was a developing 'organised' serial murderer, as distinct from a 'chancer' who simply plucks his victims from the streets on a whim. Organised serial killers trawl, select a target, home in on the target, entice their prey into a suitable killing zone and then destroy the victim. But, for all their thinking and organisation, they have a pathological and flawed personality. They are totally unable to maintain and construct a long-term plausible defence as to why they are not guilty of an offence – their inflated ego prevents this.

If John Cannan were to be truthful with himself, he would admit to being a Mr Nobody when he looks into a prison mirror. However, for all the failure of his life's ambitions and grandiose plans, he will never admit that he is fundamentally a non-achiever or that his entire mental structure has been built on shifting sands.

John has been faced with overwhelming DNA evidence in the past. His semen was found at the Donna Tucker crime scene, yet he claims he was fitted up. In John's mind, he is always right and the system has always been conspiring to get him – or so he claims.

There is a part of John that craves the publicity of being known as the prime suspect in Suzy's murder, which is why he invented the number plate SLP 386S. This is why he hinted to Gilly Paige, the ice-skater, how Suzy might have died – by placing his hands around her neck.

John's solicitor at the time of writing claims that his client is not a games player, but that is exactly what John Cannan is. He thrives on it. Today, this is his only reason for being. While he would thoroughly enjoy all the attention if he were brought to trial, he also dreads the long-term consequences of a guilty verdict because it would reduce him to the status of just a regular rapist and sex killer. Within the system, where his self-perceived status currently keeps him mentally afloat, he would at last look into the mirror and for the rest of his life see only Mr Nobody.

BIBLIOGRAPHY

FAWKES, Sandy, *Killing Time*, Peter Owen, London 1977
LEYTON, Elliott, *Hunting Humans*, McClelland & Stewart,
   Toronto, 1986
MICHAUD, G. Stephen, and AYNESWORTH, Hugh, *The
   Only Living Witness*, Simon & Schuster, New York, 1983
MICHAUD, G. Stephen, and AYNESWORTH, Hugh, *Ted
   Bundy: Conversations with a Killer*, New American
   Library, New York, 1989
NORRIS, Joel, *Serial Killers: The Growing Menace*,
   Doubleday, New York, 1988
STEPHEN, Andrew, *The Suzy Lamplugh Story*, Faber &
   Faber, London, 1988
WILSON, Colin, and SEAMAN, Donald, *The Serial Killers*,
   W H Allen, London, 1990